Dream and your dreams will fall short

Pedro Casciaro

Dream
and your dreams will fall short

SCEPTER

LONDON – NEW YORK

This edition of *Dream and your dreams will fall short* is published:
in England by Scepter (U.K.) Ltd., 21 Hinton Avenue, Hounslow
TW4 6AP; e-mail: scepter@pobox.com;
in the United States by Scepter Publishers Inc., P. O. Box 211, New
York, NY 10018; e-mail: info@scepterpublishers.org

This is a translation of *Sonad y os quedaréis cortos*, first published
in 1994 by Ediciones Rialp, Madrid, and in 1996 by Scepter.

ISBN 0 906138 44 2

Cover design & typeset in England by KIP Intermedia, and printed
in Thailand.

Contents

Foreword

This book describes the years Pedro Casciaro lived with Blessed Josemaria Escriva, the founder of Opus Dei. Reading it myself has brought back to me numerous intimate memories. Particularly notable is his account of the period from 1935 to 1940, describing the years of faith and hope during which Blessed Josemaria opened up vast horizons of sanctity and apostolate. From the very beginning, in the inter-war Madrid of under a million inhabitants, he taught his hearers to help their workmates get closer to God.

He was soon able to see the fruits of his labours, as many people began to share in the first apostolic undertakings of Opus Dei. Full of optimism, Blessed Josemaria communicated to them a total trust in divine Providence, for God 'wants all men to be saved' (1 Tim 2:4) and he wishes to involve us actively in the entire unfolding of his salvific plan.

I was not an eye-witness to Opus Dei's earliest years of apostolic activity. But I do have those events engraved in my heart exactly as Blessed Josemaria Escriva and his successor, Bishop Alvaro del Portillo recounted them to me. The sudden death of the Prelate of the Work, Bishop Alvaro, which occurred when this book was just about to go into print, has made my memories even more vivid. He left a wake of sanctity behind him, and his life was the most eloquent expression of the spirit which the founder of Opus Dei transmitted to all who flocked to him in those years. For instance, I cannot forget his account of those Sunday afternoons in the mid-thirties, in Madrid in the DYA Residence for students. Bishop Alvaro del Portillo was there together with Pedro and the most senior members of the Work. He heard from the lips of Blessed Josemaria himself an impassioned description of how in the future, the Work's apostolate would spread through all the five continents. In that same house in Ferraz Street their immediate plans were outlined – to start up in Valencia, then in other Spanish cities, then in Paris – though they were put back a few years by the Spanish Civil War and later, by the Second World War.

Blessed Josemaria outlined an enormous field of apostolate. He was very realistic about it – his feet were firmly on the ground – but he spoke with a great awareness of supernatural realities at the same time. He encouraged them to picture it all in their imaginations and to trust in God and in supernatural means. These dreams of apostolate seemed impossible to many who knew the founder at that time. And yet, thanks to a special grace from God, they always cherished the heartfelt conviction that their dreams would indeed become reality. They were certain that if they struggled to attain sanctity every day in the midst of the world, the Lord would make them his instruments, capable of spreading, among every kind of people, the awareness that God calls us all to the fullness of Christian life.

Pedro Casciaro's narrative makes it clear how busy our founder was with the formation of the first members of Opus Dei for this task, all the while keeping the atmosphere cheerful and free. I had the grace of being at the founder's side from the beginning of the fifties onwards; and I too was able to experience at first hand how the Father continually taught us to act from the motive which he considered most powerful as a stimulus to action: namely, a sense of responsibility at both the human and the supernatural levels.

The Father always attached great importance to initiative and responsibility, something which comes across frequently from Pedro Casciaro's story. When one is in command of one's own actions, each person acts spontaneously and according to his or her own judgement, not feeling as though forced into a strait jacket. From the very beginning, our founder's example has taught us to juggle the totally free exercise of our personal responsibility with docility to God's plans. *In the spirit of Opus Dei*, he used to say, *we feel free and understand perfectly at the moment of obedience: because our directors ask us to do something realising that we are intelligent people, with maturity and personal responsibility, who actively put our understanding to work and our will into obeying, and who will accept the consequent responsibility for each act of obedience* (Letter, 31 May 1954, 22).

Pedro Casciaro asked for admission to the Work in 1935 and lived side by side with Blessed Josemaria during the difficult years of the Spanish Civil War. He brings us a vivid narrative written with a tremendous sense of humour, which highlights our founder's human and supernatural traits: his cheerfulness, simplicity, sincerity, optimism, candour, cordiality, sense of Divine sonship, love for each and every person, love of freedom, and enthusiasm for all things human. The author emphasises the trust the Father always had in the members of the Work. He relied on us completely, however young we were. This trust helped us to mature more quickly and made us particularly responsible.

Although the narrative covers Pedro Casciaro's whole life, it dwells especially on the years he lived alongside Blessed Josemaria. It recounts events in Madrid, during the crossing of the Pyrenees, and in Burgos, events to which he is one of the few witnesses still living, if not the only one. As can readily be understood, these pages are invaluable.

Today when I contemplate the immense variety of apostolate which the faithful of Opus Dei carry out all across the world, I lift up my heart in thanksgiving: for those "dreams" our founder had in the mid-thirties have today become a joyful reality in the service of the Church throughout the five continents.

I am convinced that Blessed Josemaria looks down from heaven with special affection and gratitude on those first men and women who, like Pedro Casciaro and Francisco Botella (who frequently appears in this story), were completely faithful and devoted their lives in total self-giving to God's Will.

I can think of the names of so many people who started Opus Dei in different countries, overcoming difficulties of every kind, and the names too of those who persevered, year after year, in the same place. Some of them already possess God in heaven, like Fr José Luis Muzquiz (who began the apostolate in the United States), or Fr José María Hernandez Garnica (who opened up a path for the Work in several European nations). Both of them were ordained priests at the same time as Monsignor Alvaro del Portillo, on 25 June 1944.

I was able to witness the intensity with which Monsignor Alvaro del Portillo prepared for the celebration of his golden jubilee. But God knows best, and He called him into His presence three months before the day. We are left with the great consolation that he will celebrate it there with José María and José Luis, delighting in God and the Blessed Virgin, and in the company of our holy founder.

I turn to them as intercessors before God in my prayers for the Church, and for the members of Opus Dei to live in total fidelity to the spirit which our founder transmitted to us.

I hope that, in reading these pages, many people will raise their hearts in gratitude to God our Lord and our Blessed Lady who have granted us the grace of experiencing in our daily lives the profound truth encapsulated in those words of Blessed Josemaria: *Dream and your dreams will fall short.*

Monsignor Javier Echevarria
Rome, 18 April 1994

CHAPTER 1

Introduction

Don Filiberto

Back in the far-off year of 1914, my maternal grandfather, Don Diego Ramirez, a schoolmaster in Torrevieja (near Alicante, in the south-east of Spain), was seriously worried. And that was not only on account of the international tension which was soon to lead to the European War. Rather it was because of something more domestic and immediate, within the family itself: the impending wedding of his daughter Amelia, that is, my mother.

"How could you hope for a better match than this lad?", his relatives demanded. They were right. His daughter's fiance, Pedro Casciaro, was a fine fellow, honest and conscientious into the bargain. He came from a well-known and well-heeled Italian family, related to the Parodis and the Boracinos, founding fathers of half of Italy, if the truth be told! The Casciaros had emigrated from Naples to England in Napoleonic times. The Parodis, coming from Genoa at the same time, had settled in Torrevieja. The Borracinos had set foot in Spain in the eighteenth century when Charles III went there from Naples, where he was king.

"How could you hope for a better match...?" What they said to my grandfather, Don Diego, was quite true: the boy was an excellent catch. He was the son of Julio Casciaro, a cultured and very proper man with a degree in law. On coming into his father's inheritance, Julio had moved to live in Torrevieja, where the family had an estate called *Los Hoyos* (The Hollows). Pedro was the grandson of Peter Casciaro, an Englishman by birth who, after being educated at a well known school in London, had specialised in Mineralogy and Accountancy.

Peter Casciaro was also a businessman of great acumen. He had built the railway line between Medina del Campo and Salamanca (in central Spain). He worked a large number of mines from La Union in Murcia to the Urals in Russia. And he owned several urban properties and farms in Spain and in Algeria. As he did not want his children to lose their English roots, when his son Julio was born in Cartagena, he had him registered as a British subject despite having lived for such a long time in Spain.

His grandson Pedro was a well-mannered, amiable, cheerful fellow. With a doctorate in the Arts, he was a very cultivated young man, as well as being quite personable and an able sportsman. What more could Don Diego want for his daughter? Everybody told him there was no cause for worry...

My maternal grandfather was a deeply religious man. He attended Mass daily and did a lot of catechesis. What worried him was the religious indifference of the fiance's family. He had no objections from any other angle: his opposite number was a generous, clean-living man with high principles. But, alas!, he did not practise, and neither did his wife. He was a republican, of the same mould as the 'Intellectuals for the Republic', who saw the Republic as a solution to Spain's decadence. For many people at that time, the word 'Republican' was synonymous with 'anti-clerical' and often with 'anti-Catholic'.

This was not the case with Don Julio and his wife. But even so the engagement caused Don Diego serious problems with his conscience. Should be allow his daughter Amelia, a good and fervent Christian, to marry such a man however much in love they were? What kind of upbringing would his grandchildren get? And what if...?

After turning it over and over in his mind he decided to ask Don Filiberto, the parish priest, for advice.

"Don't you worry", Don Filiberto pronounced gravely when he had heard my grandfather's troubles. "The children from this marriage will dedicate themselves to God."

I do not know what possessed Don Filiberto to prophesy in such a precise and categorical way. Was it the Holy Spirit who whispered in his ear? Was it simply an excuse to pacify a worried father? Or was it just something to say, spoken at random? I do not know. The fact of the matter is that Don Filiberto was not mistaken.

Of soup and soldiers

To return to the story of the family: My grandfather agreed to give his daughter's hand in marriage, and as soon as the air had cleared my parents were wedded amid much rejoicing, in a chapel on the estate at Los Hoyos. Soon afterwards my father was appointed Professor of Spanish History in the recently-founded University of Murcia and also Assistant Professor of History and Geography at the Institute there. And all three of us were born in

Murcia. I was baptised in the parish church of Santa Engracia in 1915; then my sister Soledad appeared, but she died when she was only a few years old. Later on came my brother, named José María though at home we always called him Pepe. When the next set of exams were held for professorships in the Institute, the first one to be contested was in history and geography. My father went in for it and came second, which meant he had to opt for Vitoria rather than Murcia. Still, as he wanted to stay in the Levant area, he changed his post as soon as he could for one in Albacete, which is relatively near Murcia and Torrevieja where the family home and concerns were based.

At first my father considered his posting to Albacete as no more than temporary and wanted to return to Murcia or Cartagena as soon as possible. Bit by bit, though, he became more involved in his job and made a lot of friends in La Mancha. He was Head of the Training Centre, for which he carried out many projects, including the building of a new home for the Institute where he was now the Director. He encouraged local archaeological excavations; and he conceived and constructed the Provincial Museum, to mention but a few of his achievements. To cut a long story short, he ended up becoming very fond of the place, which for those who know it, easily happens.

It is true that politics also influenced his decision to stay in Albacete, though he had taken little interest in it during the early years of Primo de Rivera's dictatorship. However, when the monarchy toppled he took part in the republican cause with much enthusiasm. Not that he was a proponent of left-wing extremism such as communism or the socialism of that time. (That certain sectors of the public rated them all – republicans, socialists and communists – pretty much of a muchness, owing to the electoral alliances being made at the time, is quite by-the-by.) His republicanism was not of that ilk. His was a moderate form, more liberal, with a great concern for the working class. It is illustrated by the fact that he became president of one of those tribunals set up during Primo de Rivera's mandate to arbitrate in disputes between owners and workers.

These presidents were, in the main, sound men, esteemed and accepted by both sides. But the task caused my father not a few problems: he could not understand how some people, friends of his even and very well-off, could haggle over a day's pay at 50 cents with people who were frequently on the bread-line. So he distanced himself from some of them, though they belonged to the most powerful families in the city.

At that time Albacete had its small provincial society, made up of land-owners, civil servants, people in the professions, some industrialists and other members of a middle-class of modest means. Since the proclamation of the Republic, the division which already existed in the city became more marked between right- and left-wingers. As time passed my father became known as a left-wing intellectual. It was under that banner that he took part in the great rally held in the Round Theatre in the presence of Azana. My father was what you would call an intellectual with a strong social conscience. From a religious point of view he was not at all committed, although as a sign of his respect and love for my mother he used to accompany her to Mass on Sundays and he wanted to celebrate José María's first Communion in fine style. But the times did not allow for those subtleties. When his political opponents found out about the celebration they published a ferocious article in the local paper under headline, 'Laicism, but not in my family'. They then attacked him pitilessly. He was thoroughly incensed; from that day onwards he ceased going to Mass.

That reaction gives a very good picture of what he was like. He was a passionate man who had plunged heart and soul into the difficult social and political times that Spain was going through. I remember that one day, some years earlier, he arrived home thoroughly exasperated, just as my young brother was having a bowl of soup. Father was irritated in the extreme because some of the military had been appointed to government posts. He snatched off his detachable collar and tie and flung them furiously into the armchair, shouting: "They'll be putting soldiers in our soup next!"

At these words my little brother peered into his soup anxiously, searching through the bowl in vain for those soldiers who were annoying my father so much and who threatened to invade his soup. And for some time his childish imagination speculated as to what the gentlemen concerned could possibly want by sneaking themselves into our little soup tureen, and more mysteriously still, how would they manage it?

CHAPTER 2

Madrid in the Thirties

1932: Mediodia Railway Station

At that time my dream was to become a sailor and I was completely unconcerned about such land-lubberly political enthusiasms. The sea enthralled me and I had inherited my paternal grandfather's love for ships. He had owned a merchant schooner which crossed the Atlantic and had had a three-masted motor yacht built to ply the Cartagena-Marseilles route, sailing from the neighbouring port of Aguilas. During the long summers of my adolescent years spent in the sunny haven of Los Hoyos, I would dream of countless adventures at sea. And when I saw the ships and sailing boats moored along the quayside, I imagined myself dodging squalls and storms on the high seas and, in a not too distant future, joining the Navy in the flamboyant uniform of a Coast-Guard.

When my mother got wind of my desires she put my feet back on the ground – literally – and refused point-blank to let me embark on my scheme. So I had no choice but to turn to another great ambition of mine, this time well-grounded on dry land. I decided to become an architect.

Although it was a hard decision to make, I did have the right qualities for being an architect. My father had passed on to me his love of art. I was observant and reasonably able at drawing.

No sooner said than done. At the age of seventeen, having finished my schooling, I went to the Spanish capital. At that time the only universities where one could study architecture were in Madrid and Barcelona. I arrived one day in 1932 at the Mediodia Station in Madrid, looking like a raw provincial, with his hands full of baggage and his heart full of hopes. I installed myself in the Sari Hotel at 2 Arenal Street, very near the Puerta del Sol.

I liked the hotel. It was situated in the very heart of Madrid, that Madrid which shortly before had called itself 'Town and Court', (the Republic had been proclaimed on 14 April 1931), and where one could still listen to the cheerful mechanical music of street organs. I settled down to my studies.

But Rome was not built in a day. Before aspiring architects

could get onto the first year of the course, they had to sit a notoriously difficult entrance examination. It was extremely challenging: not only were we required to pass all the subjects in the first two years of the Pure Sciences degree course (which included Physics, Chemistry and Geology) but we also had to take some very demanding drawing exams in the School of Architecture itself. In other words, just to be admitted to the School took years of work, and plenty of people fell by the wayside.

But as I intended to become an architect come what may, and I had to join the School of Architecture, even though I was keen neither on Mathematics nor on Physics, I was determined to devote to them as many hours as I needed to.

I retain very happy memories of my first years in the Madrid of the early thirties. It was full of surprises, the capital *par excellence*, and it preserved a singular appeal. It was curiously traditional and noble, lordly, cosmopolitan and provincial, all at the same time, which made it especially attractive for a devotee of art and architecture such as I was. It was a real delight to roam its wide avenues of an evening, to lose oneself in the Prado Museum's many galleries, or to discover the great buildings one by one – the Bank of Spain, the Casino, the Princess Theatre, the Ministry of Education, the Church of St Jerome – or to stroll slowly down Recoletos Walk or along the Castellana, that most aristocratic of all streets, which ascended to what we used to call the Hippodrome Heights.

It was still a city with a human feel to it, in which people knew each other, especially those from so-called 'good families'. When I arrived it was a time of change: the Republic had brought new faces in with it, and a lot of the old-timers, especially from the ranks of the nobility, had emigrated. Those who stayed behind had abandoned the Castellana as the focal point for their rendezvous and now car drives in Retiro Park had come into fashion.

When the nouveax riches appeared in Retiro Park, the most snobbish of the 'good families' withdrew once more, now adopting the wooded area beyond Puerta de Hierro. There the avenue might only be a makeshift affair paved with terracotta slabs, but it was graced with cars driven by chauffeurs in uniform. I was quite well acquainted with this sophisticated scene thanks to some friends of mine who lived in a second-floor flat in Almagro Street and would drive around all over Madrid in a big cream-coloured Lincoln.

Thus Madrid was a pleasing city as far as its people, its climate, its architecture went, but less so from the social point of view.

Throughout those years there was a steady rise in disturbances, tension and student unrest culminating in outright clashes and strikes. Anti-clerical feeling was gathering strength and the political skirmishes we were going through augured worse to come. Only to some people though. I myself never thought that the whole thing would end in a blood-bath. Perhaps that was because I was only a naive eighteen-year-old. In fact, if anyone had suggested to me just how much this was going to affect my own life a few years later, I would not have believed a word of it.

Ignacio de Landecho

We must not however anticipate history. In that far off year of 1932 I was simply a young student from the provinces, anxious to fit in to university life and, like all newcomers, eager to make new friends. And in the latter I was truly lucky. One of the first boys I met was one Ignacio de Landecho who, for all his youth, was a gentleman through and through. He was strong, forthright, honest and intense. He, too, was preparing for the architecture entrance exam and was assuredly one of the best friends I had in those days.

I admired the fortitude, daring and confidence with which Ignacio moved in every *milieu*. On one occasion I remember, we were watching a military parade in the Castellana from the balcony of a mutual friend's house. Two or three floors below us, also on their balcony, were some girls we knew. When they saw Ignacio they called out: "Come down Ignacio, come down!" So, without a moment's hesitation, he leaned over the railing and grasping hold of the mouldings on the facade, he let himself down from one floor to the next until he reached the girls, while we held our breath. That was Ignacio all over.

On another occasion we were on a trip to Salamanca, and when we were going up one of the Cathedral towers, he took it into his head to climb up on the outside till he reached the iron weather vane. Truth to tell, his bravery sometimes verged on the foolhardy.

I was in the same classes as he was. These were held in the science faculty which was still in a rambling old house in St Bernard Street, although there was a temporary period when we used the classrooms and workshops in the old Areneros building which the government had requisitioned from the Jesuits. We also both went to the Drawing Academy run by José Ramon Zaragoza, the painter. As we had a lot to study, quite often he also used to come to my room in the Sari Hotel so that we could work together.

Let the reader not be taken in by the pompous name of my lodgings. In actual fact the Sari Hotel was a hotel in name alone. Despite its high-sounding appellation it was just a *pension*, with three to a room and the dynamism proper to student life. As everyone knows, university students are night-birds. Quite often Ignacio and I would stay up studying the whole night through in my room and then go off to classes in St Bernard Street the following morning after breakfast.

I will never forget those descriptive geometry lessons at eight in the morning in the big house in St Bernard Street. It was still dark, and the cavernous room lit by bare electric light bulbs used to depress me terribly. Nor can I forget Luis Vegas, our teacher, who, because of his small stature, could only just manage to reach the bottom of the vast expanse of blackboard. How many hours I spent there, side by side with Ignacio, listening to the tap of chalk on the board – numbers, letters and geometric diagrams, numbers, numbers and still more numbers...!

With the passing of the years I appreciate more clearly how lucky it was for me that Ignacio and I got on so well together right from the start and that we were such good friends. We helped each other with our studies and he introduced me into some good circles in Madrid. Also, without my realising it, he led me away from friendships which were less good for me, with students who frequented the Pinar Residence and the Auditorium in Serrano Street.

Ignacio had a much better spiritual formation than I. He was the product of a good religious school and he had some relatives who were Jesuits. I had been at secular schools, and although my mother had imparted the basics of Christian living to me, I shared some of my father's opinions on religious matters.

Meeting the Father

That does not mean that in those days I was some kind of obdurate heathen. I believed in God and considered myself a Catholic. I had faith and received the sacraments now and then. But I lacked a level of religious knowledge even minimally sufficient for my years. I had picked up a certain distrustful anticlericalism from my father and was aware of having a strong prejudice against priests and religious, almost like an allergy.

I do not know how to explain the cause of this prejudice. But it was certainly there and I wanted nothing to do with 'dog-collars' as

I called them, somewhat contemptuously. The strange thing is that up till then I had never had a face-to-face conversation with one except in the confessional. And of course I had never had a regular confessor.

This wariness had always made me keep my distance from the very few priests who had crossed my path – the odd secondary-school teacher, some parish priest or other. I used to look upon them with a critical eye and I was put off by the priestly manners of the time which struck me, no doubt wrongly, as rather unnatural.

So it was that when, in 1935, three years after my arrival in Madrid, a childhood friend of mine called Agustin Tomas Moreno spoke to me very highly of Josemaria Escriva, a priest he had recently met, and offered to introduce him to me, my response was a sarcastic remark and an ironic retort springing from my self-sufficiency.

We met again, quite some time later because we did not see very much of each other. Agustin mentioned the priest again and I put him off and carried on blithely in the same vein.

Fortunately Agustin was persistent. On one of the rare occasions when we met he came out with a few deeply spiritual comments which I supposed were not the fruit of his own experience but of the priest in question. They made an impact on me despite myself. So I agreed to be introduced to him.

Everybody is as God made him. Why did I give in? I must confess that it was out of curiosity, pure and simple. I was curious by nature. I liked dealing with older people and becoming conversant with new situations, taking everything in, right down to the last detail. Of course, I went along to meet the priest with the resolute intention of not discussing personal matters with him. I was going along to see, to observe, to analyse. No more.

Agustin and I arranged to meet one afternoon towards the end of January 1935. He took me to 50 Ferraz Street in the Arguelles district. We went up to the first floor. As always I was taking note of everything. Beside the door there was a gleaming plaque which read *Academia DYA*. We went in. The entrance hall made a good first impression on me. It was not as I had thought it would be. I had imagined a large and rambling place without any warmth. Instead I found myself in the hall of a modest, middle-class family home, tastefully decorated and, above all, extremely clean. The atmosphere was cordial and relaxed. It was a good start. I liked it.

We were shown to a little sitting room where we waited for a few minutes. Soon a young, smiling priest of 30 or so, came in. He stopped for an instant, looking amiably at me over the top of his round horn-rimmed glasses, leaning forward very slightly.

"Father, this is my friend, Pedro Casciaro," Agustin said.

Then the young priest asked Agustin to excuse us for a few minutes so that we could be alone together. He made me feel as if I were somebody important.

We sat down to talk and that conversation was enough to knock aside all my reservations at one stroke, for the Father (as we all called him according to the way of addressing priests prevalent at that time) was certainly completely unlike any idea I had formed of him. I had expected an other-worldly character or something equally strange, in accord with the caricature my prejudices had painted. I found instead a young, 33 year old priest who was energetic, cordial and kind, very spontaneous and natural. Right from the start he infused into me both great confidence and, at the same time, a respect for him far beyond what I owed simply to his years. I was particularly struck by his goodness, his infectious joy, his good humour... And I poured out my heart to him as I had never done with anybody else in my whole life.

I could not say how long we talked. It was probably not more than three-quarters of an hour. I only remember telling him as I said good-bye: "Father I would like you to be my spiritual director."

Spiritual guidance

The reader should not imagine that I had a very clear idea at that stage of what the two words together, 'spiritual direction', actually meant. I know some people, such as my friend Ignacio, had it. I had also read obituaries in the ABC newspaper, which often listed among the mourners of the deceased 'his spiritual director, Fr Joe Bloggs'. That was the limit of my knowledge on the subject.

We arranged to see each other regularly. At our next meeting I realised that the initial impact he had had on me was not just a passing impression. The more I talked to the Father, divulging my innermost self to him, the more I discovered just how fine his spirituality was, how privileged his intelligence and wide his culture. And, above all, I discovered his tremendous capacity to love and his great understanding.

That was not something only I experienced. Many other friends and classmates of mine came to know him too and said similar things. Like me they immediately felt understood by the Father. It was clear to see that he really loved us and took us very seriously. He took upon himself all our concerns. He did not confine himself only to purely spiritual matters. Week after week he proved as much. At the same time as making demands on us concerning specific points of Christian asceticism, he instilled into us a deep sense of responsibility. And almost without our realising it, he was raising our standards, humanly speaking, through our contact with his own finesse and the great consideration with which he treated us.

I recall a small but quite significant detail. A few months after making my acquaintance, the Father invited me to lunch at the hall of residence. He could have done so by word of mouth or over the phone, but he preferred to send me a card with a few lines on it, inviting me to come in a caring and affectionate manner, for all the world as if I were somebody important! Nor was I a special case. That was how he treated everybody, even if they were only first year students like me!

The chapel at Ferraz Street

One day I went to have a chat with the Father and I found him particularly happy. Normally when we met I would do the talking first. The Father would listen very attentively until I had finished, without interrupting at all. He would ask me about my interior life, my studies, my parents and so on. Then he would give me his advice. Not so that day. It was he who started talking, explaining how Don Leopoldo Eijo y Garay, the bishop of Madrid, had granted the permission which they needed so as to reserve the Blessed Sacrament in the chapel of the hall of residence.

The Father had already showed me the oratory – the chapel – on my first visit with Agustin Tomas. I remember it perfectly. It was a quiet little chapel in a room off the hall which led through to a spacious, peaceful patio. Reverent, simple and pleasing, it had obviously been done with love. On the front wall above the altar, there was a painting of the disciples at Emmaus talking to the Lord. Soon afterwards it was replaced by a carved wooden statue of Our Lady of the Pillar, standing on a bracket against a backdrop of olive-green damask. As I say, I did like the oratory; but as proof of my scanty religious formation I had not noticed that it had no tabernacle.

The Father, then, was joyfully telling me about the permission he had been given. I, in all truth, had very little idea of what he was talking about. I lacked the necessary Christian formation for understanding when and how the Blessed Sacrament could be reserved in a sacred place. As I listened to him I was wondering to myself how it could be; for if there were a single institution in Madrid where the faith was really lived out in a wonderful way – I thought – it was in that same residence, and if there were an exceptionally holy and intelligent priest, it was the one I had in front of me at that moment. So, in my ignorance, I concluded that the bishop really should have given his permission sooner!

"Father is the Blessed Sacrament left overnight in churches?" I inquired.

This question made my tremendous ignorance on religious matters only too plain. Later on I asked him how long the Lord could be left alone in the oratory, because I had noticed that in some churches at times there was nobody there at all. I kept on asking questions of this kind and others that were more simple-minded still. With tremendous patience the Father resolved all my rudimentary doubts. He spoke at length about the Eucharist in words which revealed his deep and sincere devotion to Jesus in the Blessed Sacrament.

Our Lord must never feel lonely or forgotten here, even if he sometimes is in some churches, he said warmly. *Here, in this house, where so many students live and so many young people come, he will be happy, in the midst of all our devotion. You help me to keep him company.*

I was moved by his ardent love for the Eucharist. Since I passed fairly near the residence on my way to the School of Architecture, I decided enthusiastically to pop into the oratory as often as I could, to pray for a while in front of the Tabernacle, as the Father encouraged us to do. It must have been then that he dictated to me the words of the spiritual communion:

I wish, Lord, to receive you with the purity, humility and devotion with which your most holy Mother received you, with the spirit and fervour of the saints.

Soon afterwards, on 31 March 1935, the Father was able to celebrate his first Mass in the chapel and the Blessed Sacrament was reserved in the Work's first tabernacle. It was a very simple wooden tabernacle, which some nuns had lent the Father. Mingled with his joy, he felt an acute sorrow at not being able to dedicate a more dignified tabernacle and sacred vessels to the Lord, because he always wanted to offer God *a sacrifice like Abel's*, using only the best for divine worship.

Years later he stated: *The altar and the tabernacle ought to be good, if at all possible. At first we could not manage that. The first monstrance was made of iron, painted over in silver paint: only the centrepiece for the Host was gold-plated. The first tabernacle was made of wood... an Atonement nun, whom I loved very much, lent it to me. How upset I was to be offering up such a poor thing to our Lord!*

God in everyday life

Through weekly spiritual guidance the Father was bringing me closer to the Lord, helping me to improve my relationship with God. Not all of a sudden, but little by little, patiently, with an intensity which increased with time, without rushing things but without slackening off either. He was teaching me how to pray for a little while every day; how to converse with the Lord and keep up a continuous awareness of being in His presence throughout my day as a normal ordinary student. With regard to this last, one day I brought up the difficulty I had over it.

"You see, Father, when I really get down to something, I put all I've got into it and completely forget everything else."

That was true. When I was studying, I would get so engrossed in my books that the hours flew by without a single reference to the Lord. Even while drawing I was so wrapped up with the problems of descriptive geometry that it seemed to me there was no room in my mind for anything else.

In reply the Father presented me with a crucifix, which I still have, for me to carry around in my pocket and place on my desk or on the drawing board.

Glance at the crucifix now and again, or say a few aspirations, and you will be able to turn your work into prayer.

What about remembering that I was in the Lord's presence as I walked through the streets? That was not too easy either. I loved walking around Madrid gazing at the facades, studying the structure of the buildings or analysing the architectural hits and misses which I found along the way. And the Father was asking me to do all this *and* be absorbed in God, all at the same time! But how?

Let's see, he said. *Tell me exactly which streets you go along, from Castello Street, where you live, to the School of Architecture or the University.*

I started to recall them: First of all I turned down Goya Street and went down it is far as the Castellana and... He then listed the images of the Blessed Virgin which I could locate on my way:

In Goya Street there is a pastry shop, just round the corner from Castello Street, which has a figure of the Immaculate Conception in a niche. When you reach the statue of Christopher Columbus, as you cross the Castellana, you will find on one of the bas-reliefs round the pedestal of the statue a scene of the Catholic King and Queen, where there is an image of Our Lady of the Pillar; and as you go up the Boulevards...

I was amazed. I, who observed everything so carefully, had not even noticed the existence of those images which could help me to remember God's presence on my daily round. Then I realised that this was not simply the result of the Father's keen powers of observation. Only a soul in love with our Lady could have detected them. From that day on I tried to put into practice what he told me. Little by little, my working hours acquired a new supernatural meaning, and my walks through the streets of Madrid, new contemplative perspectives, totally unsuspected until then.

The DYA Academy

By frequenting the house, I gradually came to know its short history. Nearly 18 months previously, at the beginning of December 1933, the DYA Academy had opened in a building facing on to Luchana St and Juan de Austria St. Later, in October 1934, the Academy was moved to where it now was, at 50 Ferraz St, on the corner of Quintana St, near the university campus. Rooms for student accommodation had been added.

Three apartments had been rented in the same building: two on the first floor where the hall of residence was; another, on the second floor, to house the Academy. The landlord was a man called Bordiu, a mining engineer with lots of children, some of them already grown up. He lived in the same building on the ground floor. Bordiu prided himself on being descended from the Luna family which had produced the anti-Pope whom he affectionately termed "Uncle Peter".

From the financial point of view setting up the residence had been – though I only discovered this much later – a veritable odyssey. In September 1934, a few months before I first set foot in the house, only the absolute essentials, the dining room, a sitting room for visitors, the hall and one bedroom had yet been furnished. The remaining rooms stood empty, awaiting better times, bare except for some very unassuming lamps with spherical white shades ribbed with metal pretending to be bamboo. All the kitchen equipment and the tableware were still to be bought. Even so the Father's example comforted everybody, for he overflowed with faith, security, optimism and trust in God.

One of the maddest things I've ever done, the Father remarked sometime later, *was opening a students' residence without a penny to buy all the things I needed to run it: all the linen, the furniture, the tableware and bed clothes.*

He scraped through the dearth of finances as best he could. Bed-linen was acquired on credit from a shop called *Almacenes Simeon* where an old acquaintance of the Father worked. His name was Casimiro Ardanuy and he was the son of the baker who had delivered bread to the Escriva home in Barbastro. But where could the linen be stored? *We had no cupboards to keep it in*, the Father recalled later. *So we had very carefully laid some newspapers on the floor and the linen, a huge quantity of it, on top of them. I thought then that it was a huge quantity. Now it would seem ridiculously little. And on top we spread some more newspapers to keep the dust off.*

Naturally they awaited the arrival of the students as for rain after a drought, thinking that everything would then begin to function smoothly. But at the beginning of that academic year, in October 1934, the so called Asturian Revolution broke out. As Maranon pointed out it was 'an attempt carried out according to a communist plan, to take over Spain'. It was successful only in Asturias. But it had been intended for the whole country right from the start. There was a fierce attack on the Church: fifty-eight churches were destroyed and thirty-four priests assassinated. As a result there was a general strike under the cloak of revolution which forced the University to postpone the beginning of the academic year.

Thus there were only one or two students in DYA at the beginning of term. Then, as calm was restored, a few more came, until there were five altogether at the end of the first term. The rest arrived in dribs and drabs, reaching a total of fourteen or fifteen. So the budgetary calculations collapsed completely and there were times when the Director – Ricardo Fernandez Vallespin, a young architect – preferred to take Alberto, one of the first residents, to eat in a local restaurant because it was cheaper than feeding him at home. The months passed remorselessly and the situation grew more and more difficult. Residents did not arrive but the invoices did. There was one month that they started off with fifty pesetas in the cash box. And then there was the rent to pay, at four hundred pesetas a month for each flat.

Despite these difficulties the Father remained undaunted. He continued to carry the apostolate forward day after day, full of faith and trust in the Lord. *When we seek God only, we need not be afraid to promote works of zeal, by putting into practice the principle laid down by a good friend of ours: Spend all that you ought, though you owe all that you spend,* he wrote later in *The Way*.

When I appeared in the Residence at the beginning of 1935, I obviously could not even begin to suspect anything of all this. I only know that the name DYA Academy and Residence stood for Law (Derecho) and Architecture (y Arquitectura). But it also had a deeper meaning. The Father explained: *For people generally it means Law and Architecture because we really do have lessons in those subjects. But for us it means God (Dios) and Daring (y Audacia).* It was quite clear that the Father had undertaken this apostolic enterprise trusting only in God and with great supernatural daring.

The Circles

One of those empty rooms which I mentioned before, had been turned into a classroom. There, together with some other students, I started to attend some gatherings with the Father – *Circles or whatever you want to call them (the name is the least important thing),* he told us – in which he talked to us about looking at things from a supernatural viewpoint, sanctity in the midst of everyday living, sanctifying our work, and our prayer life.

What were those classes like? I remember that at the beginning the Father would help us to go over the subject discussed in the previous Circle. There were talks about some aspect of Christian life: interior life, prayer, the Eucharist study... I retain a vivid and indelible memory of those Circles: the Father's words and the strikingly concrete and vivid examples he used. Week upon week, Saturday by Saturday, Circle after Circle, he urged us to carry out an intense apostolate with our peers, showing us how to love God, and fostering in us the desire to live a truly Christian life.

It was obvious that what he said to us did not come solely from study or from his wide experience of souls but also from his own deep interior life and prayer. Many are the times when I have been reading *The Way* that I have remembered what he said to us in those Circles.

The very first point provides an excellent example: *Don't let your life be barren. Be useful. Make yourself felt. Shine forth with the torch of your faith and your love. With your apostolic life, wipe out the trail of filth and slime left by the unclean sowers of hatred. And set aflame the ways of the earth with the fire of Christ that you bear in your heart.*

In his talks the Father often referred to *the fire of the love of God*. He used to tell us we had to spread that fire to all souls by word and example, without bothering about what people would think of us. He also asked us if among our friends we could not count a few who would understand the formation which was being given in the Residence. At the end of the Circle he would ask one of those present to read a few pages from a spiritual book such as *The Imitation of Christ*.

My doubts

Meanwhile I continued my spiritual guidance with the Father. I always tried to raise some doubt or query by way of additional material, outside my normal confession, so he could answer it for me. If I did not, I felt as though I was cheating him. However, one of the first effects of his spiritual guidance was to uncomplicate surprisingly my involved mode of being; thus it became more difficult to raise queries because, one after the other, all my doubts were being cleared up.

On one such occasion, for lack of a more satisfactory dilemma, it occurred to me to ask for advice about a family matter. My father, like all civil servants, was very attached to his rank and followed my choice of career with real anguish. "An architect!," he would say, time and again. "And what if one day there is a crisis in the construction industry? Or if you can't build up a good clientele, what financial security will you have? What you ought to do is carry on and get a Science degree as you have already done the first two years of it. That way if you have problems with architecture in the future you'll still have another string to your bow. Listen to me, Pedro, do listen to me."

Truth to tell, my father's suggestion was not much to my liking. I was willing to do the first two years of the science degree because it was a sine qua non for getting into Architecture. But 'Maths/Physics', as we called it, was for me just that: an entry requirement, and that was it.

I mentioned this to the Father. Contrary to my expectations, he thought my father's advice extremely well-founded. Even though he understood that it would mean a great effort for me, he explained what a good idea it was from the spiritual point of view to have a demanding time-table. He said that this way I would avoid the pitfalls of too laid-back or 'bourgeois' a life-style, so common then among students who had succeeded in getting into a specialised school. He talked to me about the apostolate I could do among my fellow students in the science faculty. *If you can manage it, it would please your father. But think it over.*

Those words were a kind of challenge and fired me up enough to enrol the following year for third year in Maths/Physics.

Later on I mentioned this to Paco Botella, one of my classmates from Architecture. I thought that if he signed up as well, the course would be less boring. Paco immediately took heart, for although he had greater aptitude than I had for mathematics, he had not been all that keen on it either. So we decided to do both – Architecture and Maths/Physics the following year.

My friends

Following the advice of the Father, who encouraged me to be actively apostolic with my friends and companions, I tried to talk about God with those I was closest to. Nevertheless with all my good will, I did not succeed in awakening any spiritual desires in some of them or in getting them to shake off their accustomed levity. On the other hand there were some who did come to the Ferraz St Residence. Among them were José Rebollo Dicenta, Miguel Fisac, Mariano Alvarez Nunez and several others.

Naturally Ignacio de Landecho was one of the first friends I invited along. He began coming to the Circles the Father gave and immediately became very fond of the Father. I was not surprised. I cannot think of a single person who got to know the Father reasonably well without being captivated by his cheerfulness, his constant good humour, his extraordinary way with people and his love of freedom.

Concerning this last point, I should like to observe that I was very independent. My self-reliance was due both to my character and to the way in which I had been brought up. Perhaps that was why the Father's teaching on valuing people's freedom of conscience was so dear to me. He was always reminding us that love of freedom consists above all in defending other people's freedom.

The Father was revealing the demands of the Christian life to me without forcing it into a strait-jacket, not smothering it under rigid norms or predetermined mind-sets. He helped me to live an increasingly devout life without ever diminishing or submerging any of my legitimate human aspirations. On the contrary, he made it more possible for me to achieve them.

He also helped me to see how much I had received from God in those first twenty years of my life. He enhanced my parents in my eyes and taught me to appreciate and be grateful for the sacrifices they were making to enable me to take a degree, which in those times was particularly costly. That was all part of God's providence he told me, for God our Father loves us more than all the mothers on earth.

He also talked to me about the need to be a saint, without behaving oddly, right where I was, in the world, by sanctifying my classes, the hours I spent drawing and studying, and, in the future, my professional work. He emphasised that holiness was not the sole preserve of a few, nor was it restricted to certain states in life. He put all these things over in a cordial, affable, open and expansive manner.

The reader must be wondering how I responded to all of this. There is a point of *The Way* which very fittingly reflects what my reactions often were. *How frankly you laughed when I advised you to put your youthful years under the protection of St Raphael, "so that he'll lead you, like young Tobias, to a holy marriage with a girl who is good and pretty – and rich", I told you jokingly. And then how thoughtful you became when I went on to advise you to put yourself under the patronage of that young apostle John, in case God were to ask more of you.*

As far as the last point – vocation – went, the Father never said anything about it to me, even less about a vocation to Opus Dei. I considered that I was already doing as much as I could in that department. Since I started going to Ferraz St, I had been following a kind of plan for my life: I struggled to live cleanly; I was getting regular spiritual guidance; I tried to have an apostolic influence on my friends and fellow students; and I felt very close, in a brotherly way, to those who attended the Circles with me. I had arrived at the upper limit, the loftiest spiritual ceiling that one could aspire to – or so I thought.

CHAPTER 3

Summer in Torrevieja

At Los Hoyos

At the end of June 1935 when the innumerable exams were over and the academic year ended, I went, as I always did, to spend my holidays on the Los Hoyos Estate. There the whole family came together over the summer months. It was a big place, situated on the outskirts of the village near the coast. It had one surprising peculiarity – it was surrounded by a wall several kilometres long with sentry boxes and peep holes at the correct intervals and perfectly designed for firing from. Actually it could only have occurred to a 19th century gentleman, and English at that, in this case my great grandfather Peter, to build such a rampart in Torrevieja. It surrounded the property completely, as if he had been afraid of the natives attacking. But such a long time had elapsed since the building of those extraordinary battlements that the local people had grown used to them. They were part of the countryside and people called them the Hoyos Stockade or simply 'the stockade'.

Inside 'the stockade' there was a little of everything. There was a garden with iron railings round it; a big house built in lordly neo-classical style, dating from the first half of the last century; a shrine dedicated to St Joseph, and behind the shrine, the family mausoleum. The pantheon was so near the house that the family never dared bury any of itsdead there. (Grandfather Julio used it as an arsenal for his fishing tackle, and since the crypt was pleasantly cool, as somewhere to have his siesta in the summer.) There were other constructs as well; to wit, an oil-mill for making olive oil, several granaries, and houses for the guard and the gardener, not forgetting the wine-store, the water-wheel with the typical donkeys and paddles, the ponds, the windmills for pumping water from the wells, as well as all kinds of pens with different animals in them. It was a splendid place. There were scores of almond trees, fig trees, and especially palm trees – whole groves of palm trees. The only thing that remains to be included in the inventory is my grandfather's greenhouse which sheltered thousands of cacti of different varieties and species, and where he spent many daylight hours lovingly tending his spiky plants. We enjoyed long pleasure-filled holidays there, such as, it seems to me, were only possible in Spain before the civil war, despite the political confusion current even then.

I said earlier that 'the whole family' gathered there. I mean that quite literally: my grandparents, six uncles and aunts, five of whom were married, as well as my cousins, my parents, my brother José María and I, all stayed at Los Hoyos over the summer. Often there would be more than twenty-five of us at meal times!

Summer passed slowly and peacefully. In the mornings I used to go swimming or rowing in a canoe that my Merchant Navy uncle had given me. In the afternoons I used to take part in our very long, placid, family get-together, when everybody joined in and we were lulled by the cool breeze from the east.

We talked about everything under the sun but especially about politics. Each one of us took a different position. Grandfather Julio was the living image of disappointment over the Republic that he had so often dreamed of. My uncles championed their diverse opinions and discussed daily developments. Nevertheless, even though there were many varying viewpoints among us, our conversations were always good-natured. We shared a common concern over the perilous turn of events the country was witnessing.

In the evenings I would go for a walk by the spas or along the sea-front with young men and women that I knew. Sometimes there would be dancing in the square which had a small open-air pavilion where the band played 'habaneras', the Afro-Cuban dance tunes.

Other times we would go to the cinema, which was quite good. I had a tacit agreement with my Aunt Maruja, my father's youngest sister, who was single and not much older than I was, (she had made her first Communion at my parent's wedding Mass). She ferried me to and fro, between Torrevieja and Los Hoyos. In theory, I was supposed to be looking after my youthful aunt; in practice, it was she who took care of me, running me around in her Peugeot. My aunt really furnished a rather unusual picture for those days. For it was not common to see a woman at the wheel, even less a young one, out and about, driving her own car.

I had several letters from friends from Ferraz St during the summer months. The Father used to add a few lines in is own hand and enclose a copy of *Noticias*, a little newsletter of several book-sized pages, printed with gelatine plates in violet-coloured ink.

With family-like intimacy it contained accounts of what we were all doing. Despite the passing of the years I well remember those 2 or 3 pages, printed on the rudimentary jellygraph in the Residence. Nobody knows what a jellygraph is nowadays. In an old dictionary you might find this definition: it is "a copying appliance that uses a plate of jelly in a tray".

How I enjoyed reading, and re-reading, in my room those numbers of *Noticias* posted to me! In the July number they quoted a letter of mine, half jokingly, half in earnest: "Pedro Casciaro writes, 'I have written to you many times in my head, as I think I can truthfully say that not a single day has passed without it crossing my mind.' He is in Torrevieja (Alicante) sighing for his beloved Albacete. Round about 20 August we shall see him back, sun-tanned and filled out a bit! He thanks us for the greetings we sent him, but grumbles about others who are conspicuous by their silence. 'They are a passive lot.' Just as well God keeps me bright and cheerful in spite of so much ingratitude!', he says."

Those lines from the Father, the newsletter written amusingly as befitted our age, yet with spiritual substance, and the letters from the others with their news, were all a source of much spiritual encouragement. They gave me zest for apostolate and new strength to keep to most of my spiritual plan of life, the same plan that, with the Father's help, I had managed to follow during the academic year.

Among other things, the Father urged us to use our time well and to learn other languages. That summer I remember writing a letter, in the language of Shakespeare, to a friend of mine, Mariano Alvarez Nuñez, who was holidaying in Cuellar, a town in the province of Segovia. Mariano couldn't tell them fast enough in Madrid about the letter, and my linguistic prowess was cited in the next number of *Noticias*: "Casciaro writes to him in English!, instructing him to reply in English as well. They're aiming high!" They also said that my friend, Mariano, spent his afternoons "playing the fiddle, though we are not sure if he plays it in English or not."

There in Torrevieja, in the usual enervating summer weather, the teachings the Father conveyed to us through *Noticias* were a continual reminder to me not to let myself be carried away by my surroundings. At the beginning of the August number he wrote: *Be persevering in your prayer and study and, like that, next year we will be sure that our Lord will give our apostolate a push forward*

*which will be beyond anything we had hoped for. Don't forget that
we still have a lot to do... and it would be terrible to hear Jesus say,
as the paralytic did at the Probatic pool: 'Non habeo hominum', I
cannot find anyone able to help me.*

Though the mountains

What did I know then about the Opus Dei which had been
founded seven years before, on 2 October 1928? My acquaintance
with it boiled down to the following. I had had spiritual guidance
from the Father on a regular basis. I had attended fifteen circles, and
four or five friends of mine, fellow students in the School of
Architecture, had come to Ferraz St. Nevertheless, even though I
had only been going to the Residence a short time, the Father had
got me to enter into the Work's concerns and I considered them as
my own.

I knew the essentials. I knew Opus Dei was a way towards
holiness in the midst of the world for ordinary Christians through
sanctifying their everyday work. The Father explained it to us in
these or similar words ones: *The divine paths of the earth have been
opened up.*

What did we have to do to become saints? The Father had told
us in many different ways, but it can be summed up admirably in
this one phrase of his: *Get to know Jesus Christ; make him known,
take him into every place.* It was because he foresaw the rapid
growth of the Work that he frequently urged us to learn languages,
even the less common ones like Japanese.

Although I did not belong to the Work, in a way I felt part of it;
not just one person in a small group owing its existence to particular local conditions of the moment, but part of an incipient
apostolic undertaking that would perdure for all time. The Father
shared with us his universal longing for apostolate. He had got us to
pray for the future expansion of the Work. We knew that the
learning of languages, such as German and Russian which he also
insisted on, had a compelling apostolic *raison d'etre.* Opus Dei had
to spread to all four corners of the earth.

So, although those holiday months were as pleasant and as much
fun as in past years, they also had a different quality. In that relaxed
and easy-going atmosphere, I was aware of the absence of the
spiritual striving and great ideals which the Father was passing on
to us. Caught up by his holy impatience for Jesus to be loved, I too
desired to make Him known and to take Him to thousands of souls.

This is reflected in a point in *The Way*: *So it is, so it has be, with the horizon of your apostolate: the world has to be crossed. But there are no paths made for you. You yourselves will make the way through the mountains with the impact of your feet.*

Through the mountains... I realise now that I had not queried then exactly how this future growth of Opus Dei was to happen. Nevertheless I was certain the Work *would* spread to all five continents one day. How? I had no idea. But I was convinced that one day it would be so. Of that I had no doubt. It was part of the faith I had in the Father's words. When would it happen? I thought then that its expansion would occur many years later, and I suspected I would hardly witness it in my own lifetime. As can be seen, I had understood the basics about Opus Dei. But little did I appreciate what the Father meant when he said to us: *Dream and your dreams will fall short.*

Yet, despite my lack of vision, I did want to help the Work grow insofar as I was able. Deep down, I felt an increasing desire to make our Lord known. Indeed, I too wanted to take Jesus everywhere! But I did not know how to. And I wondered how in the future I would be able to make the demands of family and profession compatible with the burgeoning desire to participate somehow in the work of apostolate. I experienced a strange yearning; it was the same old itch for adventure, except that now it was for a much higher and more noble ideal than when I gazed out across the blue sea at the steamships laden with salt, sailing out from the Torrevieja Port for unknown lands...

CHAPTER 4

The call

And what if God...

In the September issue of *Noticias* the Father wrote: *Jesus expects a lot from you in this new academic year. You will be able to give it all to him, if you are faithful to our spirit of piety and work.*

From September onwards, I was back at my books in Madrid. There I met Miguel Fisac, who had stayed in the capital all summer long and had continued going to the Residence assiduously. He seemed rather restive and, as we knew each other very well, I asked him what the matter was. He explained that he was considering the possibility of becoming a member of Opus Dei.

Being a member of Opus Dei! That was something new to me. Then I understood that at the heart of the apostolate in the Residence there was a small group of students and professional men who had given their lives to God. Here was the way to make those apostolic ideals I had dreamt of in Torrevieja a reality.

My friend was in the throes of a vocational crisis, asking himself if this was really what God wanted of him. I tried to soothe him. But, trying to calm him down, I came to feel troubled myself. I began to wonder, "And what if God should call me to take that path? What if...?"

I thought that the best way of settling my growing anxiety was to ask the Father about it. For, I repeat, the Father had never made the slightest suggestion along those lines. Nor had he given me any specific advice or directives. Even though it was he who had sown in my soul a profound desire to seek sanctity at all costs, and the urge to know and love God's will and to respond as generously as I could to the Lord, he had always left me completely free. I had never spoken directly about the possibility of my giving my life to God in Opus Dei.

I felt completely at sea. Evidently it was I who was thinking all this. But was it only I? What if it was our Lord who was behind all this chafing, and it was He who was asking me for something? And if that *were* the case, what was the 'something' He was asking me for?

I went to see the Father, and related my unease. He listened to me calmly serene. The only thing he advised me to do was to resume my habitual plan of life – which had grown rather cold over the summer – and to try to begin the term with a great desire to work hard. He also suggested leaving all my worries in the Lord's hands, since He is God of peace.

Restored to a relative degree of tranquillity, I continued visiting the Residence where some changes had taken place. The house was now full of students lodging there, many of them from Bilbao. So many university students were coming to the various types of spiritual formation which the Father offered, that the Circles took place wherever there was a free room, because there were times when we hardly fitted in the house.

Meanwhile, I went on talking to the Father, who was helping me overcome the spiritual decline which often results from summer holidays. He encouraged me to live in God's grace and not forsake a short plan of life which as yet did not include Communion daily, but just on Sundays and sometimes Saturdays.

I started to struggle with those aspects of my Christian life with renewed effort; but I found that as I grew closer to the Lord, my uneasiness about a possible self-giving to God in Opus Dei welled up once more in my soul. Then, perhaps to counteract that spiritual agitation, I tried to enjoy myself for the next few weeks. Perhaps I went too far. I went to the cinema often with friends who did not go to Ferraz St, such as Emilio Carnicero, José Jimenez Fernandez, Pepe Buso or Paco Botella. We spent more money than normal, to the point that Paco's father wrote him a letter saying that this friend of his, Pedro Casciaro, might well be a great chap as he said, but that since becoming friends with me he was becoming a complete spendthrift...!

Paco Botella

I must pause at this point and concentrate on Paco Botella. I had met him a few years earlier in the School of Architecture when we were in the same class for a term. He was tall, thin and pleasant, a lively but precise speaker. He had a high forehead and wore quite thick glasses. As often happens at the beginning of so many friendships, I do not think he was particularly inclined towards me at first: during a water-colour painting class I said, in typical student banter, that his drawing of Moses was coming out very well. In fact, he was copying a Venus. My barbed witticism evidently did not please him too much.

My attitude towards him changed when I saw him going to Communion one day in the parish church of the Immaculate Conception which was very near my lodgings. I realised that he might perhaps appreciate the apostolate going on at the Residence.

Everything favoured our friendship. We were the same age. He was from Valencia and though I was born in Murcia, I had roots in Alicante. We were studying for the same two degrees – Architecture and Maths/Physics – and we lived almost next door to each other. Paco was in a hall of residence at 39 Castello St; I in number 35, two doors down.

Paco came to see me on 11 October. He told me that he knew I was talking to the Father. He had noticed that some evenings after classes had finished in Areneros at 6.30 p.m., instead of heading towards the boulevards, a group of friends and I would go down the Alcala Martyrs' Street near the Liria Palace. He had inquired as to where we went and what we did there; and Salvador Segura, another friend who also frequented Ferraz St, had told him all about it. I said that I had been thinking of inviting him to come along to the Residence, and told him abut the work of apostolate which the Father was promoting. He asked me to arrange a time for him to go, which I did. The Father met him two days later on the 13th at 5 p.m. He started coming to the Circles on Saturdays and our friendship grew.

It was a year of hard work. We had such a packed timetable for classes that there was not so much as a free minute. Paco and I were always in a rush: from the house to the university, from there to the School of Architecture and back again to the university. We used to go everywhere together, the Ferraz Residence included.

Both of us also went, with other classmates from the School, to spend three days in Toledo. Before going I took leave of the Father. He advised me to make the most of those days, to do as much good as I could to my friends. He also said I should try to go to Mass.

It was a wonderful three days. We did a lot of sketching in the city, with its ochre-coloured buildings clustered around the cathedral and almost entirely surrounded by the riverbed of the Tagus. I thought it was splendid, as though time had stood still there. I loved the cathedral, the Alcazar, the synagogues, the famous country houses on the banks of the Tagus; so much so that, at the end of the trip, Paco and I decided to stay two days longer. During this time we talked a lot about the Father and the vocation to Opus Dei as we wandered up and down the steep winding city streets or downed coffees in Zocodover Square.

Paco's restlessness brought mine from a few weeks earlier to the surface again. Paco had been turning over the question of a vocation for years. In fact, he had come to Madrid with the inner certainly that it would be there that God would make him see his vocation. My spiritual disquiet was equally intense, though much more recent. Anyway, we were both facing the possibility, in all its radicalness, of giving ourselves completely to God.

A day of recollection

On our return to Madrid I decided to attend a monthly day of recollection which the Father preached in the Residence for those of us who frequented Ferraz St. Paco came too. Years later he recorded his impressions with some very precise details. The day of recollection was on a Sunday. "The Father spoke in the oratory on a single central theme in all the meditations and talks. That topic was vocation." He talked about the rich young man who refused to respond to the Lord's call and went away sad; the Father encouraged us to be generous with God. Paco notes that the love of God, which shone through the Father's words, "took us with a force which was supernatural." "He spoke," Paco continues, "about sacrifice, about the Lord's Cross and about mortification." And he adds a final detail which is particularly significant. "He always ended by looking for the support and courage we needed in our Lady."

The Father's sturdy marian devotion had also impressed me deeply. Through countless words and gestures, he sought to pass on his great love for the Mother of God to us as well. A text he wrote years later bears this out. In it he evokes his devotion to a small statue of the Blessed Virgin which he had on a desk in the Residence. He used to call it "the Virgin of the kisses". The Father wrote: *In the first residence we had, I never went in or out without going to the Director's room, where the statue was, so I could kiss it. I don't think I ever did it mechanically. My kisses were human kisses, the kisses of a son who was afraid... But since I've said so often that I'm not afraid of anyone or anything, let's not say I was afraid. They were kisses from a son who felt far too young and who needed all the tenderness of our Lady's affection. All the strength I needed, I sought from God through the Blessed Virgin.*

As with Paco, that day of recollection was decisive for me. In the first meditation on the rich young man I saw quite clearly that I could not do what the young man in the Gospel did – cling to what I had got or might get – and go away sad. At the end of the recollection I sought out the Father and asked him to let me be a member of Opus Dei.

Again the Father advised me to be at peace. He said it was better for me to wait a little and in the meantime to intensify my spiritual plan of life. For how long? At first he spoke in terms of one month.

A whole month! It seemed so long. I asked him to make it shorter. Could it not be in weeks? Four, three, two... It was a real battle.

"Father," I explained to him, "since I began wondering about a vocation I've had no peace. I can't concentrate on my studies, and these days I have a lot of study to do!"

I insisted so much that I achieved a shortening of the term to nine days. He advised me to make a novena before coming to a decision.

Nine days? At that moment nine days seemed an eternity to me. Couldn't it be fewer?

Do a triduum, he conceded finally. *Commend yourself to the Holy Spirit and act in full freedom, because where the Spirit of the Lord is, there is freedom.* He spoke a lot about freedom and advised me to ask God, as I received Holy Communion over the next three days, for the necessary graces so as to make my decision freely. *In libertate vocati estis,* he said, we have been called in freedom, as Scripture teaches.

I started the triduum to the Holy Spirit on Monday, 18 November. When I finished it, my decision to give myself to God in Opus Dei was reaffirmed. I decided to make a formal request to the Father for admission to the Work.

The Father had already told me that the way to ask for admission to Opus Dei was by a hand-written letter addressed to him. Naturally, people who were asking to join gave him their letters by hand. I do not know why, but I thought I had to send my letter through the post and wait for reply. Which is what I did. I wrote the letter, posted it in the Plaza de la Cibeles, as true Madrilenos call it. I calculated that the Father would get it the next day. So, I thought, that when I went to Ferraz St again to talk to the Father five days later, he would have had enough time to consider his answer.

During those uncertain and expectant days I talked things over with Paco. Years later he still remembered everything that happened very accurately. He relates in his memoirs: "Pedro and I were walking along the Gran Via in the pouring rain, with no umbrellas, talking about the Father, about apostolate. This topic nearly always came up, after class, on the way to art exhibitions, or when we went to the cinema at night and returned home slowly, on foot. That day I told Pedro I could not stand God's pressure any longer... I had to make up my mind. Pedro told me that he had almost decided already. I asked him what he had decided. And he just took the time to say, 'I'll carry on with architecture', before running off at full tilt and leaving me standing there. I turned towards home, soaking wet, not knowing what to think."

Shortly afterwards, on the same day that I was supposed to talk to the Father, Paco and I were studying together before lunch in his hall of residence. I seem to recall that we were working on some cosmography experiments. Paco did the calculations on a blackboard and I looked up the corresponding logarithms. But I was unable to concentrate. I was thinking about my vocation the whole time, constantly losing the thread and making mistakes. I could not keep my finger on the right line in the log tables, the result being that Paco ended up losing his temper with me. I apologised, telling him my mind was elsewhere because that day was the most decisive in my life. When he heard that, he became worried and asked me over and over again what was up.

"I was a nuisance, it's true," Paco recalls. "Pedro told me he had decided to follow our Lord's call to him to join the Work and that he was going to see the Father that same afternoon. What Work?, I asked. Very briefly, but perfectly clearly, he told me what the Work was: to live one's Christian life authentically, giving oneself to the Lord totally, while continuing in the world as before, more committed to it than ever, yet carrying the Lord in one's heart at every moment of the day, while at work, and while doing apostolate, which he explained as being like that of the early Christians. The Father was its founder. The Work had been born in 1928," and, Paco concludes, "now I understood what the Father was doing in those few square metres of the Ferraz Residence. I realised it was the beginning of a universal enterprise."

As soon as I had explained the Work to Paco, I asked him what he thought of my decision. As he had much more religious formation than I had, I realise now that his answer could have had a lot of influence on me, for better or for worse. But he refused to comment. He only listened to me with great interest, and asked various questions.

I kept on insisting: "But, Paco, what do you think? Tell me clearly."

He was not to be drawn. That surprised me. When we said good-bye, he became very thoughtful.

After lunch we met again in a Maths lecture. We left before it ended and continued talking about my vocation as we went along the boulevards in the direction of Ferraz St. It was then that Paco told we that he too was going to ask for admission to the Work.

"You as well?"

I felt great surprise and a great joy. But first of all he had to talk to the Father, and Paco wanted me to tell him. When we got to 50 Ferraz Street he kept insisting.

"Tell the Father that I want to join the Work. Tell him. Pedro, tell him!"

That night I telephoned Paco to tell him that the Father would see him at 6 p.m., three days later. And so it was, three days later, that he talked to the Father, who let him ask for admission to Opus Dei immediately.

The speed of it was quite a surprise to me. Later I understood that it was perfectly fair, taking into account Paco's deep religious formation and his long desire to give himself fully. And so, thanks to this chain of circumstances and apparent coincidences, we both ended up asking for admission to Opus Dei at practically the same time.

Before going off to spend Christmas with our families, Paco and I broached to the Father the possibility of our going to live in Ferraz after the holidays. He thought it was a good idea, but first we had to sort out a few problems. Paco depended on a cousin of his who lived in the same Hall as he did. I had to get permission from my parents to arrange the financial side. The Father told us he would pray for satisfactory solutions to our difficulties.

During the Christmas holidays Paco received an apostolic assignment: the Father asked him to inform the auxiliary bishop of Valencia, Monsignor Javier Lauzurica, of his wish to begin apostolate in that city.

The holidays over and family difficulties overcome, at the beginning of 1936 I went to live in the Residence. Paco came as well; he lodged in the flat at number 48 in the same street, as part of the Academy had just moved there.

We were beginning a new life. As the Father had said, it was the beginning of a marvellous adventure.

CHAPTER 5

First steps

The first members

What was Opus Dei in that January of 1936? Now the Work has spread throughout the five continents and there are thousands upon thousands of people, single, married and priests, who have followed the Lord's call and strive to sanctify themselves in their work, in the middle of the world. We can also count in thousands the apostolic undertakings which have developed as a result both of that spirit which God entrusted to the Father and of Opus Dei members' personal apostolate. But then, there were only a few of us around the Father, very few indeed. Just a handful of young men, mainly undergraduate, and one or two who had recently graduated. The apostolate with women which had begun in 1930, was also taking its first steps.

Who were we? Among others, I remember Alvaro del Portillo, who was then just a young twenty-one year old Civil Engineering student. The director of the Residence was Ricardo Fernandez Vallespin, a twenty-five year old architect. Then there was Juan Jimenez Vargas, a medical student. He was twenty-two, active, resolute, a man of few words. There was José María Hernandez Garnica, an engineering student, whom we called by his nickname Chiqui. He was twenty-one, almost my own age. José María Gonzalez Barredo was a chemist and little older: he was twenty-nine, and doing a doctorate. There were others, but only a few. At that time I also heard them talk a lot about Isidoro Zorzano, another member of Opus Dei. He was a young engineer, of the same age as the Father, who had been in the same class as him at secondary school. He lived in Malaga where he was working for the Andalusian Railway Company.

The Father was young too. He was thirty-three, and he did not refer to himself as the founder. Even though he did not like to use the expression, it was clear to everybody that he was the person chosen by God to carry out the Work; as clear as was the fact that there were still very few of us for the thousands upon thousands of men and women whom God wanted to call to Opus Dei. Neverthe-

less, though we numbered so few, we did not form a closed circle.
The Father continually encouraged us to open out like a fan and not
to isolate ourselves from our friends and fellow students.

One day, at the beginning of 1936, I asked the Father how many
of us there were altogether, and in consequence what rank I held.
Detecting the lack of humility which my question implied, the
Father replied with an answer which impressed rather than
disconcerted me. This is what he conveyed to me:

*I have met, I have come to know deeply, and I have guided
many souls of gravely and terminally ill people, on my rounds in
the hospitals of Madrid. Among them are some men and women
who have understood perfectly what the Work of God is attempting
to do. Some of them have offered up their pains and their death for
the Work to go forward. Others have offered up not just their
suffering but their very selves, that last bit of earthly life which still
remained to them, and I accepted them into the Work... I can think
of one man, a young fellow in good health; and not only in good
health but in a good position too, socially and economically. His
name was Luis Gordon. But our Lord carried him off unexpectedly.*

I do not remember the exact words he used, but that is the
substance of what he said. He went on talking to me about Luis
Gordon, a young industrial engineer who had died on 5 November
1932. *Maybe our Lord wanted to take him so that the Work could
be born really poor, without any financial assets of its own, as it
never will have,* he added. *He had already come into a lot of money
which he wanted to leave to the Work; but heeding an inner
inspiration, I dissuaded him from doing so.*

Years later I have reflected that if the Father had not opposed
the Work's receiving that inheritance, we would not have suffered
the economic straits we endured in Ferraz, or subsequent ones. But
then neither would we have known extreme poverty which was for
us an invaluable training-ground in virtues.

Paco and I accompanied the Father twice to visit Chamartín de
la Rosa, an old cemetery which now no longer exists. I remember
going by tram. Some of those first people in the Work, of whom he
had spoken to me, were buried there. First we prayed a response for
the dead at the grave of Fr José María Somoano, a young priest who
had died on 16 July 1932, the feastday of Our Lady of Carmel. As
Chaplain to the King's Hospital, he had worked closely with the
Father as the Work was beginning. The Father mentioned that it
was widely held that Fr Somoano had been poisoned simply

because he was a priest.

Then we went to pray at the grave of María Ignacia Garcia Escobar, one of the first women members of Opus Dei, who had died three years earlier on 13 September 1933. She was seriously ill with tuberculosis in the King's Hospital when she asked to be admitted to the Work. That was on 9 April 1932. She died offering up all her pain for the Work. I found out all these details later. At that time the Father only told us that María had been very good and very faithful to the Work. There was a simple iron cross and a little railing round the grave, to mark the spot.

Family warmth

Those months from January to June in 1936 were, from all points of view, particularly intense. I was launching out in my vocation and experiencing the joy of living in a centre of Opus Dei for the first time. I was following a spiritual plan of life proper to a member of the Work. As I was studying two degree courses simultaneously, the Maths/Physics course and Architecture, the number of classes I had to attend had multiplied. These included three hours of water-colour painting under Antonio Flores Urdapilleta. I did not get out of the School of Architecture before 6 or 6.30 p.m., and I still had lots of jobs and hours of study left to do.

In the midst of all that hard work there were some especially heart-warming moments every week, when we particularly experienced the Father's loving care and the family warmth which is a hallmark of Opus Dei. These moments came on Sunday afternoons when Paco and I would be alone with the Father. We would sit around his work-table and he would talk to us about Opus Dei. Meanwhile other members of the Work would begin to appear and then we would have a get-together.

Alvaro del Portillo was often the first to arrive. I can still see that room in my mind's eye. There was a desk, a bookshelf with some tomes on it, a book cupboard, a sofa-bed, two Spanish-style armchairs, and one or two chairs in the same style. That was the office where the Father used to work. At times Ricardo used it as the Residence Director's office. The Father kept some hand-written notebooks which reflected the spirit and rules of the Work in the bottom of the book cupboard.

What did the Father talk to us about? I find it hard to sum it up succinctly. In his energetic way, he opened our eyes to the richness of Christian life as children of God in Opus Dei. If I had to summarise it, I would use his own words with which he repeatedly exhorted us: *personal holiness, personal holiness*.

I have no other recipe, he used to say. *We are here to become saints, for vocation demands holiness.* He reminded us that God expected *heroic sanctity: that is a demand in the call we have received. We have to be really, properly saints; and if are not, we have failed. If anyone is not fully determined to be a saint, let him leave.*

He had us share in his dreams and plans, and in the development of the apostolic ventures. For instance, he begged us to ask St Nicholas, the Work's special intercessor on financial matters for the following intention: he was in the process of acquiring a house, also on Ferraz Street, to which the Residence would be moved, and we had to scrape together enough money to pay for it.

The Sunday afternoon get-togethers were very supernatural and dynamic, and at the same time enjoyable and entertaining. The Father would talk of the future expansion of the Work as well as of more immediate plans. He wanted to begin the work in Valencia the following academic year, and in Paris the year after that. And then, the whole world would follow...!

Since these get-togethers used to happen around tea-time, I remember introducing the English custom of taking afternoon tea, (which we used to have in my own family). And as the British sense of social nicety stipulated that little cakes or biscuits should be consumed with the tea, we had the brain-wave of toasting the bits of bread left over from lunchtime and spreading a little syrup on them. Hey presto! Cakes! As can be seen, we had no money, but we made up for it by ingenuity and good humour.

Our cosy little tea-room, lit by a lamp over the desk which left the rest of the room in shadow, had other uses apart from serving as Ricardo's office. It was there that the Father attended to the spiritual needs of the people who came to see him. I remember another small but significant detail. When he was alone, he always left the door ajar so that anybody who wished to would find it easy to go in and have a chat. At that time we used to go to other priests for confession, so that the Father could say whatever he wanted to us without being hampered by the seal of the confessional.

Almost the whole weight of the apostolate fell on his shoulders. He gave all the Circles, of which there were many, and a lot of undergraduates came to him for spiritual guidance. Other older people also came, such as José María Albareda, then a professor at the Institute, and Angel Santos who was a Reader in Biochemistry in the Pharmacy Department. There were also Eugenio Selles, a lecturer at the National Institute of Toxicology; Luis Vegas Junior, Professor of Building Materials in the School of Architecture; Francisco Navarro Borras who taught Mechanics on the Architecture and Maths/Physics courses; Juan Manzano, then an assistant lecturer, and many others who were well embarked on their careers.

Some priest friends

Now and again some priests also came to visit the Father. Among others I remember Fr Lino Vea-Murguia. He was from Madrid, young, tall, strong and almost the same age as the Father. There was Fr Blas Romero Cano, from La Mancha. He was about fifty-five and, if my memory doesn't fail me, he was a curate in the parish of St Barbara. Fr Blas taught us Gregorian Chant because the Father wanted us to care, with the utmost attention to detail, for everything related to our Lord, especially when pertaining to the liturgy.

I shall never forget those classes in the early afternoon with Fr Blas. He came on Saturdays, before the Residence began to fill up with students. Before he arrived we would get a cap and a good dose of sodium bicarbonate ready for him. Those two elements were much more important to the singing lessons that might appear at first glance. No cap, no lesson: for Fr Blas said he would get a cold without his cap on. As for the sodium bicarbonate, he could not sing without it. He often asked us for it: we would give it to him and between hymns he would take it, first sprinkling some on to his hand and then popping it down his throat, continuing all the while to conduct the choir vigorously, as we began our rendering of the second psalm:

> *Quare fremuerunt gentes...*
> *Quare fremuerunt gentes...*

Fr Blas did his level best to combine and harmonise our voices; but despite his efforts and ours, only very rarely did he achieve the desired rendition. And when the class came to an end, we would still be repeating for the umpteenth time...

> *Quare fremuerunt gentes...*
> *Quare fremuerunt gentes...*

There was another room in the Residence which was put to diverse uses. One of its functions was as a visitors' dining room. It had a homely round table, a small bookcase, a violin for purely decorative purposes, and a piano which Don Alejandro Guzman had given us. He was a heavily bearded old gentleman, of elegant bearing, who wore an old-fashioned Spanish cape and frequently came to visit the Father. On the walls of the room there stood out a small picture of our Lady and a piece of card bearing the words of the evangelical exhortation to fraternal charity: *Mandatum novum do vobis...*

Every Wednesday the Father used to invite a diocesan priest of about fifty to lunch in this room. There were many things that surprised me about this invitation. The Father normally only used trams and the underground. But, by exception, he would go to fetch that particular priest by taxi. Whenever he came, the Father endeavoured to present fare which was better than our normal, and to offer him some little extra: perhaps a dessert or a cup of coffee. While several of us who were in the Work, enveloped in white overalls, prepared the meal in the servery, a bell-boy served at table. When we had finished we whipped off our overalls and went along to entertain the guest.

Sometimes I had lunch with the Father and I was moved by the consideration he showed in dealing with that priest. For instance, before he arrived he would suggest topics of conversation which might interest the priest, so he would enjoy himself. It was not an easy task. I found that particular guest rather hard work. To be totally truthful, I found him tedious in the extreme. When he did take up the conversation it was in so inane and in so self-satisfied a manner that I could not bear it. After lunch there would be a short get-together, which, though actually not long, seemed interminable to me. When it was over, as the Father had to attend to other people, he would ask one of us to accompany the priest home, again by taxi.

As these invitations continued invariably every Wednesday, I became more critical. Besides I felt they supposed a considerable sacrifice for the Father, not just in time and patience, but also financially, as we had no money for those little extras and still less for taxis. So I dared to suggest to the Father that he stop them or at least space them out. He told me then that the good priest was in poor health and had very few friends and that we should show understanding to priests who were lonely.

I did not fully understand his answer until years later when the Father remarked to me that we had to teach people who came to the Work to live in God's presence, giving them a new light every day. On Thursdays they could consider Eucharistic piety and on Fridays, the Passion of our Lord. Saturdays could be dedicated to our relationship with the Blessed Virgin Mary. He added that it was a good idea to make some sacrifice every day with the same theme in mind. *For example, on Wednesdays in honour of St Joseph: it is a good idea really to exert ourselves in charity and patience with someone who has made us suffer or whom we find particularly difficult.*

It was only then that I finally realised why the Father had lavished so much on that priest who, as I later discovered, had made him suffer a lot, some time previously.

The poverty of Opus Dei

As I said earlier, we were going through serious difficulties from the financial point of view. I have to acknowledge that, over the years, when I have heard opinions casting doubt on the spirit of poverty of Opus Dei I have had to make a real effort to react with meekness and patience. So many memories related to poverty come to mind. From the very beginning the Father suffered many privations to get the Work of God on its feet.

It was not a showy, superficial poverty. He always taught us to live a *bashful poverty*, as he called it, a kind of poverty which hides itself from the view of other people. You could guess its presence in his person and in everything he used. For instance, since first meeting him I had an agreeable impression of decorum, of cleanliness, even of distinction. But as time passed, I observed that immaculate though it always was, he always wore the same cassock.

I also discovered that a gesture he used to make frequently, putting his pocket-watch to his ear, was not simply a habit as I had thought, but another manifestation of his poverty. That old watch of his would stop every second day, and every first day as well, and he had no money to get it mended. Later I discovered that he called his guardian angel *my watch-mender*, as he asked him to make sure the blessed watch did not land him in difficulties by stopping just at the time which would prevent him from carrying out his priestly duties punctually.

I also realised that when he celebrated Holy Mass with that big gothic-style chasuble that he used, he genuflected in such a way that his right foot was always hidden under his cassock and alb. Similarly, when he knelt at the foot of the altar to say the prayers after Mass, he ensured that the alb would cover the soles of his shoes. Later I discovered why: those shoes, for all that they were spotlessly clean, urgently needed re-soling or, better, entirely replacing by a new pair. It was not surprising that he wore his shoes out, for he used to walk miles from one end of Madrid to another, from St Elizabeth Street to Ferraz, from the Salamanca district to Vallecas.

I stumbled upon lots of things like those, during the first months I lived in the Residence. For instance, the food served was healthy and every effort was made for it to be varied and plentiful. However, in the servery not a scrap went to waste, as witness the ends of bread converted into tea cakes, which more often than not was all we had for tea. I am quite sure that very often they were all the Father had for tea-cum-dinner.

In the Residence there were two boys who worked as bell-boys (three in the third term): they served in the dining room and did the cleaning. An elderly lady did the cooking. She came for just a few hours daily. Some goods nuns, the Handmaids of Merciful Love, who lived at 17 Ferraz Street, took care of the laundry and ironing. Their congregation, founded by Mother Esperanza, whose Cause of canonisation is now under way, was at that time suffering what is called 'the incomprehension of good people'. The Father used to go to the convent to visit Mother Esperanza from time to time. I accompanied him on a few occasions and came away with the impression that he went there to give her encouragement. He told me that she was a very holy Religious and that the Lord was allowing her to go through some very difficult trials.

One of those Religious members remembers how the Father said to them: *The Cross can be very heavy, but on you go! The Lord managed his. Saints do not turn back. Saints reach the end of the course. On you go! A day without the Cross is a day without God.*

The unassuming normality of the supernatural

There was nothing strange or artificial in the Father's conduct. Quite the opposite. As Paco too recalls, the Father behaved eminently naturally. He possessed that unaffected natural supernaturalness which is a characteristic of men and women of God. We, who were close to him, tried to respect his privacy, so that when something supernatural happened it would be as little externally evident as possible. Besides the Father repeatedly reminded us that our sanctity was to be found in ordinary things, and that we did not need signs and wonders to shore up our faith in the supernatural nature of the Work.

Nevertheless, God did want the supernatural to make itself felt in his life now and again. For example, some years previously it happened that a stranger one day made as if to attack him in the street in broad daylight. Another stranger as mysterious as the first came to his defence and, having warded off the attack, turned to him and repeated the words, "little donkey, little donkey" in his ear.

At that time, apart from his spiritual director, no one knew that the Father called himself in *Intimate Notes*, his private diaries, by that very name *little donkey*. In his humility he added *mangy little donkey*.

Do you understand now?

Still, let us return to normal life. As I said before, Paco and I had a lot of classes and not a minute to spare. We used to leave the Residence first thing in the morning in a great hurry to arrive on time for the 8 a.m. lecture by Navarro Borras at St Bernard's. We spent the whole morning until 2 p.m. either at the university or at the School of Architecture.

However one day, I forget why, we stayed at home and discovered something which amazed us: the Father was going around, making the students' beds, sweeping the floors, cleaning bathrooms and generally tidying up. We realised that the bell-boys who were young and inexperienced were not enough and that the Father had been doing this for some time without our being aware of it.

Of course, we set to work immediately to help him. It was no small task for there were twenty-odd beds and some twelve rooms. But we could not help him every day. We could not afford to miss Technology, Mechanics and Planning in the School of Architecture, and in the afternoon, from 3.15 to 6.30, it was very risky to skip drawing lessons. In the maths department the time-table was even more demanding. We decided to take turns attending classes so that one could make notes for the other. Like that we were able to help the Father some mornings with the housework.

The domestic chores did not finish there. There were jobs to be done in the evenings after the cook had left. That was when we went into the kitchen to do the washing up. Paco recalls, "The Father would come in and don a white overall. Pedro and I had our overalls on too, and we would all set to, each to his own specific job. That was our routine day after day and we enjoyed being there with the Father. And at the appointed time everything was ship-shape."

The last thing we did in the kitchen in the evening was to leave breakfast laid out ready for the next clay. For milk, we used Nestle's powdered milk. Paco or I saw to that very necessary duty, alternating by the week. I weighed almost 80 kilos then, while Paco was all skin and bone as he always was. The Father used to refer jokingly to 'the fat cows and the lean cows' as he shared these tasks with us. I have memories of him in the kitchen with Ricardo, washing plates, polishing apples with a cloth and doing other humble tasks.

Naturally the residents who were not members of Opus Dei had not the slightest inkling of who it was who did those jobs. And though we in the Work tried to make sure the Father did them as rarely as possible, our time-tables often did not comply with our solicitude. Thanks to his example we learnt then that there is no task however material which, when done for love of the Lord is unworthy of God's children or which cannot please him.

The housework once gave rise to an unusual event. On a certain occasion a prestigious lecturer in Mechanics in Architecture and Maths/Physics called Francisco (Paco) Navarro Borras, to whom I have already referred, came to lunch. Paco and I were students of his at both teaching sites. Lunch was served in the 'piano room' and the Father and Ricardo, in his role as director of the Residence, lunched with him. The Father asked Paco and me to come along for coffee.

In the ensuing conversation over coffee, in answer to a question by (Paco) Navarro Borras, the Father began to explain how we put real poverty into practice in Opus Dei. However, our lecturer did not seem particularly disposed to understanding what the Father was saying.

As the situation was becoming a little awkward, Paco and I decided to leave the others to it. We excused ourselves and slipped off to our jobs in the kitchen. A little later, as we were washing up the crockery and coffee cups, the Father and our lecturer suddenly appeared. He was struck at seeing us so involved in a task so far removed from the Kinetics which he taught us at the University.

Then the Father who was very much at ease with him, inquired: *Do you understand now, Paco?*

Nevertheless, all this must not give the impression that the Residence was like a poor-house. It was a welcoming and dignified house, where we all felt at home. The Father taught us to combine dignity with poverty, a cheerful poverty which always sought to pass unnoticed.

Opus Dei's first co-operators

As I have already said, many members of Opus Dei were

students, and there were very few people at that time who were able to reap the benefits of their professional work to help the Father in his apostolic initiatives. A few friends and acquaintances of his did help, but the donations of those first Co-operators of the Work were few and could not have added up to much.

I have already mentioned Don Alejandro Guzman. Doña Concepción Ruiz de Guardia was another person who helped. The Father told us she was a very generous woman. I knew her and could see that she held our founder in greater esteem and veneration. Paco and I accompanied the Father to see her on some of his occasional visits. They always had a specific apostolic aim. On one occasion, I remember she installed a figure of the Sacred Heart in her house. The Father said the customary prayers simply and fervently, slowly, dwelling lovingly on each little detail. "He followed the order of the ceremony with as much care as if we were in a cathedral full of people," Paco notes.

Doña María Francisca Messia y Aranda, Countess of Humanes, was also generous with her support. She was an old lady who had never married and who had been completely blind for many years. She lived in an old house with a housekeeper, the aunt of a friend of mine, and the servants. The house had a private chapel where the Father would sometimes go to say Mass and renew the Blessed Sacrament.

The Father asked me to go with him on some of his visits as he knew I loved antiques, and she had a quantity of pictures and objects in her house which testified to the ancient lineage of her family. She herself had been a bosom friend of Princess Isabel, popularly known in Madrid as 'Chata'. On occasions, after thanksgiving following Mass, we went through into the dining room to have breakfast. I still recall gratefully the York Ham and special preserves with which Doña María regaled us, before the usual milky coffee and sponge cakes. After breakfast she would show us round the elegant rooms of her house, pointing out very accurately each picture and each object, saying, "Do you see this picture? It is of one of my ancestors, painted by Vicente Lopez." And so she would continue, without ever making a mistake, in spite of her blindness.

Where the banisters began by the staircase, there was a dark metallic statue. I suspect it was made of calamine, a zinc alloy imitating bronze. One day I said so. The Countess confirmed my suspicions and began to talk about the statue as if it were an old family friend: "Ah, you mean the calamine gentleman?"

This little episode later gave rise to the Father pulling my leg at times. *Perico, do you remember the calamine gentleman?*

Yet those first benefactors' co-operation, with all the good will and the affection they had for our founder, constituted neither a continuous nor an adequate support for our apostolic enterprise, and the Residence was running at a huge deficit. How did it keep going? One day I asked the Father directly. With some demur he told me that he had to appeal continually to his mother, Doña Dolores, whose small capital it was that we were spending.

Doña Dolores

I had yet to see the Father's mother. From those days onwards, we members of Opus Dei have all referred to her as 'the Grandmother', out of love, respect and gratitude. My first meeting with her took place in rather painful circumstances. She lived in the Saint Elizabeth Foundation where the Father was Rector. This ancient foundation had been set up by the Austrias and it comprised a public church, a convent of enclosed Augustinians nuns, the chapter house, a school dedicated to the Assumption and the Rector's house, where the Father lived with his mother, his sister Carmen and his brother Santiago.

The immediate area around the Foundation had become unsafe. The house was situated in Saint Elizabeth Street, very near the Saint Carlos Faculty of Medicine where students regularly took to the streets to demonstrate. It was also near the Mediodia train station, the station in Atocha, where there were numerous sweatshops. It was one of the districts of Madrid most affected by street riots which had been on the upsurge since the victory of the Popular Front, which had led to Manuel Azana being made president of a left-wing Republican government on 19 February 1936.

The Ferraz Residence was on the other side of the city, immediately outside the university campus which was still being built. This meant that the Father had to go miles, from one to the other, every day either on foot or by tram, in addition to the trips he made all over the city in response to the apostolic demands of the Work.

It is easy to imagine the fears and worries Doña Dolores had for her son in such a violently anti-clerical climate. She also suffered for her other two children. Carmen was a still a young woman and Santiago was turning seventeen. Judging from the number of times I saw the Father stay the night at the Residence or the late hour at which he set off for the Foundation after preaching, giving Circles or having a string of confessions and taking into consideration how slow, few and far-between those old trams were, one can imagine the time he must have arrived at St Elizabeth and the long hours, Doña Dolores must have spent awaiting him, anxiously thinking about him and praying for him.

Her fears were not groundless. A few historical facts will suffice for us to appreciate quite how justified her anxiety was. With the triumph of the Popular Front the most violent and aggressive parties had come to power. In the months that followed, a series of bitter strikes and arson attacks took place, followed by a breakdown in public order where the Church became the main target. Anticlericalism flared up in the press. Hundreds of churches were burnt down and large numbers of Catholic centres and convents were forcibly taken over. Worship was banned or restricted in many places. Sacrilegious robberies and outrages and anti-religious attacks proliferated. Everywhere a terror was unleashed that made it dangerous for priests to step out of doors in their cassocks. Yet the Father continued wearing his priestly robes all the time, setting an outstanding example of courage.

However, seeing the way things were going, the Father must have realised it was not prudent to keep his family on in the Rector's house at St Elizabeth. He decided to more them into a rented apartment in King Francisco Street very near Ferraz Residence. So one day, perhaps because of a certain flair I had for moving furniture around, the Father asked me, if classes permitting, I could lend a hand with the removal from his mother's house.

One Saturday I went along to the Foundation with Paco, needless to say. I was introduced to the Grandmother. Although she was about 60 and had prematurely white hair, her face was still young. She radiated dignity, serenity and gentleness, and at the same time there were traces of interior suffering. I was under the impression that her eyes were tearful.

Paco explains in his memoirs the cause of her tears. The Father wanted a bed to be left there. The Grandmother realised that her son Josemaria did not want to abandon the nuns, whose Chaplain he was, in such dangerous times.

I was very shy at my first meeting with the Grandmother, just as I have so often felt when I met people who were also shy and well-mannered. I did not know how to address her. I settled for Senora. She was very much a lady in all her expressions and gestures and in her way of speaking. She had a gentle, very quiet, voice.

After that first day, when Paco and I helped her with the move, we had many opportunities to meet her. From then on she would always refer to the two of us together – 'Pedro and Paco' or 'Paco and Pedro'. All the others of whom she was so fond, each had their names to themselves: Alvaro, Ricardo, Isidoro. Our names, on the other hand, always formed an inseparable duo as far as she was concerned.

At the St Elizabeth Foundation the situation had become untenable for the nuns. A little earlier, at 10 o'clock one night, a big crowd had gathered outside the convent. Some of the mob sprayed the big front doors with petrol and tried to set fire to them, until the police arrived and dissuaded them. That resulted shortly afterwards, on 17 May, in some of the enclosed nuns being forced to move to a private house in Angel Square, where they lived in secular dress because of the circumstances. Others went to live with their families.

On those occasions when the Father went to visit them in their new abode, Paco or I would go with him. Occasionally we both went. We saw how in such difficult circumstances, the Father comforted them and gave them spiritual encouragement. Paco notes in his jottings that one of those nuns would kneel down every time she saw the Father, and bow her forehead to the floor as a mark of respect. This was a custom practised in some monasteries, but it made the Father suffer a lot as it hurt his humility.

Violent days

From February 1936 onwards many religious houses were burned down. The atmosphere throughout the land was becoming more and more anti-clerical. As a consequence it became normal for Catholics to form voluntary vigilante groups to watch over convents and churches. The general situation became more polarised and chaotic. On 19 February the President of the Government, Portela Valladares resigned. March saw an increase in strikes, and large numbers of country-houses and estates were requisitioned. In April, Prime Minister Alcala Zamora was dismissed, which caused an internal rift in the army. Later there was an attempted insurrection...

In the midst of these difficulties the Father instilled us with serenity. His reflective balanced attitude was in total contrast to the polarisation all around us. He never discussed political matters. His judgements of events were always exclusively priestly ones. His feet were firmly on the ground. But at the same time he had an unshakeable faith in the fact that the Work would become a reality, even though the circumstances did not appear to favour the apostolic expansion for which he had us pray so much.

He suffered a lot, for the Church and for the situation in his country, which he loved so much. He respected any opinion, relating to public life, which a Christian could legitimately hold. Among the members of the Work and the undergraduates whom his apostolate reached there were, of course, very diverse political views. The Father taught us to have a great respect for each person's freedom. As the Father said to one of the boys: *Look, nobody will ask you about your political views here. People from all sectors come here: Carlists, people from Popular Action, Spanish Renewal Monarchists. Yesterday, the President and Secretary of the Basque National Students' Association were here,* he remarked by way of example.

On the other hand, he went on, *you will be asked many other 'awkward' questions. You will be asked if you pray, if you make good use of your time, if you keep you parents happy, if you study, because for a student studying is a serious obligation.*

Emiliano Amann, one of the residents in DYA and not in the Work at that time, remembers how the Father continued to propel the Work forward constantly, despite the critical state of affairs. In a letter to his parents he wrote: "More and more people come to the Academy for lessons in architecture, medicine, law and science. By next year I am sure there will be preparatory classes for the School of Agronomy."

Like a lot of others at that time, my friend, Ignacio de Landecho, became quite fanatical in the politico-religious conflict. He spent many nights on guard duty with other student militants in CEDA or other monarchist parties. They aimed to protect nuns in a particular convent who feared an attack by Marxist militia.

Around that time I put it to him that God might be calling him to Opus Dei. I admired his bravery in the current situation and I broached the possibility that our Lord might be asking him for something more: his whole life. I suggested he think about it quite freely. It seemed to me, and I told him so, that we ought not to limit ourselves only to trying to solve the particular situation we were going through then, for all that it was so immediate and harrowing. God expected from us another kind of heroism as well: our total self-giving in serving Him and the Church.

I can remember our conversations perfectly. They were quite heated sometimes for we got very hot under the collar. We drew a clear line between a religious situation which was specifically Spanish and the universal call to holiness and apostolate which the Work declares. Although Ignacio did not see his vocation to Opus Dei clearly at that time, when I remember those discussions I consider that one truth particular shone out from them: namely, that Opus Dei was not the result of any concrete historical circumstance, however grave, such as ours. It also became clear that though its members were still very few and though we all lived in Spain, we were fully aware of the Work's universal mission to serve the Church world-wide.

The Father, who loved Ignacio very much, told me that he was a fine lad and that he needed the impetus of grace to grasp our way fully. In spite of these divergencies, Ignacio did not lose his admiration for the Father or for our self-giving. Nor did our mutual friendship grow cold; quite the contrary.

On 19 March the Father had the joy of using a new, more dignified tabernacle for the first time. It had been made by the sculptor Jenaro Lazaro. Soon afterwards, at the end of Holy Week, from 10 to 13 April, we held a retreat in the Residence. It was my first as a member of Opus Dei. "We were not all in the Work," Paco records. "As soon as Pedro and I arrived the Father pointed out to us a rather plump boy wearing baggy trousers. He wanted to join the Work. That was Vicente Rodriguez Casado. He walked around the flat in a state of euphoria, which he has been in ever since." About 20 boys attended. José Ramon Herrero Fontana, Lahuerta, Dean, Isasa, Vega de Seoane... A week later the Father, left for Valencia with Ricardo to start the Work there.

The oratory carpet

One spring day, I do not know why, I did not go to class. At about 11 a.m. I was coming out of the oratory of the Residence when I met the Father in the hall. He was saying his Breviary sitting on a bench under a wall-hanging worked with the motto *per aspera ad astra* (through the arduous reach up to the stars). I said nothing so as not to disturb his concentration. But as I was passing he forestalled me with a motion of his hand, his eyes never lifting from the book. He finished the psalm, marked his place in the breviary with one finger, and looking at me with love in his eyes he asked me something I did not expect in the slightest. *Pedro, would you be willing to be a priest if you heard God's call?*

I was dumbstruck. It was the last thing I expected to hear at that moment. But I answered him immediately, "I think so Father."

I went back into the oratory. Shortly afterwards the Father came in. He knelt beside me and, pointing to the red carpet which covered the raised altar area, he said in a whisper: *A priest has to be like that carpet. Over it the body of our Lord is consecrated. It's at the altar, it's true, but it is there to be of use. Furthermore, it is there so that everyone else can have something soft to tread on and you see how it does not complain, it does not protest... Do you understand what the service of a priest is? You will see that later on in your life you will reflect on these things.*

From that day on, I often spent my time of prayer contemplating first the tabernacle and then the carpet. That was all the topic I needed.

A camp in Rascafria

May and June flew by occupied with study owing to the imminence of exams. I remember little about that period except for the Father telling us in May that the people who would be going to Paris and Valencia were already starting to get ready. On 17 June the deeds of the new house were signed. It was in the same road, in 16 Ferraz St, and we moved in there early in July. Before that, at the end of June as soon as the dreaded exams were over, the Father wanted us younger ones in the Work to have a few days break in the mountains outside Madrid. That would help us to recover our energy, to rest and to strengthen ourselves in our vocation.

Off we went, led by Juan Jimenez Vargas: Paco Botella, José Ramon Herrero Fontana, Vicente Rodriguez Casado (whom we called Vicenton) and I. Vicenton, cheerful and in festive mood as always, had asked for admission to the Work on 12 April.

By and large we were good at sports. Juan was an expert climber. Vicenton knew a lot about camping. He had been a Spanish boy scout, and had managed to get hold of a big tent and most of the necessary equipment. I was more of a sea-farer than a mountaineer, but I did have a bit of camping experience because I belonged to the Spanish sea scouts years earlier. I suspect that Paco was the one who enthused least over the delights of the great outdoors.

Rascafria was our destination. We set off by coach on Saturday, 27 June at 3.30 p.m. as José Ramon specified so precisely in his diary. We arrived at almost 7 p.m. Those were other times and other speeds! We picked a spot near the River Lozoya which runs near the monastery at Paular, and there we pitched tent.

Before settling down we went to see the parish priest in the nearby village. He was pleased to learn that a group of under-graduates wished to attend weekday Mass, and he was delighted to accommodate his timetable to ours to enable us to get there in time in the mornings.

We had some amusing adventures typical of every excursion. Paco tells how on my saint's day (29 June) we tried making a rice pudding and ended up inventing a new dessert: rice pudding with enamel chippings, which insisted on getting in on their own initiative. We played a lot of sports. We swam in a nearly lake; some of us, Paco included, had to scarper from it at top speed when the guard suddenly arrived with his dogs.

Paco records half-humorously half-pathetically: "What I cannot forget is how we went into the lake as well. With Juan and Vicenton in the party it was impossible to get out of those dips, and it was as cold as ice. Nor can I forget going back from the lake, when we got lost. We even got a bit worried because it was getting dark on us. As we prayed the Rosary we had to go through a herd of bulls which stared at us more than we liked."

So Paco evidently did not cherish very happy memories of the trips we did over those days. To go by the notes he wrote, they must have been pretty tough for him. "Pedro got back exhausted. He got tired out on the hillsides, and was panting. I can see him now in his dark, nearly black, mackintosh... Vicenton ran down the slopes. Juan was for ever shouting after him, 'Vicente, Vicente!' It began to rain and we speeded up. We got back to the tent late. It was pouring with rain and we piled inside without having had any dinner, utterly exhausted. But after a while we had to go out again to loosen the tent cords, as Vicenton advised, otherwise the tent would have burst on us."

Despite all those little mishaps, which provide the stuff of amusing anecdotes in all youthful escapades and give them a certain flavour of adventure, those days proved to be an unforgettable experience. We consolidated our vocations. We were able to pray peacefully and breathe in the fresh air. We came back physically and spiritually renewed. It was the first of thousands of excursions of this type for young people, which now take place all over the world. It was also my last memory of a Madrid in the mid-thirties which would witness, petrified, the appalling outbreak of the civil war a few weeks later.

CHAPTER 6

The Civil War

The Happy Levant

The move from 50 to 16 Ferraz Street began at the beginning of July. The new Residence was very near the Montana Barracks. On 2 July we were in the middle of the move: three loaded lorries had left for the new site and there were three more to go. On the following day, 3 July, Paco and I left Madrid to stay with our respective families for a couple of weeks. Paco went to Valencia, and I to Albacete from where I intended to go on to Torrevieja as soon as possible. I was planning to spend a while there and then return to Madrid.

The truth is that I was not very keen on going to Albacete. My father had worked on the propaganda which had helped the Popular Front to victory in the last elections. As that coalition had adopted a mode of persecuting everything religious, I feared a confrontation with him, something I wished to avoid at all costs. When I told the Father that he put things straight. He said I really ought to go and see my family and that I should put filial piety first. He recommended I pray for my father and not get embroiled in politics with him.

Paco journeyed to Valencia with another job: to find a place suitable for setting up the future Residence at the beginning of the next academic year. As soon as he found one, Ricardo would go from Madrid to see it. Thus a long-term desire of the Father was set in motion.

In those circumstances of general instability and political turbulence the Father's serene attitude and way of focusing on the supernatural dimension to things were particularly remarkable. Ten days after we left, on 13 July, the press reported the assassination by the police of Calvo Sotelo, the National Front leader. But these external difficulties did not daunt the Father. He had written: *The Work of God comes to fulfil the Will of God. Therefore, have the profound conviction that heaven is determined it should be accomplished.*

On 16 July, three days later, Paco sent a telegram to Madrid announcing that he had found a place to set up the residence. Next day, 17 July, Ricardo headed for Valencia. His journey marked the first expansion of the Work in Spain. The Father gave him a blessing before he left. And that some day news came through of the Army revolt in Africa. The Civil War was beginning.

I was in Torrevieja that day. My parents were still in Albacete and, from one day to the next, my father found himself suddenly plunged into a complex political scenario. He was Deputy Mayor of the city and an executive in Azana's party. A few days after the uprising he was elected Provincial President of the Popular Front and forced to accept the post.

His situation was complicated, from the family point of view too. As befell so many Spanish families, mine embraced divergent political leanings. One uncle was a radical socialist mayor; others were socialist, moderate republican or monarchist councillors. As the conflict developed their fates too were diverse. Some of my cousins who were naval captains and officers were shot or thrown into the sea alive. Another cousin who was in the Falange was jailed in Alicante with José Antonio Primo de Rivera, the Falange founder. Another uncle, a judge in Hellin, was himself tried for refusing to sentence someone to death. Another cousin was a volunteer in the International Brigade.

In spite of the position my father held in the new political set-up, confused and chaotic as it was, he wholeheartedly deplored the dramatic turn events had taken. I remember his bitterness the day he learnt of Calvo Sotelo's assassination. When the war began shortly afterwards, he managed to save some lives, especially of priests and religious. There is a piece of furniture, now in a Centre of Opus Dei in Madrid's Diego de Leon Street, which used to be in my father's house. The Blessed Sacrament was reserved in it and my father wanted there always to be a lamp burning in that room.

A librarian had just been appointed to the Institute at Albacete and, unbeknown to almost everybody, he was actually a priest. Thanks to my father's protection he was able to attend to many sick people and administer the Viaticum to them.

I was not able to participate directly in the conflict. When I was called up, the military authorities declared me unfit for active service.

In the first weeks of the war, anti-clericalism worsened and the Church was terribly persecuted. I will recall one statistic which is particularly eloquent: in just one day, 25 July, the feast of Saint

James, the patron saint of Spain, 95 ecclesiastics were assassinated throughout the country. I remember that day particularly well because it was the last time I was able to go to Mass in Torrevieja. It was celebrated in a temporary parish hall as the church had been burned down. From then on, I had to cycle to Mass in a nearby village called Torrelamata, where a priest continued to say Mass. Getting there was not easy. I needed a pass and then...

Before going on I had better explain about the pass. I do not know if readers nowadays have an idea of just how essential it was in those times of war to have a safe-conduct pass. You had to carry it on you to make any journey whatsoever. Without a pass you could not even go out of doors. One's entire life depended on that piece of signed and sealed paper which stated who you were, why you were there and how long for, and where it confirmed that you were not 'an enemy of the people'.

So for a while, with my pass at the ready and showing it endlessly at the numerous checkpoints, I managed to get to Torrelamata and attend Mass.

The parish priest of that little village was an old man who had recently returned from Mexico after many years of priestly ministry there. He had a great devotion to Our Lady of Guadalupe, whom I had never heard of. A few days previously he had been hauled up before the Village Revolutionary Committee, but he had not backed down. Mentally he turned trustingly to Our Lady of Guadalupe and, surprisingly, he was allowed to go free. Not long afterwards he was forbidden to celebrate Mass. Even so, I was able to go to him for Confession and to receive Holy Communion. Meanwhile all kinds of conflicting news was getting through to Torrevieja. Most came from the capital. It spoke of thousands of assassinations in Madrid. The figure swelled from one month to the next, producing a climate of disquiet. Later we would learn the precise death toll from the anti-clerical brutality which swept towns and villages during those months. In August alone, 2077 priests, religious and nuns were murdered, some 70 per day. Lots of lay men and women were also murdered for the mere fact of their being Catholics. The assassination and persecution of priests continued. I prayed for the Father the whole time. What had become of him? For in those long nerve-racking weeks all communication with Madrid had been cut.

Almost two months later I received my first postcard from the Father. What joy! What a relief! So many uncertainties disappeared when I read it!

Nevertheless, with all the hardships we experienced, living as we did in Valencia, Alicante and several other Spanish Mediterranean provinces, life was easier by far for us than it was for people in the central region of the Peninsula where the Father was. In the Levant cities, surrounded by market gardens, watered by the Turia or the Segura, there was nothing like the hunger or the terror which reigned over the civil population crowded into Madrid. The capital was being steadily drained of supplies of every kind. That explains why the Father refers to 'the happy Levant' in some of his letters.

His letters were very short, often just a few hand-written lines signed *Mariano*, his fourth name, instead of Josemaria. When he was baptised he had received the names José, María, Julian, Mariano. He joined the first two together out of devotion for our Lady and Saint Joseph. He wanted them to be always both together in his heart, as they were in his name. He signed himself by his fourth name, Mariano, out of devotion to our Lady. He had been given that name in memory of an uncle of his, a widower, who had later been ordained priest. In those days he also used it to avoid putting us or himself in danger.

The Father encouraged us to be very united to our Lord during those times, not to neglect our prayer or abandon our plan of life. He urged us to plead with our Lord constantly to cut short that terrible time of trial. He advised us always to commend ourselves to the most Blessed Virgin Mary, our safe path, asking her to protect all our lives, our faithfulness and perseverance.

Juan, Isidoro, José María and Alvaro were still in Madrid with the Father. And what of the other members of Opus Dei? Where were they? What were they doing? Had they been killed? At first we received very confused reports. Later we were able to find out about each other through Isidoro Zorzano who, being Argentine, had not been forced to hide or seek refuge in an embassy.

In his tiny copperplate handwriting, Isidoro would transmit ideas from the Father's preaching to us. Little by little, without our having fixed upon it together (we had no opportunity to do so), a kind of private language spontaneously developed among us. It contained certain key words enabling the addressees to understand it all. When the Father mentioned "Don Manuel", he was referring to our Lord. "Don Manuel's Mother" was the Blessed Virgin; the Father was "Grandfather", and he would refer to himself as if he were an old man writing to his children and grandchildren.

For some time I had no idea of what had become of Paco. Later

I had news of him. The outbreak of war had caught him at home in Marquis del Turia Street in Valencia. He had got a job in the mornings in the Municipal Institute of Public Health. He took part in vaccination campaigns with his cousin, Enrique Espinos, and a friend, Amadeo de Fuenmayor. So they managed to acquire certificates from work allowing them to move around freely. Though we were quite near each other geographically speaking, we were incommunicado for quite a while because of a tiny error. I received a letter from Paco; but he gave his address as 'M. del Turia' (M., because Marquis was not a term which went down well in those highly politicised times). I misread is as 'H. del Turia', that is Hotel del Turia, and sent the letter there. Naturally, he never got it.

Thanks to my family circumstances I enjoyed a certain freedom of movement. But in those moments of confusion nobody was unaffected. Despite my father's position, militiamen would come round to requisition things on the estate. We all did our best to save our skins.

Attempts at escape

In those dramatic circumstances, my grandfather Julio recalled that he had never renounced his British citizenship, his birthright as the son of a British subject. He also knew that he was registered as such in the British consulate in Cartagena. That consulate had closed and its files had been transferred to Alicante, which had acquired the status of consulate-general during the war. He went off to apply for his British passport. At the time a document such as that was a life saver. I myself went to Alicante several times with the same aim, and at last obtained the desired passport in which my grandparents figured as Julio and Mary Casciaro.

The consul gave us some posters to stick on the doors of our properties, guaranteeing that they were owned by a British subject. He also gave us a medium-sized Union Jack. My grandfather thought it ludicrously small, so we had to design and make up a new one, which turned out absolutely enormous. Soon afterwards we ran it up from the highest point of Los Hoyos, on an old pigeon-loft in the form of a turret complete with its battlements! We thought that living under the protection of the United Kingdom would give us relative security.

We were not mistaken. Having a foreign passport was, at the time, the best pass and the surest guarantee to a relative freedom of movement. Even the most ignorant and cruel revolutionaries knew that it was dangerous to take the life of a foreign subject. Meanwhile, various members of the family turned up at Los Hoyos looking for refuge. The atmosphere there was one of typical wartime anxiety.

'I heard on the radio that they have killed...', said one. 'Somebody told me that so and so has been shot too.' 'In Torrevieja people are saying...'

Though at first some people thought it was just a short-lived uprising of a few weeks duration, the war dragged on. I started looking for a way to earn some kind of living in the turmoil. What could I do? I was 21 and still at university. Fortunately I got a job in a laboratory at Las Salinas de Torrevieja. The head of Department, Chuno Chorower, a Russian Jew who had done a doctorate in Germany, discovered I was reading Maths/Physics and employed me as a maths assistant.

The enabled me to join the U.G.T. (the General Workers Union) with the other employees. I also found an old FUE (Federation of Spanish University Students) membership card, which I had joined at sixteen. I managed to swop it for a Socialist Party card. My documentation now allowed me to travel to Valencia, Alicante, Alcalali (where Rafael Calvo Serer was in hiding after tremendous adventures) and other nearby towns.

My comparative freedom also meant I was able to send some food and other necessary supplies to those left behind in Madrid. I remember those parcels which I sent to Isidoro perfectly. They were called sample packages and contained dried cod, coffee, sugar, soap and other items from my grandparents larder because they had built up a stock of provisions for the war.

Considering the situation in general, my own circumstances were not too bad. Nonetheless, in view of the fact that months were passing and the war still dragged on and on, and nobody could tell when it would ever end, and seeing also that travelling to Madrid was out of the question, I decided to leave the country.

There were two reasons for my decision. I knew that my mission in life was to carry out Opus Dei; so I thought that if I went abroad I would continue the Work with total freedom. In Spain it seemed that all opportunities for it had been barred. Most of the churches were destroyed. Christians has gone underground, as to the catacombs. To declare oneself a priest was to sign one's own death warrant; possession of a religious object was sufficient motive for its owner to be put in front of a firing squad. Alone, cut off in that small Mediterranean enclave, what could I do? I thought the best thing would be to go abroad. During the spring of 1937 I started planning my escape.

My first attempt entailed asking one of my uncles to lend me a boat so that I could get from the spa of San Pedro del Mar (which belonged to my family) to an English cruiser anchored in the port of Cartagena. My uncle refused. He reckoned that the cruiser would only take freemasons aboard. My heart back in my boots, I began thinking of something else.

Another possibility would be to get to the United Kingdom with my grandfather. I persuaded him that as a British subject he could do that. It seemed feasible. We even obtained an invitation from the British Consul in Alicante to attend King George VI's coronation ceremony. We asked for permission to travel, arguing that because of my grandfather's age and state of health, I had to accompany him. Everything seemed to go smoothly until I applied to the Civil Government in Albacete for a passport. There the plan fell through. We were told we were crazy to attempt such a thing, and I nearly ended up in jail.

Now I devised a new escape. It consisted in casting off from one of the beaches near Alicante at night, and making for a German ship anchored just offshore. I began looking for contacts and putting out feelers. My link was one of my fellow students from the School of Architecture who lived in Alicante. But in the end, after many shots in the dark, it all came to nothing.

In the midst of this instability, my comings and goings, the rumours and gossip, the anxiety to hear the latest news of the war, my successive plans for flight, and the constant and vain search for solutions, I tried to follow my Christian plan of life proper to a person of Opus Dei. Likewise, I tried to make the most of my time, as the Father had taught me. This surprised my family quite a lot.

"Why are you studying if you don't know what is going to happen?" they inquired. My logic went the other way round. It was precisely because I did not know what was going to happen, that I thought the best thing to do was to make the most of my time and continue being apostolic. As the Father had taught me to do, I began with my own family. I spoke to my brother Pepe, who was finding his feet as a growing man in the midst of all that convulsion, the tensions and the agitation. I advised him to use that time well, especially since we did not know how long it would last, from the human as well as the spiritual point of view. I wrote him out a plan of life.

Pepe recalls: "One day my brother, Pedro, suggested a plan of life to me. He gave me a Thomas a Kempis to help me pray for a while every day. He gave me a Bible in French, by L'Abbe Crampon, for me to use for spiritual reading and practise my French at the same time, and he lent me a book by Chateaubriand called *Le genie du Christianisme*. He recommended I take up French and told me always to keep busy. I put all this into practice in a rather unusual fashion. As all the young men on the estate had been called up, we had to stand in for them as best we could. It fell to me to look after the sheep and cattle. So during those months I spent many hours reading Chateaubriand among the sheep, in the shade of the almond trees."

Now and gain I had news from the Father through letters which he sent out to all of us in the Valencian zone, or which he sent directly to me. On 7 April 1937 he wrote to me asking me to do all I could to help José María Hernandez Garnica. The Father was very worried about him, for he had been arrested and after spending some time in the prisons of San Anton in Madrid and San Miguel de los Reyes, he had been sent to the Modelo prison in Valencia. Writing in code, the Father asked me to take him if possible *to the Alicante countryside to recuperate* after he came out of the sanatorium (that is, the prison).

I remember those letters so well. He would often begin with an affectionate touch. For instance he would draw the initial 'P' of my name in an artistic manner, with long curling strokes. He gave us news of each other and asked us to pray. In a letter which I received on 6 June he evoked, in our established code, our visits to the Countess of Humanes where I had lectured them on El Greco and Velazquez. *Did I tell you that hardly had the good lady died when an armed group invaded the house and looted everything, right down the floorboards?* Then he told me about a possible trip to Valencia, which cheered me up no end. *Though nothing is definite, it looks as though Josemaria will probably leave quite soon. If he goes to Valencia, Ignacio* (that is, Isidoro) *will write and ask you if you could go and see him.*

Meanwhile the months had been passing, and in June 1937 I was called up. As I said before, at the beginning of the war I had been passed unfit for all active service and destined to auxiliary service. But as things got worse the auxiliary services were mobilised too, and I had to go to the Army Recruitment Centre in

Albacete, where I was registered.

It was a real adventure. From Albacete we were taken by lorry to a military camp at Torre Guil, a farm five kilometres from Murcia. The house was big, like Los Hoyos, but it was absolutely inadequate for the 4,000 recruits concentrated there. Chaos reigned. For instance, we were supposed to be grouped into three companies: people with tuberculosis, people who had trachoma, and the 'glass brigade' – those of us who more spectacles. In actual fact we were all mixed up. We slept on the floor and, needless to say, there were not enough mattresses for everyone.

One night it happened that I was sleeping beside a tubercular man who began to vomit blood. Thank God, he survived. The food was very wholesome given the circumstances: rice, oranges and wine, plenty of wine. Outside the military camp there was an inn where you could drink as much as you could pay for. Discipline was very lax; so much so that on one occasion I escaped and went to Murcia on foot. I had an aunt there, so I went to her house to change my clothes and have a bath (in Guil there were practically no latrines and no way at all to wash). Afterwards I returned to the military camp the way I had left it.

I met some acquaintances from Albacete there. One of them was permanently semi-drunk. One day he confessed to me perfectly openly that he tried to be sozzled as much time as he could in order to more or less bear the appalling situation in which we found ourselves. It was the only way he had found of not sinking into deep depression.

A medical committee came to give everyone cooped up there a very superficial check over. Some were freed and allowed home due to ill health. Some from the 'glass brigade' were declared fit for any military service and a third set, myself included, were destined to medical services, military offices etc. In effect, I was sent to the Headquarters of the Remounting Unit, a cavalry section which had been transferred from Madrid to Valencia and was installed in a big house near the Turia River.

My final destination must have been at the personal prompting of my Guardian Angel; because, after so many vicissitudes and comings and goings, after so many frustrated efforts to escape, I once more came together in Valencia with, of all people, Paco Botella.

In Valencia

I lived in Valencia from July 1937, working in the head office of the Remounting Unit, directly subordinate to a cavalry major. This particular major or commander was not the product of any military academy; he had gradually worked his way up through the ranks, from corporal to sergeant to sub-lieutenant and so on. That meant long years of service and living among the troops. He was about fifty, a big rough fellow with a kind heart. Above him was the colonel-in-chief, a good man who had taken voluntary retirement during the regime of Azana. The critical circumstances of the war had forced him to rejoin the army and take up that post. He was very distinguished looking; a tall, slender man of fifty plus. He looked on me with a certain benevolence.

Every evening when I finished work at the office in the Barracks I would go and spend a goodish while at Paco's parents' house. Their names were Don Francisco and Doña Enriqueta, and I became very good friends with them. Paco had two younger sisters Enrica and Fina. Fina had TB which was a very serious illness then. I also took advantage of my visits to the Botella household to do some of my Christian plan of life which I followed as a member of Opus Dei.

During that period I was able to go to Communion every day. Paco kept some consecrated hosts under lock and key in a desk in his house. I was also able to go to confession regularly. Paco informed me that there were two old priests (dressed as country folk, of course) in Parterre, who dedicated themselves to administrating the Sacrament in spite of the risk it involved. If anyone informed on them, they would be arrested and very possibly shot. Outwardly they looked like two old men who, in common with many others, were sitting in the sun and minding their grandchildren... there were lots of children playing round about. The system for going to Confession was very simple. You approached one of them, gave the established greeting, and after a short walk received absolution. And off you went, until the next time.

As to my accommodation on my arrival in Valencia I had no choice, but to take what I could get. The only place where I could find shelter was in a rundown lodging in the old part of the city in a seedy area. At the best of times those lodgings would hardly have been considered delectable, but it was a case of any port in a storm. Due to the war Valencia was overcrowded, and that combined with my slender finances prevented me from finding anything better.

Gradually news of the others filtered through. Fortunately, José María Hernandez Garnica was freed in July 1937. Some months previously, Ricardo had also been in Valencia. He had then been forced to go to the front at Teruel on the Republican side. From there he managed to slip over to the other side on 17 May; so we did not coincide in Valencia.

On 6 October 1937 Paco and I had a surprise. Juan Jimenez Vargas, in person, had come down from Madrid to visit us. He was very thin. His hair was very short and his features were more pronounced than usual from the privations of the war. Dark glasses did not help. Briefly Juan told us, for he had always been a man of few words although precise and clear, that the Father was coming in two days time with several others on their way to the Pyrenees. From there they would try to pass to Andorra, through France, to the Nationalist-held part of Spain.

We quickly made plans to put them up. Juan would stay with Paco. José María Albareda, Tomas Alvira and Manolo Sainz de los Terreros would stay with me or in the house of Eugenio Selles, an acquaintance of the Father, who lived in 16 Eixarchs Street. I did not know all the people coming, as they were not all members of Opus Dei. We thought it best that the Father should also stay in that house as it held out the best hope of safety. The house in Eixarchs Street belonged to Don Mariano Bosch, the father of a good friend of Selles and Albareda called Paco Bosch. He had managed to get out of Valencia the previous June.

Juan encouraged us to be very faithful to our vocation in the midst of tribulations, and made us see how much our perseverance mattered for the survival of the Work. As night fell, he told us in his almost telegraphic language, what had happened to those who had stayed in Madrid during the fifteen months. A little we already knew from the letters we had got. I have filled out what he said with what I learned later. Basically, it was like this: The Father had been living in his mother's house in Doctor Carceles Street since 21 July 1936. It offered very little security and they were afraid of a search party; so on 9 August he went to Manolo Sainz de los Terreros' house. There he heard the news of the assassination of Don Pedro Poveda, founder of the Teresian Institute. He was a holy priest, a close friend whom the Father loved very much. The Father also heard of the arrest of Don Lino Vea-Murguia in his home while saying Mass, and of how he had been taken out and killed.

Juan also told us that weeks later, on 30 August, when he and the Father were hiding in a house in Sagasta Street, some soldiers had come to conduct a search. The Father, Juan and somebody else managed to hide in the loft. They were in great danger. But inexplicably, after searching the building and the other lofts, the soldiers did not enter the one they were in. After that they moved on, from one place to another. They spent September in Herrero Fontana's house, in José María Gonzalez Barredo's parents' house, in a house belonging to Eugenio Selles, in a small chalet in Serrano Street with Alvaro del Portillo. In view of the situation the Father had no choice but to take refuge in a clinic which belonged to a family friend, a Doctor Suils. It was a clinic for the mentally ill, and was situated at 492 Arturo Soria Street. He was there from October 1936 until March 1937. But the Father was not safe there either, and he had to seek asylum in the Honduras Legation where he stayed several months from April onwards.

That was a period of great suffering and hardship. The Father bore it in a very supernatural way. We, in Valencia, had heard news of some these events through the Father's letters. Paco had received one dated 28 March 1937, the twelfth anniversary of the Father's priestly ordination, in which he called himself the little donkey of God, his Friend, 'since he always carries him'.

The Father wrote from the Honduras Legation: *Here you have this poor old man evacuated to Widow Honduras' house, sleeping on the floor in the dining room (great fun) with four members of my family. Now I'm really feeling my age. I have lost nearly 30 kilos and actually I feel better, though I was ill in bed (what a luxury!) for more than a month. I am awaiting Ricardo with great anxiety because I need him. When he comes I will write and tell you.*

I am on tenterhooks not having news of my children who are away, but I'm always hopeful that I'll be able to embrace them all again when the war ends.

As for Josemaria, I must tell you that he assures me that it is precisely in these disunited times that he manages to be most closely united with his friend whose little donkey he is, as he carries a lot on top.

At last – Juan went on to relate to us in broad strokes to which I am adding more precise details – in August 1937 the Father had obtained a document which allowed him to move around fairly freely in Madrid. He was living in lodgings in Ayala Street, and he very bravely carried on the apostolate despite all adversities. He heard Confessions in the street; he attended to some nuns who had sought refuge in private houses; he preached retreats, changing the location continually to avoid being discovered, until the possibility of crossing the Pyrenees to the other side came up.

Two days later, on 8 October, when I arrived at Paco's, his father told me with understandable alarm that there were some gentlemen, our friends from Madrid, waiting for me in the sitting room. Paco was with them. I entered the room lit by the evening light coming in from the balcony. I could make out Juan and someone else whom I did not recognise. It was a very thin man, very properly dressed in dark grey. As soon as he saw me he clasped me in his arms saying, *Perico, I am so happy to see you again!*

I was perplexed. It was the Father. The voice was the Father's, but he had changed so much! When I was sure it really was him, I began to shake and to cry with emotion and joy. He had to calm me down.

While he was talking to me I was observing the striking changes wrought in the image I had in my memory of the Father of fifteen months ago and the figure I now had before me. I had always known him wearing a cassock and looking energetic and healthy. Instead, now he was very thin; he must have lost more than 30 kilograms – and he was dressed as a country-labourer. In Madrid he always wore his hair very short around a large tonsure which he would cover with a black cloth calotte. Now his hair was relatively long, with a side parting. Where before he used narrow-rimmed round spectacles, now he was wearing oval ones with much thicker frames. His cheeks were sunken. His high forehead was more prominent than ever and his eyes more penetrating. I especially noticed a small detail which seemed to me, who knows why, very significant: his tie was knotted very neatly. The only thing that had not changed was the tone of his voice.

While I was observing him attentively, the Father was talking about fulfilling God's will. He said it was not easy to understand God's way of working things out in those circumstances, nor was it easy to see all the good we were going to draw out of that tragedy. But he conveyed to us his conviction that God our Lord was determined that the Work would be realised and that He would not fail to help us. We had to try to regain the freedom we needed in order to be able to talk about God anywhere and everywhere. But we also had to pull our weight and do everything humanly possible to get out of that hell and to continue our apostolate, putting all our trust in God, for the Work belonged to Him. He told us that it seemed to be possible to cross to the other zone from Barcelona; other people had managed it. He had made this decision after a lot of prayer, he said.

They explained the plan to us. They hoped to leave the very next day by train for Barcelona. From there they would send news to Paco and me. May be they would then be able to arrange something there so that we could go with them.

After such a long separation, that first meeting with the Father seemed very short. But we left early because we did not want to worry Paco's family. An unauthorised meeting of young men in those circumstances was pretty dangerous; it could arouse suspicions. For the same reason the Father did not let Paco and me accompany him to the house where Eugenio Selles lived. We arranged to meet next day for lunch if we could, where it would not be rash for a relatively large group to gather.

After going back with the Father, Juan returned to Paco and myself again, and we strolled along Marquis de Turia Avenue for some time. He talked about what the Father had just been saying,

stressing the transcendence of those moments in the history of the Work. He spoke about maturity on the human level, the importance of looking for the divine meaning in things. He explained to us how the Lord's call had to be placed ahead of everything else. We could not use our youth as an excuse. Despite our age we had to be aware that amongst all of us, we had to carry out the Work, overriding other plans and commitments, however pressing they seemed.

A farewell

While Juan was talking to us, Paco and I realised that he was passing on to us the ideas he had heard from the Father in Madrid and during their journey. Maybe he was obeying a specific request from the Father to prepare us for what would happen afterwards. When Juan went back we asked each other what the main idea was that each of us had come away with. The synthesis was very simple: henceforward we were fully adult in the Work. One of us said good-humouredly: "Get it into your head that, as from today, we have stopped being a couple of carefree youngsters and have no choice but to start being responsible men."

The next day, 9 October, the Father celebrated Mass in Selles's house. I could not attend because of my timetable at the Barracks. They said that the Father even wore sacred vestments. The family had managed to lay their hands on some, which people had hidden during the persecution. Despite the risk they were running, because at any moment there could have been an unexpected search, they had even put out a pair of candles.

The Father asked us to give the children a present of some sweets in gratitude for all the family's attentions towards him. It was not easy to fulfil his request. In the end we took them some enormous sweets of the kind that were traditionally distributed during Holy Week processions before the war. We also took them a few toys for their youngest daughter. Selles remembers a coincidence from that time. In the same building, some floors higher up, there lived a young student called Amadeo de Fuenmayor who, after the war, was to ask for admission to the Work. He was not to meet the Father until later.

The doorkeeper of the house was a priest in hiding. Selles told the Father. After some initial hesitation the Father wanted to reveal his own identity to him. Selles writes: "He did not want to deprive him of any service he could offer."

At midday we met as discreetly as possible in a very modest restaurant patronised by soldiers and militiamen. It was situated in the old town, near the market and the warehouses, and on the first floor. I used to go there sometimes, so I knew the place well. Something happened there which was common enough in wartime. We were having lunch when some militiamen came in asking people for their documents. They didn't ask everyone, just a few at each table.

There was a moment of great tension. I went pale. Little by little the militiamen got nearer to our table and I started shaking. If they asked the ones from Madrid for their documents, they would probably have been taken away on suspicion. Juan had abandoned the warfront and had managed to get an emergency pass for himself. The Father and Tomas Alvira had permits of uncertain reliability to reside in Barcelona for fifteen days. That was quite out of the ordinary and if the militia set themselves to investigate the matter... Actually, I myself was the only one whose documents were all in order, so to speak. The Father realised this and he whispered to me: *Stay calm. Pray to the Guardian Angels.* When the militia came to our table the only documentation they asked to see was mine. They looked at it and left. I heaved a huge sigh of relief. That night Paco and I went to the railway station to see our visitors off. The train came in chock full of that human cargo so characteristic of wars: soldiers (in more or less standard uniform), bearded militiamen, militiamen with no sense of decency, smugglers dealing on the black-market, decimated families, people evacuated from their homes. The Father and the others spread themselves out through different compartments and corridors all along the train, partly out of necessity (it was useless to look for seats together) and partly not to attract attention when their documents were checked. Paco and I said our good-byes on the platform in the midst of this heterogeneous sea of travellers, feeling a mixture of affection and uncertainly. Would they reach Barcelona without mishap? Would they find the necessary contacts to cross into France? Would we both be able to go with them? The Father inspired us with courage and hope from out of a window, communicating trust and security just by his look and his smile.

The last few passengers clambered onto the train and it shunted away. Then the Father put his right hand slowly into the left side of his jacket. We knew that at that moment he was giving us his blessing, discreetly making the sign of the Cross with his hidden hand, while he soundlessly formed the words of the blessing spoken by Tobias senior, preceded by a prayer for the intercession of our Lady: *Beata María Intercedente, bene ambuletis...*

I felt utterly bereft at the departure of the train, as if my heart were holding back its beats. However optimistic we tried to be, we did not know when or where we would see the Father again. Once again Paco and I were alone in Valencia. Then we took up again our routine from the preceding months: my daytime hours in the Cavalry Barracks; the nights in that desolate boarding-house in the old quarter; the daily visits to the Botella household.

Some time later, I learned that that night hearing the continual blasphemies of the passengers, the Father had decided, after making many acts of atonement, to consume the consecrated Hosts he carried on him so that they were not exposed to further irreverence. He had to do so, with great heartache, in the toilet aboard the train. I heard him recount the details many times, always with the same pain and the same love for Jesus in the Blessed Sacrament. He never forgot that first trip to Barcelona: the people, the train, the night time.

How I deserted

Not even a week had gone by when I got a telegram from Barcelona at my unsavoury lodgings. It said the Father was expecting me next day in Barcelona. It was signed by either Mariano or

Ricardo, I do not remember which. I do not mean Ricardo Fernandez Vallespin. In the undercover language of our wartime, we called Juan Jimenez Vargas 'Ricardo'.

Getting from Valencia to Barcelona was quite a tall order in those circumstances. I did not even consider the possibility of obtaining a permit to travel from the Headquarters where I was posted. The idea was as absurd as it was impossible. Paco and I, telegram in hand, deduced that those laconic words meant that I should join them on the expedition which was on the point of crossing the border.

In such in circumstances, I concluded, it would not be wise to leave any trace of the route which I had taken out of the country. So I decided to do so in the time-honoured fashion, and got everything ready to make a quick getaway without uttering a word to my military bosses.

Of course I needed a safe-conduct pass. Fortunately, that was not a problem. Two days previously I had the brilliant idea of 'absentmindedly' walking off with a few blank but already stamped permits from Headquarters. In addition, taking advantage of a day that I was on guard alone in the office and that through the major's negligence I had within my grasp the authoritative rubber stamp of the no less authoritative colonel-in-chief, I had taken care to stamp them all in due form. Now all that was needed was to write the appropriate words on one of them, granting me a few days' leave and authorising me to travel to Barcelona. With that, and the minor matter of imitating the signatures of the major and the colonel, I was all set up.

I say 'imitating the signatures' as I consider it the best verb to describe the action in question. In normal times it would have been a clear case of forgery – but times were anything but normal. I should remind the reader that those legal certifications were handed out by the most fantastic and shadowy organisations, acting in the most arbitrary fashion possible. That's why when the man in the street was not able to get in with them in order to be able to move around or simply to survive, there was no help for it but to try to fabricate documents for oneself. The action certainly did not trouble my conscience, especially not when every day of the week I saw the real passes were being signed and sealed by people who, for the most part, had taken authority into their own hands.

As soon as this hurdle had been surmounted, I gave the remaining certifications from Headquarters to Paco, in case we might need them in the future. That very might Paco accompanied me to the same railway station from where the Father had set off for Barcelona a few days earlier. Paco was happy for me, but he too felt the understandable pain of being left by himself in Valencia.

Next morning I arrived in Barcelona without any difficulties. The Father and Juan were waiting for me at the station. It was an emotional day. As soon as I arrived I was able to attend Mass said by the Father in the house where he was lodging with Juan, Tomas and Manolo. It was a cosy flat on the Diagonal Avenue, on the corner with Via Layetana. A widow called Rafaela Caballero Cornet lived there with her mother. There was a small sitting room next to the bedroom which the Father was using. On a chest of drawers the essentials for Mass were laid out. The Father celebrated without vestments for, of course, there were none; but he fulfilled the rubrics lovingly, spoke the Latin text slowly, and celebrated Holy Mass with such fervour that I completely forgot all else. I felt myself transported back, for moments at a time, to our beloved oratory in Ferraz St. It was the first time I saw him use a small hand-written missal which contained the text of the votive Mass of Our Lady. Soon I understood the real meaning behind the telegram they had sent me. They had already managed to make contact in Barcelona with somebody they called Mateo the milkman. They told me that this unusual individual was going to help them cross the border in the Pyrenees. They wanted me to memorise the procedure and then return to Valencia and, from there, try to organise another group which could get out together.

The Father reminded us to put our trust in the Lord who would not forsake us. In those hazardous times, when one could only receive the sacraments in concealment and rarely even then, he insisted that we follow faithfully those parts of our plan of Christian life which could be done anywhere and in any circumstance: mental prayer, the Rosary and aspirations.

The Father appeared cheerful and optimistic, as good-humoured as ever. He was quite convinced that, if we trusted our Lord and at the same time took a prudent care over all the details of our journey, everything would work out. But you could see that he was undergoing great ferment on the inside, thinking of the people who had stayed in Madrid.

I was familiarised with everything, and at nightfall the Father, Juan and I went for a long walk down to the area around the port where the station is. There were still several hours to wait for the

Valencia train, so we filled in the time by having dinner in a sailors' tavern. It was so sordid that the pewter cutlery was chained to the tables so nobody could not walk off with it.

Suddenly a ferocious air raid began. The lights went out. Sirens wailed and everybody feared for their lives. In the midst of the panic and the exploding bombs, and with a flickering tallow candle as our only light, the Father started teasing me to calm me down:*If people could only see you now, Perico!*, he said, laughing, recalling my appearance in Madrid when I was always perfectly turned out, to the extent that I would sport an enamel tie-pin in the shape of woodlouse. For this was the fashion in those days. *Where is your 'coccinella septempunctuata'?* he asked me humorously, using the nomenclature of Linnaeus to designate my woodlouse. Indeed, if people could have seen me at that moment! My only garments now were a pair of none too clean army dungarees, an army belt and a barracks beret...

The Father and Juan accompanied me to the station when the bombing was over. A noisy crowd was waiting on the station platform. Lots of people were lying down on the ground, waiting for their trains, beside the most colourful baggage: huge suitcases, sacks of potatoes, baskets with chickens and other animals, all kinds of victuals, bundles and soldiers' knapsacks.

The train came in. This time there was no room for sadness or long drawn out good-byes because to board the train I had quite literally to storm the carriage. It was so full of passengers that the windows were being used as auxiliary exits and entrances, and at times they offered more hope of getting in or out than the train's real doors.

It was later on, during that long might on the train on my way back to Valencia, that I had more than enough time to think. Up till then I had not thought of the possibility of returning, so I had not contemplated what might happen if I returned to my post after taking french leave. No matter how hard I tried to find a justification for my absence, none occurred to me.

I arrived in Valencia with my nerves completely on edge. I went to Headquarters, and after a lot of official shuffling I was instructed to go into the Colonel-in-chief's office.

I can still see Colonel Lopez Dominguez while he was reprimanding me and shouting at me. He was very heated, stalking up and down his office not understanding the excuses I gave him (which is not at all surprising because they were quite farcical). He condemned my conduct roundly. Underneath I could see he wanted to spare me. However, he had to carry out orders and he needed to give me a punishment proportionate to my offence, which was very serious: missing role-call four or five times in succession and being away for 48 hours without permission in wartime, added up to full-scale desertion. In some cases the offender ended up in a punishment battalion; in others he went straight in front of a firing squad.

In the end the colonel found a benevolent solution which he pronounced with all the energy of somebody sentencing someone to death.

"Military Prison."

He explained severely that the sentence cancelled out any chance of promotion in the ranks of the Army. He had given me the minimum sentence: 16 days, which would also figure on my record.

It was a sentence of such unheard of leniency for those times that there was not a single cell in the whole of Valencia with a lockable door to put me in. I had to wait a whole day, guarded by an armed soldier, until one had been tailor-made for me, using a small windowless store-room in the San Anton Barracks beside the Turia. I could only communicate with the outside world through a small window in the door.

I was not in solitary for long, in that cell barred only by a very minimal door and an even more minimal lock. Once its existence became known, other prisoners whose presence was vexatious to the army came to keep me company. Almost all of them were legionnaires from the Third Army who had crossed over Nationalist lines to join the Republican Army, and had been arrested for the usual offences in the red-light districts of Valencia. Paco often came to visit me. To see me the poor chap had to line up with the other prisoners' visitors: often they belonged to that group of women who will precede the Pharisees into the kingdom of heaven.

How I deserted for the second time

In my made-to-measure prison, unexpected events continued to occur. I still had a week to go to complete the sentence when Paco came to see me one fine day in the company of none other than Juan Jimenez Vargas. At first we talked through the window in the door; later, thanks to the clemency of my gaolers, in a corner of the barrack courtyard. They brought me up to date on the news. The Father was worried about us and Juan had come to take us both to Barcelona.

It seemed as though the circumstances had been specially prepared by our guardian angels. The time was right. Paco had been called up and was to present himself for service on exactly the same day that I was to come out of prison.

Even so there was still a week to go. What were we to do?

On our own initiative, and on our own heads, we decided to go and collect Miguel who was in Daimiel, so that he could come with us. We drew up the following plan: Juan would go to Daimiel using a stamped certificate from the Headquarters of the Remounting Unit which Paco had stashed carefully away in his house. If he found Miguel he would give him the necessary military documentation. They would come back to Valencia, and from there the four of us would leave for Barcelona.

Providentially, everything turned out well and on the day I was set at liberty, instead of slinking into the office at Headquarters with my tail between my legs (for I was still posted there), I fell into recidivism. That is to say, I deserted all over again. But this time I was not alone – Paco deserted too. Our passes certified us as being soldiers in the cavalry on postings to auxiliary services attached to the above-mentioned Headquarters. We were taking a few days leave and were going to Barcelona to sort out some 'family matters'.

CHAPTER 7

Days of waiting

In Barcelona

Paco takes up the story describing our departure from Valencia. "In the station, there was a notice up stating that the Ebro had burst its banks and the train would only go as far as Amposta. Juan said we could not afford to postpone our journey; so we set out at two p.m. To look more natural, Juan suggested we should sit on the carriage-steps for part up the journey, like veteran militiamen.

Due to the circumstances of the Ebro's flooding, the passenger controls and checks must have suffered a minor collapse, for no one asked us for our papers during the whole trip from Valencia. When we got to Amposta the train stopped. The flood extended over a wide area of several kilometres, and that was the end of the journey! As it was late, we looked for a house to sleep in. The next day, 1 November, we crossed the Ebro in a little cart pulled by a very diminutive donkey. The water was not deep. At midday we got to the other side and we looked for a house, near the station, where we could have lunch."

Something amusing happened at that point. When we asked where we could get something for lunch somebody pointed out a woman's house to us. She said she would make lunch for us, but first we would have to catch one of her chickens, which were pecking around at liberty in the next field. Paco got the job of pursuing and catching the creature, haring after it and perspiring freely. And did it make him pay dearly for its capture!

We arrived at the Francia Station in Barcelona at eleven o'clock at night. It was too late to negotiate the city, which was totally blacked out because of the air raids. Neither was it advisable at that hour to go to the houses where we were supposed to be lodging. So Juan decided we would stay, and sleep in the station itself. We lay down on the ground and did our best to appease sleep. We turned over and wiggled around on the freezing paving trying to get comfortable; but it was no good. There was no chance of even a wink of sleep in that place. It was too cold, and travellers were constantly coming and going up and down the platform, from one place to another. Paco and I decided to spend the night walking around, smoking our last cigarettes 'conscript killers', much worse even than the ones people called 'best coffin nails' which cost 25 centimes a packet...

In the morning, after praying for a while, we went to the place where the Father was staying. He was saying Mass. We had some hazelnuts for breakfast while we related the adventures in which the palpable way God had safeguarded us shone clearly through.

We had to wait around for several tense days, which seemed interminable to me for various reasons. We were divided into three groups. Some were in Rafaela Caballeros' house; others, such as Tomas Alvira and José María Albareda, were with relations of theirs. Still others, of which I was one, were staying in a flat, in Republica Argentina Street; it belonged to the nephews and nieces of Vice-Countess Brias who was married to the politician Portela Valladeres.

The days passed and still the intermediaries who organised the expeditions to cross the Pyrenees would not come up with a definite date. They kept on putting it off, and more and more time elapsed.

Matters were urgent too. The papers which some of us had from the Headquarters of the Remounting Unit soon expired. In wartime, permits were only granted a few days at a time; to avoid giving rise to suspicion we had filled ours out accordingly. We tried to get round this problem by carefully scratching out the first or second figure of the date, substituting for instance a 'one' by a 'two'; it was not easy. Before we could do anything we had to try and find a typewriter with a similar typeface, no easy thing in the midst of our enforced isolation.

In addition, the small amount of money which the Father and the others from Madrid had managed to scrape together to finance the adventure, dwindled with every passing day. 'Crossing cover' cost money too. The people who acted as guides did not risk their lives out of lofty patriotism or philanthropy. They demanded the money of the highest bidders; and the money was to be paid in Spanish Bank notes with a serial number corresponding to the time before the military uprising. It was said that the Government in Burgos had put it out over National Radio that only notes issued prior to the terrible inflation then gripping the country would be exchangeable at the end of the war. One must bear in mind that many of the guides had been smugglers before the war. Though some of them were surely good people, the fact is that in many cases the normal contraband had simply been replaced by a new kind, more humanitarian perhaps, but much more lucrative as well.

Hunger

Another factor which made those November days seem everlasting was hunger. We were hungry, very hungry, ravenously hungry, in Barcelona. We had no ration cards and it was not prudent to try to acquire them to buy food. Neither did we have money to buy food on the black-market. The money we were keeping back to pay the guides was untouchable.

To give some idea of just how hungry people were, it will suffice to record that where we lived in the flat in Republica Argentina there was a dog which was so famished that, in a moment of carelessness on my part, it ate my leather belt leaving only the metal buckle. It also ate Paco's socks, which he had left to dry in the bathroom, and the only piece of soap we had. The poor animal was foaming at the mouth for a whole day!

Perhaps what made us suffer most was the state of some children who were also living in a house in Republica Argentina near Lesseps. They were related to José María Albareda. His mother had also sought refugee in the house. She had come to live in Barcelona after the killings in Caspe where her husband had also been murdered. The Marchioness of Embid lived in the same building. She was mother-in-law to one of José María's brothers. There were also two nephews of José María aged between 5 and 6. The family was so hungry that, despite his tender years, the older of the two children would queue up for hours to buy tobacco. A trooper would then give him in exchange a ration of bread, such as the army gave out to guards to have with lunch.

Those children touched the Father's heart. We saw them everyday because the house they were temporarily living in was between Mrs. Cornet's flat and the one in Republica Argentina. Commenting on this sad situation he said, *I feel very sorry for them. It shows up how cruel revolutions are. Their parents had to run away without them and now they have to be cared for by their grandmothers, two old and sick ladies who are terrorised by the assassination of their nearest and dearest. They cannot help it that the children live in the street and go hungry.*

We were not able to do much to help these children. Our breakfast consisted in a little watery beer with 2 or 3 revoltingly salty biscuits, which we swallowed in a local bar. The Father, however, saved up his biscuits for the children and, when he could, he also gave them part of his miserable lunch. As he had nothing else to give he tried to make up for the little creatures many wants with affection. He would say to me, *Amuse them for a while. Play with them.* That way he also tried to get me to enjoy myself because he had realised that those children kept me entertained.

On our occasion, to amuse them, I told them I was going to draw something for them. I asked them what they wanted me to draw: a dog, a car, a picture? But with one voice they begged me to paint a plate with a couple of fried eggs on it. I did so, and for good measure I added some tasty looking sausages. The children jumped for joy and licked their lips at the sight. At that moment the Father walked in. In a whisper, so the children would not hear, he said: *My son, don't you realise that for hungry children that drawing is mental cruelty?*

As well as the hunger it was the long wait, with its element of uncertainty, which drew out our days in Barcelona so agonisingly. We were powerless to do other than wait; wait and hope and pray that one fine day, one of those mysterious figures, Mateo the milkman, or whoever it might be, would inform us that we could finally get under way and which direction to take. On more than one occasion we lost contact with those possible intermediaries who were helping with our flight. Yet the Father kept trusting that the Lord would help us. He encouraged us ceaselessly and did his best to make sure that we did not fall prey to a state of nerves as it would have been so easy to do in those circumstances.

In Paco's words: "And so it went on day after day. To begin with the plan was for us to be in Barcelona for only a few days before beginning the journey over the Pyrenees. But things started to get more complicated. Around that time a party was detected when, finding themselves inside Andorra, but only just across the border, they broke out into shouts of joy and gave themselves away. The guards crossed into Andorra and machine-gunned them down. Some were killed, others injured. The rest were taken prisoner. The event was reported in the Press."

An old friend

One day, when reading the newspaper, the Father discovered that a former classmate of his from Saragossa University, called Pascual Galbe Loshuertos, was in Barcelona. He was a magistrate in the Courts of Justice there, representing the autonomous government of Catalonia. The Father went to visit him. Galbe did not believe in God and probably held anti-clerical views; but he esteemed the Father highly. He found the Father so changed that at first he did not recognise him. Then he embraced him with deep feeling and said, "How marvellous, Josemaria! The number of times I thought you must have been killed!"

Without hedging the Father hold him that he intended to cross the Pyrenees into France with a group of young men and asked him to do his best to save them if they were captured. "Don't do it, Josemaria, don't do it," Galbe advised him vehemently. "I wouldn't be able to do anything to save you or your group. Orders have just been given to the guards to shoot people and not to take them prisoner. A few days ago they caught a party and not a single one was left alive."

The Father explained his motives. As Galbe really was fond of the Father, he began to try to dissuade him. Galbe then suggested another possibility to him. He could stay in Barcelona working alongside him as a lawyer. The Father flatly refused. *If I didn't practise law when the clergy and the Church were not being persecuted because I had to dedicate myself totally to the priesthood, even less will I use that loophole now just to save my skin, and serve under an authority which is persecuting my mother, the Holy Church.*

Seeing his attitude, Galbe told the Father to come back another day so they could continue talking. When the Father appeared again, he took him into an office from which they could see into one of the courtrooms. Some fugitives who had been caught trying to cross over to the other side were on trial. At its conclusion the terrible sentence was passed:

"Death!"

The Father was deeply affected. But he would not change his mind. Galbe realised then that he was not going to be able to persuade him; and, even through he knew he was putting his own life and his family's in danger, he told the Father that if he was stopped at some point in the escape and was not killed there and then, he could lay claim to being a relative of his.

From then on the Father often prayed for him. He was always very grateful to him and prayed that God would grant him the grace of conversion.

Moments of anguish

I have mentioned before the hardship and hunger in Barcelona. That will serve as a point of reference to imagine the physical state the Father was in. He had not come from the 'Happy Levant', as I had, but from Madrid, where he had been subjected to innumerable privations during the previous months. I was thirteen years younger than he was; and while I was healthy, the Father had experienced bouts of fever. And, during the time he was hiding in Dr. Suils' lunatic asylum, he had endured a crippling attack of rheumatism in all his joints, which kept him prostrate in bed for some time. He was worn out, and since the beginning of the war he had lost almost half his original weight.

In Barcelona we could not have more than one meal per day which, moreover, was extremely meagre. Our finances only allowed us to go to two very modest eating places which we had discovered after several attempts: one of them was called the 'Red Eagle' and was in Tallers Street. There were tablecloths on the tables and the cutlery was clean, but the food was so sparse that we were hungrier after lunch than before it. I remember the menu: donkey meat and lots 'frincando amb bolets' (stew with wild mushrooms).

In the other place the food was more abundant but its cleanliness and tone left much to be desired. We, younger ones, preferred the second, and the Father in deference to us willingly accompanied us there, until we realised that he preferred the first one. From then on we decided to frequent that one; with his kindness and good humour he would make the best of the circumstances and make life pleasant for us. To save money we walked everywhere, which was also useful because it got us in training for the long walks ahead of us.

We were really worried that because of all these privations the Father would not be able to cope with the hard days in store, especially as he was already so weak from prolonged malnutrition. With the few means at our disposal we did our best to fortify him. One afternoon we nearly wrecked everything.

What happened was this. Manolo Sainz had seen a sign in a small restaurant in Las Ramblas advertising yoghurt, a new product which was to be served that afternoon, from such a time to such a time. As a doctor, Juan Jimenez Vargas considered it worthwhile spending a bit of money on such a healthy nutritious food. So off we set.

We were enjoying ourselves, savouring this untoward delicacy. Suddenly the police appeared, checking peoples' documents, table by table.

There was a moment of panic. We realised at once that some of our passes were no longer in order. In the midst of this situation the Father stayed calm and carried on the conversation as if nothing were happening. Once more our guardian angels – devotion to whom the Father had instilled in us – bailed us out. Our table was the only one the police did not stop at. If they had done so who knows where we would have ended up. (Needless to say, from then on we stopped trying to pep up our calories with yoghurt.)

Another worry was to avoid giving rise to suspicion among the neighbours in the place where we were staying. We tried to give the impression that we had been evacuated from our houses and had found stable employment in Barcelona. So we would leave our houses at the normal working time with the accustomed hurry of people who were off to work. What did we do then? There was no help for it but to keep walking around the city streets ceaselessly. The Father would suggest occupations which would help us to overcome the cancer of demoralisation.

Since most of the churches were burnt or closed we normally prayed while we walked. We also said the different mysteries of the Rosary a number of times, counting on our fingers. He suggested, too, that every time we passed a church where there was no worship, of which there were many, we should make acts of abandonment and spiritual Communions.

In order not to arouse suspicion, we would also not all go everyday to the Mass the Father celebrated in the house in Diagonal Avenue on the corner with Via Layetana. The Father would give Communion at another time in the same house or in the one in Republica Argentina to those of us who lived there. He did the same for José María and his family. He also ministered to a lot of other people in Barcelona whose names he would not mention so as not to compromise them.

Not having much else to do, those of us who studied architecture dedicated ourselves to making notes, and sketches, of buildings around the city. On one occasion this caused the Father several hours of anguish. He went to see us in the flat in Republica Argentina and Manolo Sainz, who had just moved in with us, told him: "The architects have gone off to make some notes on the building at the old International Exhibition Centre."

We did not know, as the Father did, that some of those building had been designated as munitions stores and powder magazines. The Father thought that if we were caught making sketches there, we could easily have been taken for spies and arrested. So when we got home from our unwitting excursion, and he saw we were all right, he hugged us jubilantly. He told us he had been praying all that time to our Lady for nothing to happen to us.

Once again I understood that he really loved us *with a heart both fatherly and motherly.*

CHAPTER 8

Crossing the Pyrenees

A Password

One day, at long last, we were informed we could leave and the days of impatient waiting in Barcelona had come to an end. The exhilaration I experienced when I found out that we could now set off must have been so great that I can remember nothing of the events themselves! The only thing I do recollect is that very soon after getting the news on 19 November we were aboard a mainline bus which ran between Barcelona and Seo de Urgel.

We sat discreetly apart inside the bus, forming two groups. The Father, Juan and José María were in seats at the front. Paco, Miguel and I settled down at the back. We had agreed that the missing two, Tomas and Manolo, would join us a couple of days later, so as not to give rise to suspicion.

The Father wore brown corduroy trousers, fastened at the ankles, a navy blue polo-necked jersey of wool or cotton, a black beret and some brown sheepskin boots with rubber soles. Juan had got hold of them for him and they looked, but only looked, ideal for climbing mountains. Paco and Miguel wore khaki army trousers and shirts which I had acquired using a procedure which I had better not divulge. The author wore the grey dungarees with multiple pockets that he always wore. The guides' intermediaries had advised us to take two pairs of rope-soled sandals each. This we did, except for José María who, by then, already had walking boots which we called 'pork-fat soles'.

We had practically no baggage, just soldiers' rucksacks and knapsacks. I realised then that what we consider absolutely essential can be reduced, at times, to so little, almost nothing in fact. Among the few objects which we had in our bags were the necessary things for the Father to say Mass: a few small corporals, several purificators, a small glass, a little bottle of altar wine and the hand-written missal. The Father had prepared all these things personally, with that heightened attention to detail so characteristic of him, especially in anything relating to the Holy Eucharist. His love made up for the poverty of the things. In his shirt pocket, under his blue jersey, he carried the Blessed Sacrament in a silver cigarette case.

Juan had realised that there was hardly one of us who was physically up to the long walk ahead, and had foreseen the remedies we might need. He was particularly worried about the Father. We were afraid that the damp and the cold of the Pyrenees – worse in the second half of November – might bring on his rheumatism again. Juan carried a wine-skin which had as much sugar as wine in it, in case the Father should collapse from exhaustion or something similar. As a good physiologist he knew that a mouthful of sweetened wine would help the Father to recover from a moment of general weakness.

We arranged for not all to get out at the same place. The road which leads to Seo de Urgel was near the border area. It was probable that the Father, Juan and José María, because of their age and the papers they were carrying, would get through the police and civil guard checkpoint just outside Oliana. It was wiser that those of us of obvious military age, (Paco, Miguel and myself), should get out before then. So we alighted at Sanahuja, some distance before Pons and Oliana.

We had arranged that a guide would be waiting for us there, and that one of us would be carrying a rolled-up newspaper in his hand and use the password 'Pallares' to establish contact with him.

There were several people waiting where the bus stopped. We started to investigate. Our password was perfect. The problem was that, I do not know why, but I arrogated to myself the mission of carrying the newspaper and pronouncing the auspicious utterance, without bearing in mind that when I get in a state I stutter and find it very hard to say words beginning with labials. I had several shots at it: 'Pa. Pa. Pa...'; but the magic word 'Pallares' would not come out. At last I managed to enunciate it and, as if I had waved a wand, a red-haired individual passed us and, without looking in our direction, said "Follow me".

We followed him at a discreet distance until, having left the bridge far behind and finding ourselves amongst bushes, he tried to communicate with us. It was not easy, for he was Italian and spoke neither Spanish nor French. He must have been a smuggler by profession. I don't think he even spoke proper Italian but some southern dialect; and, to put the tin hat on it, he had had one too many. In the end he and Paco managed to make themselves understood in a very sorry Catalan on both sides.

We started walking up into the mountains. I must confess that our mountaineering debut did not augur very well. In fact, it was a total disaster. Our Italian guide got lost around midnight and we went round in circles. Five, six, seven hours went by like that. Paco helped him time and again to find his bearings by pointing out where the sun had set. After walking for 12 hours we were exhausted. Our guide was lost. There was no solution but to continue walking. The fact that we kept on our feet without stopping for more than 24 hours, was thanks to Paco who kept our spirits up all the time, treating us firmly and energetically, as a captain does his troops. At last, on the point of collapse, we arrived at our destination: a hay-shed near Peramola.

An middle-aged Catalan farmworker was waiting for us there together with a boy of about 12 or 14. They gave us a letter from the Father which he had written a short time previously. In the letter he told us that they had got the through the Oliana checkpoint without incident and after using the River Segre they had arrived at the hay-shed, which they had left a few hours ago. He also said that we would soon be meeting up and he asked us to do a portrait of the boy in pencil and give it to him as a souvenir. Obviously the Father was willing to show charity to everybody and manifest his gratitude with some little present, no matter how critical the circumstances were. We had an extremely welcome lunch in the hay-shed, and did as the Father had asked. We slept for a couple of hours stretched out on the hay, despite the rats; though we had not been formally introduced, they took unwarranted liberties with our persons and scurried about, right beside us, as if we were life-long friends.

We were awakened still stiff from the terrible walk, feeling a strange mixture of sleepiness, tiredness and repulsion at the rats. Then, marshalling resources we did not know we had, we climbed for three hours more or less, until we reached a typical Catalan country-house or masia. We found the Father and the others there. I do not remember what time it was. I think the Father had already celebrated Mass in a small room in the house, and he gave Communion to those of us who had just arrived. The Father introduced us to 'en Pere' (the Pedro), a Catalan country man of about 50, owner or the 'masia' called the Masia Vilaro. He was surrounded by his whole family.

At that moment my reactions were awkward and disoriented. Tiredness had so clouded my senses that I was unable to feel the joy one would have expected, given that we were nearly all reunited with the Father well into the mountains, in a safe place where we could set off on our journey across the Pyrenees.

However, I did notice that the Father was serious and not as cheerful as he usually was. I attributed it to his concern for the people of the Work who had stayed behind in Madrid and for his mother, sister and brother. Tiredness impeded me from being very alert to what was going on around me. Shortly after our arrival at the Masia everything was ready for lunch. They had evidently been waiting for us three stragglers because it was very late. In my trance, I thought they had made us rice with chicken and I greeted it enthusiastically as such, but they explained at once that it was boiled wheat with squirrel meat, one of the few foods available to those poor people.

I thought we were going to spend the night in the Masia, but I saw Pere talking to the Father and Juan. He told them we were in danger there: the civil guards might find us. We should go on somewhere else as soon as it got dark. I was bitterly disappointed, not at hearing that we were still in danger, but because we had to keep on walking again, that same evening. Fortunately the place was near, just over half an hour's walk away. It was a house-cum-shrine, now uninhabited and tumble-down: the parish church and presbytery of Pallerols.

When we arrived at the shrine it was already pitch dark and I could not really get my bearings. Not even there were we allowed to sleep peacefully in one of the rooms. Instead we were put into a kind of kiln near the ruined church. At least that is what the small smoke-stained room with its low arched roof seemed like to me. In spite of its appearance, there was room for all of us. We were told that we would not be so cold there, but it was quite clear to us that was just an excuse to keep some of us calm. The kiln had a small window which was boarded over with some planks. Before saying good-bye, Pere warned us not to open the door no matter who came.

When we were all inside the kiln, dimly illuminated by a greasy candle which we had lit while we were settling ourselves down on the floor, I could glimpse through the shadows the Father's dejected face. I had never seen him like that. He and Juan were whispering together as though they were arguing. I could not hear anything. I asked Paco, who was closer, what the matter was. He muttered that the Father thought he ought not to abandon his children who had stayed in Madrid, exposed to all kinds of dangers. I interpreted the

few words Paco had said, as meaning that the Father was now uncertain what the will of God was and his heart was as though torn in
two. On the one hand, he saw the need to cross over to the other
side in order to continue the Work and exercise his ministry. On the
other, he wanted to go back to Madrid where some of his sons were
in gaol or in hiding, and where his mother, brother and sister were...
Suddenly I thought I heard Juan saying something that disturbed me
even more: "Alive or dead we are going to get you over to the other
side."

I was flabbergasted. I had never heard any one of us speak to
the Father in anything like that way or even address him other than
in tones of great respect. Distraught and afraid, I began to pray.
Meanwhile I could just hear the Father holding back his sobs. That
made me feel a deep anguish. I invoked our Lady once more, and
fell asleep overcome by immense tiredness from the long walk and
the unaccustomed emotions.

A rose

I slept like a log. I don't think anybody else did. When I awoke
next morning the Father and a few others had left the kiln and were
wandering around the house. What had happened I wondered and
what was going to happen? I went out and met the Father. His face
was radiant with joy and peace. I understood even less than I had
done the night before.

Paco told me that in those moments of doubt the Father had
turned to the intercession of the Blessed Virgin, asking her for a
clear and unmistakable sign – a rose – as a signal that he should
push on forward. In short, he wanted something which would
confirm him in his decision and which would comfort him in those
moments of agonising doubt. That was something he had never
done before, because he never sought anything out of the ordinary.
It was an inspiration from God. And when he entered the ruined
church near the kiln where we had slept, he saw the gleam of a
guilded wooden rose.

That rose which had come from a reredos in the church, set on
fire by the militia, was probably from behind the altar of Our Lady
of the Rosary. It confirmed that he ought indeed to go on.

Years later the Father himself said: *It is simply an insignificant
little gilded wooden rose. I held it in my hands for the first time
there, near the Catalan Pyrenees. It was a present from our Lady,
through whom all good things come.*

He was to speak very little about the rose in future, partly out of humility for he was the protagonist in that story of God's grace, and partly because he was no friend of signs and wonders. He would very often say. *Don't forget my children, that for us the supernatural is to be found in ordinary things.*

I acknowledge that I ought to deplore having slept so soundly that night. However, if I am to be sincere, I must admit I am glad. Whenever I have seen that something supernatural, something out of the ordinary, was at hand in our founder's life, I have felt a particular kind of fear which has perturbed me greatly.

I give thanks to our Lady with all my heart for having that night confirmed the Father on the way he should take, and for having enabled him to overcome that bitter doubt; because, just as I have never seen the Father as stricken as on that night, neither have I ever seen him as elated as on the following morning.

Saint Raphael's Cabin

Our brief stay in the house-cum-shrine of Pallerols ended as soon as the Father finished Mass on a makeshift table in a room next to the kiln. Although we were used to witnessing his piety when he celebrated the Holy Sacrifice, on that occasion, due to the extraordinary circumstances which had preceded it, it was even more emotional for all of us.

When Mass was over, Pere led us on foot four or five kilometres northwards, and we went deeper into the Rialp forest with its oaks, pines and fir trees. He walked along very much on the watch in case he came across a possible catch for the daily 'paella'. The paella (a fabulous rice dish, native to the Levant, made normally with chicken, seafood and spices) was mostly made of wheat and squirrel meat. Pere left us in a cavern half-dug into the ground and covered over with logs and branches. It was perfectly camouflaged in the wooded surround. The other two from the group still to come, joined us a few hours later.

It was noticeable that there had been other groups of refugees in the cavern before us, because there was some straw left on the floor with which our predecessors had tried to combat the cold and the damp. Until we suffered its consequences, we did not know that those gentlemen had also left us another bequest of a rather less pleasant nature – a repulsive culture of lice!

To protect ourselves from the cold, Pere provided us with thin cotton blankets, one for every two people, which were hopelessly insufficient. We spent the nights shivering. Once, we lit a tiny fire inside the cabin at night; but it was not much of a solution, as we had to make sure no smoke escaped. So we ended up with a dense cloud of smoke forming inside and choking us.

Neither could we light fires or cook anything during the day for fear of being spotted from afar. Sometimes availing himself of a donkey, Pere would bring us provisions; there was not very much of them but he charged us for these provisions as if we were in a grand hotel.

The Father christened that cavern, St Raphael's Cabin, as a sign of his devotion to the Archangels, whom he used to invoke as patrons of Opus Dei. To St Raphael he entrusted the apostolate with young people. Now, after all these years, I find it hard to believe that we were only in the Rialp woods for five days: it seemed to me more like seven or eight.

During our stay in the Cabin, the Father ministered to some priests in the area who were hiding in another cave higher up the mountain. They had been there for many months. Pere showed the Father the way to their hideout. Those good priests were very grateful for the chance to be able to talk to another priest who could tell them what had been happening over those months in Spain and in the world. In spite of everything, even their precarious situation, they had reason to thank God. Twenty per cent of the priests in the diocese of Urgel ended up dead. Of the 540 secular priests with parishes in 1936, 109 were assassinated during the war years. And to that figure must be added members of different religious orders.

Maybe we, too, could have hung out in the woods indefinitely without being discovered by civil guards or militiamen. At some point the Father said it was then that he truly understood the meaning of the word *emboscado* (ambush, from 'bosque' – woods), which was a term frequently used in those times.

During those days the Father often insisted on our living a set time-table which did not leave us a minute to spare. He asked us to keep the Cabin clean, as well the area around it. He wanted us to put our hearts into keeping everything in apple-pie order. In fact he had us busy ourselves about things which I thought were completely unnecessary. After hearing Mass, which the Father celebrated in the mornings on an improvised altar in the middle of the woods among the chirping of hundreds of birds, he suggested that we should listen to a lecture given by one of us, José María Albareda for example, on a topic of cultural interest. The Father got other people to keep a diary and the Architecture students to draw. There was even a period for sports. I did everything he said; but I did not really comprehend the sense behind it.

Only with the passage of time did I come to understand the reason for acting in that way. The Father wanted to avoid the characteristic mentality which saps the will of people laid up in hiding. They dream of freedom, but end up clinging on to the comfort of their refuge because they do not want to make the effort needed to break out of their circumstances. In this way he had us occupied for days, keeping any hint of edginess, impatience, laziness or discouragement at bay. It was yet another sign of his strength of character, wisdom and serenity when faced with the multifarious circumstances life presented him with.

Under way again

In spite of the Father's efforts to keep us occupied throughout, our inner impatience to get going again grew with each passing day. At last the long-awaited day dawned. But it took me, at least, by surprise. On 27 November we were waiting for Pere to bring us our evening meal when he turned up without it; he said we had to be off immediately. We packed up hurriedly and set off due north. Pere stayed with us for a couple of hours.

When it was dark we halted to await some other people who were supposed to be joining our party. Juan recalls that 'while we were waiting, the Father was stricken again by doubts and decided to turn back... That was a fresh trial. He could not see what to do, as though he suddenly felt abandoned, as though God had withdrawn his help, as though that was a trial God was allowing to come his way, which required a tremendous effort from him to overcome his temporary torment and drive himself on in spite of himself. Realising that it could be an irrevocable decision I panicked. I grasped him firmly by the arm quite ready actually to prevent him from turning back.

The groups we were waiting for appeared at long last and Pere said good-bye to us: 'God speed and the best of luck!'

A man nicknamed 'El Mora' took over from Pere. He was small and talkative. He led us to a cave in the corb, about two kilometres north of Peramola. There we met a new guide who told us his name was Antonio, although later we discovered it was really José Cirera.

The new guide was a smuggler. Juan recollects that he was 'very sure of himself, tireless and daring, as we soon learned'. We went on into the depths of the cave and, once there, he harangued us by the light of a single candle. "I give the orders here and the rest of you do just as you are told. We'll be walking in single file. And keep your mouths shut. I don't want any noise. When I have something to say I will say it to the man behind me, and each person will pass it on to the person behind. Nobody is to stop or dawdle. If anyone gets ill and can't go on he'll be left where he is. If someone wants to stay with him, he'll be left as well."

It was a gloomy scenario. After his speech we all emerged from the cave into the night, behind our guide. We scrambled up a precipitous path among pines and mountain oaks. Our guide was young and as strong as an ox. It seemed as if God has bestowed upon him an anatomy which had been specially designed for picking his way over boulders with extraordinary agility. He soon acquired a reputation as a leader, which he well deserved, a prestige founded principally on his legs and being resolutely taciturn, surprising in one so young.

From then on a long line of refugees began to form, its numbers swelling at every cross-roads, as a river builds up from its tributaries. So our initial small group soon became a long human chain. The Father was walking immediately behind Antonio, and José María was not far behind him. From my position some way back I could see how the Father had very soon made friends with our young guide. Once again I saw that no one could resist the Father's kindness and his way with people.

From then on I lost track of time, even of night and day. I do not know how to explain it. It was a sensation rather like making your first transoceanic flight, except that it lasted several days, and was infinitely worse and more excruciating. The fact that we normally walked by night so we would not be seen, and that we rested when the sun was high, somewhere where the guides knew it was safe, only added to my confusion. Even so, safety was very relative as there had been many cases of the contrary. Besides all that, none of us had a watch on and there were no mealtimes to mark off each day's journey into stages. The result was that I lost all sense of time. I had no notion of what day or what time it was. The night-time marches seemed endless, and tiredness, sleepiness and hunger drew them out even further. The rough path did not help either, though we never followed what you could call a real mountain path; rather we clambered and struggled up crags and scrambled our way with great difficulty through the undergrowth in the woods.

Now again we could see the lights of a hamlet twinkling in the valley below, and we would ask the guide which village it was. But we discovered that he invariably told us the wrong name as a security measure to avoid anybody's informing on him.

At last, after an interminable march, we came to a deep ravine in the Ribalera gorge, at the bottom of a mountain of reddish-coloured rocks. There, before we rested, the Father said he wanted to celebrate Mass. The place chosen was not in the hollows itself, but nearby, in the open, a little below a baby waterfall formed by water seeping through the rocks.

During the previous night's march we had heard some blasphemies as there were all kinds of people in the group. In addition to twenty or so Catalan men there were also some professional smugglers. Even so the Father wanted everyone to know he was a priest and he got ready to say Mass. The group was still not all that large, but at least twenty people attended who would surely not have heard Mass since the beginning of the war. Everyone behaved very respectfully.

I shall never forget that Mass. There was no rock high enough to serve as an altar. But there was a lower one which was flat enough. So the Father had to celebrate the holy Sacrifice kneeling the whole time. In spite of fatigue and the untoward circumstances, he celebrated Mass with such fervour that we were suffused with his piety and devotion. Two of us had to kneel down as well, on either side of him, to hold down the corporal so that no hosts would blow away. Our guide, half hidden among the trees, observed it all from a respectful distance.

I especially noticed one particular Catalan lad who heard the Mass with real devotion. He looked like a university student. His name was Antonio Dalmasses, and later we became friends. He wrote in his diary: "A priest who is with us celebrated Mass on a rock kneeling, almost lying, on the ground. He did not say it as priests do in churches. His clear, devout way of saying it went right to the heart. I have never heard Mass said as it was today. I am not sure if it was because of the circumstances or because the priest is a saint.

Holy Communion was particularly moving. It was difficult to distribute because we could hardly move even though we were all grouped round the altar. We were all dressed in tatters, exhausted, dishevelled, and with several days' growth of beard.

One person had ripped his trousers and the whole length of his leg was exposed. Our hands were bloodstained from scratches. Our eyes were tearful. But more than anything else God was there with us."

After those few hours' rest we struck out again around mid-afternoon while it was still light. After a long steep climb, there was a more gentle slope, almost like a plateau, but long too; then, again, another exhausting climb, up to the summit of Aubens.

Our strength began to fail. José María and Tomas were on the verge of collapse. Juan recalls that "the gradient was steep and at times we had to scramble up screes. We had hardly begun that part when Tomas Alvira slumped down... He was in such a state of exhaustion that he was utterly spent. In his hopelessness he felt sure he would not be able to make it." We tried to revive him, but the time came when our leader gave the order to push on as we had to reach the peak before nightfall. He told us to leave Tomas lying where he was. It was a harsh decision and we were not prepared to accept it; but Tomas was at the end of his tether. Then the Father took the guide by the arm, spoke to him for a few minutes and then turned to Tomas. *Take no notice. You'll be coming with us like everybody else, to the very end.*

With hindsight, I can now understand that if José María and Tomas were able to overcome their exhaustion, it was because God wanted it so, and because the Father intervened with extraordinary charity and strength of mind. In both cases, the Father supported them with tremendous kindness and took our guide aside to speak to him. The wind carried his words to our ears and they went, in reference to José María, more or less as follows: *Antonio, you have to think that he is a very worthwhile person. He is a really brilliant man and internationally renowned for his scholarship. He has done a lot for his country and he still has a lot left to do. You are a kind-hearted man. Be a little patient and let us help him until we get to the top of this mountain. I assure you that as soon as we get to the first stop and he can rest a little, he'll get his strength back and he'll be able to carry on normally. In time to come you will have the satisfaction of knowing that you saved the life of an exceptional person...* Incredibly, our inflexible guide gave in in both cases, and we pressed on.

From then on our group took it in turns to help José María, who had gone absolutely rigid, with a blank, faraway smile on his face. He must have been suffering from some kind of altitude sickness. If we took him by the hand, he kept on walking but very slowly. As soon as we let go, he stopped, showing no reaction whatsoever to our words of encouragement. He seemed not to hear.

We were surprised that it was precisely Albareda and Alvira who collapsed from exhaustion. Being a soil geologist, Albareda was used to climbing mountains and going on long walks and scientific field trips. Alvira was one of the youngest of us all. But the months of hunger in Madrid and Barcelona had taken their toll.

The day we climbed Aubens was one of the worst. Juan was close behind the Father all the way up. We were all convinced, Juan especially so, that our principal mission was to take care of the Father's life in those critical moments. By saving him we were assuring the continuation of the Work which was God's will. That was absolutely clear to us, without anybody's having had to spell it out. Fortunately the Father reached the top of Mount Aubens and managed the other stages with surprising energy. He systematically refused the sugary wine that Juan offered him, arguing that other people needed it more than he did; but when he finally did give in, Juan squeezed the wineskin so hard that he was forced to drink more than he wanted.

The way down Mount Aubens on the northern side was less strenuous, but it was very uneven. We were walking through pine woods and finding our way down between crags. Some of us took tumbles but no damage was done. It was well into the night before we were down, and after crossing a road with the utmost caution we stopped in a house in Aunas to rest. It was a big country-house with stables for farm horses.

By then the group of fugitives had considerably increased in size. New groups had joined us, especially of country people. Sadly, that meant more swearing and more blasphemy too. The old superstition, so prevalent among peasants and carters, that animals only obey blasphemies, had gained ground notably in the long years of anti-religious revolution. That was the reason why the Father decided to consume the Sacred Hosts.

We spent all day on 29 November in Fenollet House, hiding in one of the byres. One woman, the *mestresa*, took care of the house along with others who helped her, including a nun who had sought refuge there. We were tired out when we arrived and I fell asleep at once. Nevertheless, for one reason or another I woke up several times and I noticed that the Father was not asleep. That made me cross inside. I thought to myself that if he did not make the most of these hours to rest, he would succumb later.

Afterwards I found out that, around mid-morning when I was fast asleep, we had been in great peril. Juan recalls: "Two militiamen came to the house asking if they had seen anyone. They were patrolling the area looking for runaways. The housekeeper, mustering great level-headedness, convinced them that she was more than ready to collaborate in the persecution of rebels. Meantime she plied them with wine and tasty ham, and when they had finished their lunch, off they went without investigating further."

The women at the house made some emergency repairs to our clothes, and at midday they gave us the only really nutritious meal we had on the whole journey: mutton and beans. At six we set out again, and the Father advised us to get rid of everything we had been carrying on our backs so that we would be lighter on our feet. During the ascent of Mount Aubens we had already shed part of our load, but now we abandoned the lot. Even Manolo's shoes were left behind in the byre.

As we were leaving we were told that there was no more food. I think it was then that the guides gave us a fresh cheese and a chunk of bread as our only provisions. They said it had to last for eight rations, that is to say until we got to Andorra. It humiliates me that I still remember that cheese vividly. It was round and white, and must have been no more than 12 cms in diameter and 4 cms thick. After climbing a mountain we stopped on a little plateau to rest for a few minutes. Manolo began to joke about the cheese, and to my great surprise he drew a slide-rule from his pocket and half-joking, half-serious, began to calculate using pi (π), exactly what proportion of cheese corresponded to each meal. The Father welcomed Manolo's running commentary in good spirit. Not so Paco and I: we retaliated against Manolo's calculations, and devoured our whole allowance of bread and cheese for good and all.

Hunger drove us to determine that the best place to store the food was in our stomachs rather than carrying its small weight around in our rucksacks.

In contrast to us, with our minute cheese and minimal piece of bread, Antonio Dalmasses was fairly well stocked up. As well as other provisions he had a lunch box, full only of delicious roasted chicken legs. We did not know his name at that stage. The Father remarked kindly and good humouredly that he was a clever lad for he had discovered a new species of animal, a cross between a farmyard fowl and a centipede: a centipede chicken. From then on we would jokingly call him 'the centipede boy'.

At dusk we started out again, downhill this time. We crossed a river and approached a road. We were told to be extremely careful and not to make any noise with our feet as we walked or with the sticks we had cut from branches. We had to climb two mountains, Santa Fe and Aras, which were 1200 and 1500 metres high, respectively. Between the mountains there was a valley at an altitude of 700 metres. It was quite dangerous crossing the valley because, according to our guide, the farmhouse dogs might raise the alarm and warn the militiamen in Organa. That was what had happened recently, and the militiamen had shot the fugitives.

We managed the two mountains; after that I cannot remember anything more with any clarity. I only harbour an image of thirty men, bent almost double, creeping along in single file without setting their sticks to the ground. It could almost have been a dream sequence. My memories of later events are all muddled up. Once, we crossed a road and were dazzled by a car's headlights. Juan notes: "The fright rooted us to the spot, but the imperturbable guides only said that if we were caught by headlights again, what we had to do was freeze and keep quiet."

"It's all right," they said confidently. "They can't see us."

Then came the worst part. We had to cross countless rivers. Later I found out it was always the same one, the Arabell, but we crossed it over and over again. At times we would walk in the water, at times on the bank. We discovered, then, that the boots Juan had got for the Father were a complete swindle. He had been assured that they were waterproof; but the water got in as through a sieve, but with the added inconvenience that they took ages to dry. The Father did at least two days' march with soaking wet feet.

At dawn on 1 December we camped, utterly sopping and frozen to the marrow. Hardly had the sun risen when a snowstorm threatened. We spent the whole day among the scrub and stones, wet through without being able to move about, so we would not attract attention. The ground was wet and slippery. During the night we heard some drums which warned us how close the Civil Guard or militiamen were, and we grew anxious. But in those moments I, at least, cared more about the cold than I did about being caught. It was a frightful cold, a merciless and bitter kind of cold, which ate right into my bones and made me shiver, on top of the physical and mental exhaustion which had been weighing me down for the last few days. Although I was totally empty-headed from weariness, I did wonder to myself, if that was what I felt like, how must it have been for the Father. These considerations helped me to pray and, particularly, to pray for him.

At the same time some of the things I saw the Father do irritated me; for instance, he did not protect himself from the cold by putting newspapers in his clothes and under his jersey, as the rest of us did. He tried to eat less, so that we could have more. He hardly slept when we stopped in those caves or byres. I guessed that he was doing all that in order to mortify himself and pray more. Though I was moved by it, I did not understand it, and because I loved him so much I would have liked to stop him.

During the long climbs up the mountains we each tried to say the Rosary going along, at least in our hearts, as the Father had taught us. Our gasps for breath alternated with the Our Fathers, Hail Marys and the Litany. We counted the decades in our heads, our hands having more than enough to do with leaning on our sticks and clutching at hand-holds. So we would lose count easily and end up saying 20 or 30 Hail Marys to a mystery. Then a strange phenomenon enveloped me. It was a tangible example of the physical tiredness and mental fatigue caused by having to scrutinise the ground at every step in total darkness. During one of the last get-togethers we had in the Cabin, the Father had entertained us by singing a delightfully ingenuous carol which the good nuns in the St Elizabeth convent, at the foundation where the Father was Rector, used to sing at Christmas time. The carol went like this:

> *What a lovely baby*
> *St Joseph has today*
> *Every time I see him*
> *I come all over fay!*
> *Oh oh oh*
> *I come all over jay!*

Surprisingly, those simple words, the tune with its childish rhythm, became an inseparable part of my strained breathing for hours on end; 'Every time I see him', 'every time I see him...' I repeated the tune so often, and the tunes were engraved so deeply in my memory, that I am sure I would forget my own name before I forget that Christmas carol sung by the Augustinian nuns at the St Elizabeth Foundation.

Another phenomenon brought on by exhaustion was that sometimes we would see the lights of a village shimmering in the valley far away like a kind of midnight mirage. In reality there was no village there at all.

That afternoon after a freezing day it started to snow before we set off. So without having been able to rest at all, we renewed our journey northwards.

Later we compiled our recollections of that part of the crossing. There was a critical moment near the Civis gorge. The guide warned us that a patrol was on the prowl. He had heard their footsteps clearly. He had us pass on the message:

"Total silence and keep still."

He disappeared to go and investigate. We were in a damp spot. Soaked to the skin, we stood there for two hours fighting tiredness, cold and sleep. One or two fell asleep on their feet. When the guides returned they told us that when the patrol was some distance from the point where we were to cross the road, we were to run for it, as fast as we could, up the Cabra Morta pass, on the far side of the river.

We waited in silence. The patrol went by, and when the guides was satisfied that they were far enough away, we started to sprint up the mountainside as fast as possible, hanging on to whatever we could and getting scratched by hundreds of thorns in the process. Then, after getting up a steep slope above the river, we crossed a rift, skirted round a jutting crag and went almost to the peak across open terrain. The guides told us later that the ground was so rough, that most people would not have dared to traverse it in the daytime for fear of falling. Suddenly we pulled up in the middle of a wood. The guide told us to hide. 'Each one behind a tree. Stay absolutely still. Keep Silent.'

In the midst of such hush, that stop seemed interminable to me. We could see a light on in a house and the glow of a fire. We thought a patrol was near.

I had forgotten many of these things. But together we later jogged each others' memories as we reconstructed events, and Juan, who returned with one of the guides to these places years later, recollects that we passed near a house, Llusia's Cottage, which had a light on. It must have been a carbide lamp. Some dogs got wind of us and started barking furiously. We got a terrible fright, but the guides took no notice. Later we crossed the Argolell River and from there, scared stiff, we heard shots.

Juan recalls: "They realised too late. Maybe they thought that we were still on the way up, and they wanted to knock out the tail-end of the party. But we were already out of range." We had crossed in front of Mas d'Alins when in total darkness. Now the guides told us we were over the border. We were in Andorra!

The Father said a prayer. It took me some time to react and realise that we had made it. May be it was the elation itself which stopped me from altogether believing it. The guides pointed out the way we should head, and then vanished.

We waited for daylight and then began walking. I was only convinced that we really were in Andorra when a beautiful village, Sant Julia de Loria came into sight in the valley before us. It was 2 December 1937.

In Andorra at last

After that long nightmare, we were free at last. As soon as we were by ourselves, the Father intoned the 'Hail Holy Queen' again in thanksgiving. This time we recited it slowly, aloud, with profound fervour and gratitude to our Lady. Thus we gave voice to our joy in an act of love to our Mother who once again had manifested her mercy towards the Work.

We arrived at the village. Before entering it we had to undergo a procedure which some of us objected to: the police proceeded to disarm us, that is to say, they took away the rough and ready staves which we had selected from branches. They considered them unsuitable arms!! Moreover, they classified us as political refugees. That also irritated me quite a bit, because our escape from Spain had not been motivated by politics.

We had hot coffee in a bar at the entrance to the village and looked for the church. Then we continued on foot to Les Escaldes, a small habitation in the Principality of Andorra, very near Andorra la Vella, the capital.

I have to admit that some of my first memories of Andorra are not so spiritual. In particular, I refer to having a bath with hot water and soap in the Palacin Hotel at Les Escaldes, where we stayed, and our first normal meal which we had there. Since our bodies had lost the habit of digesting food at regular intervals, and we younger ones did not have the sense to eat only a little like the Father, who hardly had anything at all, we had rather a bad time after that first meal. I can remember exactly what Paco and I had: Steak and chips, white bread and fruit. I can also remember the discomfort and downright pain they produced. We shared a room and we had to open the window to let in some fresh air to soothe ourselves.

The Father's hands swelled up alarmingly and he began to be

racked by pain. Juan was worried. He thought it could be the beginning of a rheumatic attack like the one he had gone down with in Madrid. When he examined him he discovered that the inflammation was due to masses of thorns embedded in his skin. During the climbs he had kept grabbing hold of the scrub which had been full of thorny brambles. He had said nothing so as not to worry us and so we would not try to help him. Even in those critical moments the Father had wanted to live as he always taught us to do: *'Non veni ministrari sed ministrare'* – *I have not come to be served but to serve.* Juan pulled the thorns out for him, one by one. Next morning the Father was much better, and we were all able to go to Andorra la Vella for Mass. For the first time in almost a year, the Father was able to celebrate the Holy Sacrifice wearing vestments again. He said the Mass in a chapel which the Benedictine monks of Montserrat, escaping from Catalonia, had made on the ground floor of a house near the hotel. Before beginning the Mass the Father asked us to pray for those we had left behind in Madrid. I imagine he said Mass that day for them.

Our plan was to leave Andorra as soon as possible, because the pass which the French Gendarmarie had given us as 'political refugees' was only valid for forty-eight hours – just the time it took to reach the Spanish border at Irun. But as we arrived at Andorra la Vella, it started to snow heavily. Thank God it did not catch us in the middle of the Pyrenees; Andorra was totally cut off. Envalira Pass was closed because of the snow; so, naturally, in those conditions we could not get through to France.

Time passed and the snow ploughs did not arrive. A day passed, and another, and another. We toyed with the idea of getting snowshoes, but that came to nothing. Besides, Colonel Boulard roundly forbade us to try to cross the border in such deep snow. He was staying at our hotel and was in command of the detachment which France had sent to Andorra to defend the Principality against incursions by the Spanish militia.

However, the days went by and the road was still blocked by snow; the weather forecasts were not good. 'Monsieur le Colonel', a heavily built man, had his mind made up and refused to let us leave. He was very considerate to the Father when he discovered he was a priest. After a week we prevailed upon the colonel to let us set out for France on foot and on our own responsibility. It seemed to be the best solution. After all, we were already familiar with the Pyrenees and besides that we had a very good reason for leaving:

we simply had no money left to continue paying for the hotel room.

On 10 December 1937, after attending Mass celebrated by the Father in the parish church of Andorra la Vella, we set out as early as we could. We were accompanied by almost everyone in the party which had crossed the border with us. We were able to travel part of the way in a lorry with makeshift seats and stout chains on its wheels. Then, as the lorry could not get any higher than Soldeu, we crossed Encamp Farm on foot. We walked for about 15 kilometres, sinking into deep snow, higher than our knees. The landscape was breathtaking.

At first the walk seemed easy enough, especially when compared to the preceding days. But before long our enthusiasm waned, especially when we began to feel our feet getting frozen. We were wearing the same footwear as we had used during the crossing. The Father's boots were in tatters and we had not been able to buy any more for him for lack of money. Now and again we would wrap our feet in newspapers to protect ourselves a little from the snow, but the damp soon turned them into a useless sludge.

In those arduous circumstances we climbed up the Envalira Pass at an altitude of 2,400 metres, and continued along the road to the mountain refuge which we reached after 11 a.m. At midday we set out again, this time for Pas de la Casa, used as a summer post by the French Customs. Here all 25 of us in the party squeezed into a fourteen-seater bus. Like that, crushed and weary, we arrived at L'Hospitalet, the first town in France.

There the paperwork took from 2 to 5 pm. We then squashed into the taxi that was waiting for us. It was an old hired Citroen which some friends of José María's had sent. It would have picked us up at Les Escaldes if the snow had permitted. And eight of us huddled into the vehicle which was relatively big. Packed in like sardines, and frozen with the cold, we began our journey on French soil.

Thanksgiving in Lourdes

Yet we did not go directly to Hendaye. The Father wanted to stop off in Lourdes to say thank you to our Lady. My memories of the visit are very vague, due to the exhaustion of those days. There was a biting wind. We were soaked through and our teeth were chattering in the cold.

During the drive we kept quiet so that we could do our afternoon prayer. The only thing I managed to do was to offer up the misery of being cold and wet, and at the same time beg our Lord not to let the Father fall ill. I was sitting beside him and I could not think of anything to say which would make the journey more pleasant. Yet the Father, for all his tiredness, tried to cheer us up. When we passed through Tarascon he referred cheerfully to that well-known character in Daudet's novel, Tartarin de Tarascon. He had often mentioned that character when preaching about being realistic in one's interior struggle. We were not to behave like Tartarin who went to hunt lions in the corridors of his house, he told us.

We spent the night in a modest pension in Saint Gaudens. It was rather pompously called the Central Hotel. I did not stop shivering until I had dragged my wet clothes off and snuggled down under a pile of blankets. Next morning, on 11 December, we got up before daylight and set off again.

We left for Lourdes very early. The Father was silent, very composed and devout, preparing for Holy Mass. We prayed and said the Rosary. When we got to Lourdes we had a few contretemps in the sacristy of the shrine. The Father had not been able to get a cassock and they did not want to let him celebrate Mass. But then they gave him permission to do so, properly vested in a white chasuble in the French style. He said Mass at the second side altar on the right of the nave, quite near the door to the Crypt. I served. The others knelt nearby. At the beginning of the Mass, as I raised my hand to make the Sign of the Cross, the Father turned to where I was kneeling, on the step and whispered to me:

I suppose you will be offering up this Mass for the conversion of your father and for our Lord to grant him many years of life as a Christian.

I was very taken aback. Actually I had not offered the Mass for that intention at all. More than that, I was not concentrating very much and was feeling the natural lassitude of someone who had got up very early and not yet had breakfast. I was also struck by the fact that the Father should have such a big heart as to remember my family problems at that precise moment when he was about to give fervent thanks to our Lady and commend so many important things to her. Deeply touched, I answered him, also in a whisper: 'I will, Father.'

Then he added quietly: *You do that, my son. Ask the Blessed Virgin for it and you will see what marvels she will grant you.*

And he began the Mass : *In nomine Patris... Introibo ad altare Dei...*

CHAPTER 9

Pamplona

I don't want to hear your story

We only spent two hours in Lourdes. We went on to San Juan de Luz which we reached between 6 and 7 o'clock in the evening on 11 December. José María Albareda's brother was waiting for us there. The border between France and Spain was closed, but we were allowed through over the international bridge. Paco recalls: "I cannot forget the Father's deep happiness as we crossed the International Bridge at Hendaye. He recited the 'Hail Holy Queen' and then aspirations which we echoed intensely and fervently. The Father continued praying when we set foot on Spanish soil, where we had complete freedom of movement. We did not shout aloud for joy as people often did in such cases. We did shout on the inside, though, thanking God and the Blessed Virgin. Our voices were at one with the Father."

As soon as we got to Fuenterrabia we were obliged to make multiple statements because of our condition as refugees. The Father tried to phone the Bishop of Vitoria, Monsignor Javier Lauzurica, but he was away, in Rome.

Then the Father spoke to Monsignor Marcelino Olaechea, Bishop of Pamplona, and he was able to vouch for us to the civil authorities, which cut down on a lot of official delays.

Before going on I wish to explain something, so that what comes later can be understood. It was wartime and people were very impassioned. Opinions, especially political ones, were held and defined, with fire and fury. People who had escaped from the other zone often fell into resentful reprisals, which were understandable because of what their families had been victim to, or because of the sufferings they themselves had been through. Nevertheless, even in that climate, not once did I ever see or hear the Father say or do anything that was not in keeping will his universal serenity, prudence and charity. Of all of us who were closest to him then, may be no one was as aware of this as I was, because of my complex family situation.

I would immediately have detected a wounding comment, a

contemptuous gesture or allusion. But he never made one. The Father never talked about politics. We wished for and prayed for peace and the freedom of consciences. Open to everybody, and with real greatness of heart, he longed for everyone to turn to God and get closer to Him. It hurt him when he heard an exclusively political evaluation of events which ignored the bloody persecution and the numerous sacrileges being committed. That explains why, as soon as we got to Fuenterrabia, the Father asked me to write out a list of my father's efforts to save lives and avoid sacrileges, and hand it in at the Information Office there. Thanks to his job as Provincial Director of Historical and Artistic Monuments, my father had been able to hide a lot of sacred vessels, tabernacles, religious images and so forth, unbeknown to almost anybody. He had hidden them in some store rooms in Albacete and in a cellar in the village of Fuensanta. *It is only fair that the good done by so many good people independently of their political views should be made known some day*, the Father said to me.

Those words are an example of his magnanimity. He never expressed resentment. And in those days it was not easy to combine love of justice with charity: but the Father knew how to do it admirably.

There was another characteristic typical of that time: it was that many people would speak of themselves in inflated heroic terms. Relating the whole tale of one's wartime hardships to other people became so fashionable that the following phrase was coined: "I don't want to hear your story, thank you very much." By contrast the Father, who had so many hardships to recount, never did so. Neither did he rely on officialdom for solutions. He went on as usual: working, keeping quiet, praying and trying to avoid attracting other peoples' attention.

He advised us never to harbour hatred in our hearts but always to forgive, even in those febrile times. One has to realise what things were like then, in order to understand the whole radical meaning of these words. The Church in Spain was undergoing the greatest persecution in its history, in which almost 7000 priests and nuns, as well as numerous lay Catholics, died for their faith.

Some of those who lost their lives for the faith in the conflict were close friends of the Father. Don Pedro Poveda, founder of the Teresian Institute, and now also beatified, was one of them. Don Lino Vea-Murguia, arrested on 16 August 1936, was murdered and his body dumped by the wall of the East Cemetery. Many other priests the Father knew were also killed, among them his godfather. Remembering him years later, when a woman who had suffered cruel persecution in her own country asked him a question, the Father recalled: *He was left a widower and became a priest after that. He was martyred when he was 63. I was called Mariano after him. And the little nun who taught me how to read and who had been a friend of my mother before taking the veil, she was murdered in Valencia. I am not horrified by it; it fills my heart with tears... They are wrong. They have not known how to love.*

Still talking to the same woman, the Father added: *I have recollected those events to console you, my daughter, not to talk politics because I do not understand politics. I do not talk about it, nor will I as long as our Lord lets me live in this world, because that's not my job. But tell your family, from me, to join you and me in forgiving them.*

The Father knew how to forgive and he also taught us how to do so always.

But, let us go on with our story. We spent all day on the 12th in Fuenterrabia, and the next day we went to San Sebastian. We had begun to disperse to different places: some to work, others, those of us of military age, to our posts in the army. Juan, for instance, joined the medical corps on 15 December. In the afternoon of the 17th, Paco and I boarded a dilapidated freight and passenger train to Pamplona in the company of two civil guards. After many hours of bone-shaking and struggling through a heavy snowfall in Alsasua, we arrived at our destination, the Miners and Sappers Regiment in Pamplona. We had said good-bye to the Father and he promised to come to Pamplona and spend Christmas with us.

In the Sappers Regiment

When we arrived in the Navarese capital, another pair of civil guards led us to the Engineers Barracks, the Regimental headquarters. It was at the easternmost point of the military camp, north of the fortress. As soon as we crossed the threshold, a rookie took us to our Company, on the other side of large esplanade under a thick mantle of frozen snow. I felt as though I was in Moscow. I had never seen a landscape or building like it, except in Russian engravings.

Our company was on the first floor of a building, on the left hand side, and when we entered our escort called out to the soldier on guard duty in a weary voice. A drowsy and lethargic recruit appeared, enveloped in a cape, with little more than the tip of his nose showing. That nose rang a bell with me. It belonged to José Luis Fernandez del Amo, one of my fellow students. We used to call him 'birdy', which he did not mind at all. José Luis used to come to the Circles in the Residence in Ferraz Street as well.

Our first night in the barracks was quite an adventure; there were not enough beds, straw mattresses, or blankets, and the cold was really Muscovite. Paco put a brave face on it and prepared to accept the shortages with an ascetical resignation. I wanted to survive, and I fought for permission to sleep outside the Barracks as soon as I could. Fortunately we had a good mentor in José Luis who taught us the various little ploys of barrack life. They were far more useful than the drill we did every morning with a terrible sergeant, who bombarded us with left right left right, continually bawling 'Com...pan...y!'

Poor sergeant! In spite of all his yelling, and all his efforts, he did not manage to lick Paco or me into the requisite military shape. Nor did we ever manage to hit anything during rifle practice.

We were not provided with uniforms; but we were told to have our heads covered so as to be able to salute properly. With the paltry sum of money we got weekly, we were able to buy pen and paper to write letters and begin our epistolar apostolate, as the Father had recommended.

The days passed like that until 24 December. Paco and I were on guard duty. Suddenly we heard great shouts calling us to come down to the big gate at the entrance. There was the Father, who had turned up at the barracks without letting us know beforehand. He was wearing a cassock and cloak and a shovel hat, which priests used to wear at that time. The Teresians in San Sebastian had provided him with shoes and some clothes. The Bishop of Pamplona, Don Marcelino Olaechea had offered him hospitality in the Bishop's Palace and had given him the cassock. The hat was the Bishop's own, and he had taken off the episcopal symbols, the cord and the green tassels, so that the Father could use it.

Just before midnight that night the Father came to the Barracks again. Paco remembers it in detail. While he was on duty at the Arsenal, the Father appeared with José María Albareda who had arrived in Pamplona that same afternoon. They were permitted to go right up to the munitions store because priests were held in such high trust and esteem at that time. Paco recalls: "They spent some time there with Pedro and me. We shared some turron they had brought to celebrated Christmas Eve. José María had acquired some money, so we were able to buy some things to eat. Living, as we were, through such extraordinary circumstances, those signs of affection, of family warmth, were engraved on my heart. I felt very happy and my dedication to God was something full of joy."

We were able to spend Christmas Day with the Father and José María. It was an intimate day. After lunch we went to the Father's rooms in the episcopal palace. We told him stories from our life in the Barracks. He told us how in those circumstances we could pray while on guard duty, and he reminded us that we could and should turn our work into prayer and into an occasion for doing apostolate. He also said that we had to be very human in order to be very holy.

From then on, and during the first week in January, the Father would often come to see us as soon as we came off duty in the afternoons. Like that he made friends with a corporal called Garmendia, with whom he would talk while awaiting us, and for whom he would bring a cigar whenever he could, out of the ones Don Marcelino kept for offering to his guests. The Father remarked to us: *He is a good husband and a good father. It is a shame that the war keeps so many men like him away from their families.*

The Father told us he was going to settle in Burgos. The main reason was that from there it would be easier for him to get around to visit the members of Opus Dei who were scattered about because of the war.

He would also be able to meet up with many of the boys to whom he had given spiritual direction in Madrid. It would have been much more comfortable for him to stay in Pamplona or in Vitoria, where the bishops had offered him indefinite hospitality. But the apostolate carried more weight. Added to this was the fact that probably José María would also be able to live in Burgos with him or at least spend long periods there. So, from then on, Paco and I did our utmost to get transferred to Burgos, especially as we had been posted to auxiliary services and there were lots of organisations and military dependencies there.

Doña Micaela

Before closing this account of my stay in Pamplona, I want to mention Doña Micaela Pinillos, even if only in passing. Paco and I had eventually gained permission to sleep outside the Barracks, and we lodged in a pension, in 6, Pozoblanco Street, on the fourth floor. The landlady was Doña Micaela. We came to an arrangement with her: we would just go there to sleep, as we had no money for anything else. But Doña Micaela very generously gave us dinner many times at her own expense. I do not know how old the good lady was, but she was of a generous age, well into her fifties at least. Very soon she took a liking to us and she particularly venerated the Father who came to see us there from time to time.

Doña Micaela had keen powers of intuition, sharpened further by her having known quite a few people who had dedicated their lives to God, and by having several relatives in the religious life. So she quickly detected 'something very special', as she used to say, in the Father. "You can see from miles away that he is a saint", she told us several times. She also said that in the two of us – Francisco and me – there was a bit of that 'something'. One day, when she was making a remark along those lines, I tried to forestall her:

"Of course he is a saint", I said. "Of course we have a bit of him. He is our spiritual director."

"Is that all? Only spiritual direction?" Doña Micaela inquired.

Her intuition did not stop there. On one occasion she said, "I am praying a lot for the foundation that Don Josemaria must be setting up." I was particularly surprised by that. Maybe she had heard something. Certainly we had not said anything to her about the Work; she was a very devout woman, of rare and accurate intuition.

CHAPTER 10

The months in Burgos

From Pamplona to Burgos

As he had said he would, the Father moved to Burgos. He settled into modest lodgings at 51, St Clara Street. From there he made several apostolic forays to Valladolid, Avila, Bilbao, Leon, Saragossa and Pamplona in January and February. Meanwhile I began to negotiate my transfer to Burgos by writing to my uncle for help. This was my mother's youngest brother, Diego Ramirez Pastor, who was the editor of a newspaper in Bilbao and writing under the pseudonym of Jorge de Claramunt.

One day I fell ill. When the Father heard this he came to see me at Doña Micaela's pension. He was with me when a soldier came in to tell me that all leave had been cancelled and I was to present myself in the Barracks immediately. I was frightened. In those days the news from the Teruel front was alarming and rumours were going around that the whole lot of us might be sent there. Many young men were being killed at the front.

At first the Father was worried too. He gave me his blessing and told me he would pray to the Virgin Mary. He told me not to worry: I would be all right. And so it was. At midnight restrictions were lifted, and those of us who had permits to sleep outside the Barracks returned to our lodgings.

When I got back to the pension I found the Father still there, waiting for me. Doña Micaela's pension was a good information point. He had not wanted to return to the Bishop's Palace until he knew what had happened. He welcomed me as a father welcomes a son who has survived a great peril. His affection moved me, and we prayed a Salve to our Lady in thanksgiving.

At last I was posted to Burgos. Paco had got a posting there as well. On 8 March 1938 I was able to go and live with the Father, José María and Paco, all sharing the same room in the pension in St Clara Street. It was a small house, now long since demolished, near the railway line. From one window you could see the austere facade of the Home run by the Sisters of the Poor. It had some fine escutcheons with episcopal emblems sculpted in stone.

My posting in Burgos was to the Headquarters of Mobilisation, Instruction and Recovery (M.I.R.). When the military commanders realised that I had nearly completed a degree course in Maths/Physics they assigned me to the Cipher Section, commanded by General Orgaz. I had the job of encoding and decoding the telegrams which were being sent and received.

There I got to know Pedro de Ybarra MacMahon. He was a young soldier, slightly built, fair complexioned, with horn-rimmed spectacles. He stood out for his good manners and his kindness. Pedro briefed me for my new job. That was the beginning of a long friendship, which has lasted all our lives and which, in those days, helped me to endure the interminable hours we spent in the office every day.

There was no shortage of work. When there were no telegrams to decipher, I was ordered to draw up staff plans or to do some typing. Pedro was proficient in several languages. His job was translating foreign manuals, which were later reprinted as texts for the Provisional Academies run by Orgaz. After work, I went back to the pension in St Clara Street.

We did not stay long in that pension. While we were there the Father sometimes celebrated Mass in the Monastery of Saint Clara nearby. Soon he began to say Mass in the Teresian Chapel at 5 Merced Street. He offered to give a retreat or the occasional meditation there because of the great affection he had for Fr Poveda and the institution which he had founded. He tried to support them in their loss and sorrow at the death of their founder. In those times of want, in spite of his absolute penury, he made a heroic decision never to accept Mass stipends.

Navarro Borras (the former professor Paco and I had at the School of Architecture in Madrid) also lived in our pension for a while. He had known the Father from before the war. There were several other uncommon characters there too. The strongest and most curious of them all was an English lady in her fifties who worked as a news reader for National Radio. She was the only person in the pension who had tea. Between ourselves, Paco and I called her Miss Wiggy because of the texture of her hair. At first she did not take to us at all. She used to complain about the noise Paco and I made pounding up and down the wooden stairs in our big military boots. But the Father reconciled us to her to such an extent that she ended up affectionately calling us 'Peguico and Pacuito'.

No man's land

When I arrived in Burgos, in March, the Father was really ill. I was informed that he had been like that since February. As always, he did not wish to give any importance to his health. But as soon as you touched his hand you could tell he had a high temperature. Every evening it would go up. He had a persistent dry cough and was very hoarse. Paco was deeply perturbed. He told me the Father had even vomited blood.

Time passed and he did not get any better. The Father was never given to worrying; but he must have started to bother as well, for his were the typical symptoms of advanced tuberculosis, then an illness which had no cure.

Besides being incurable it was contagious. If it really was tuberculosis, the Father asked himself, how could he live with us and do apostolate with young people in general. Nevertheless, in the midst of this uncertainty he was perfectly peaceful. He had put himself totally into God's hands, accepting his will.

He delayed going to the doctor for a check-up as he did not want to spend money we did not have on his health. Thanks to Ricardo's suggestions and Paco's insistence, he eventually consented to go to the doctor's on condition that he stayed no longer then it took for the doctor to examine him. He wanted José María Albareda to go with him. Later he confessed, with his typical humour, that he chose José María because, being a professor, he was more likely to be absentminded enough for the Father to give him the slip and enter the surgery alone! That is exactly what happened. Later, while the doctor was looking him over, and in an attempt to get him to divulge the interim diagnosis, before he got round to taking the X-rays, the Father said jokingly:

Well, doctor I have come for you to sound out my cavities. You know I'm a cave-man don't you?

Floored for a moment by the Father's witticism, the doctor recovered and proceeded to a more detailed examination. Then he said, "You haven't got, nor have you had, a lesion in your lungs." After further explorations by an Ear, Nose and Throat specialist, the doctors still had not found the cause of his illness. They came to the conclusion that the lesion was in "no man's land".

Sigfried's vest

However, the fact that the doctor had ruled out possible consumption did not mean that the Father got better. The material conditions in which he lived did not favour his recovery very much. We were going through one of those harsh Castillian winters which the Father faced out by eating little and dressing lightly, out of poverty and mortification. He usually wore a lightweight cassock around the house – it was the only one he had. When he went out he put on a clerical gown and the felt hat given him by the bishop of Pamplona. He would not allow us to buy him a jersey and a scarf. On one of Ricardo's visits from the front, he asked Paco and me really to put ourselves into caring for the Father's health. But as the reader will soon see, that was not an easy commitment to take on.

First of all, one has to take our material circumstances into account. We were trying to cope with extreme financial hardship and often we did not even have enough money for the most rudimentary requirements. For instance, we had only five pairs of pyjamas for all of us. This meant that the extra pair had to be washed quickly, so the next in line could change his. And we boasted only one warm vest between the four of us. It bore the initials of its original owner, embroidered on the front, in laboured gothic lettering. It was quite thick and made of good quality wool, second-hand, but in a very reasonable condition. We had been given it on our way through San Sebastian.

One day when I was wearing uniform trousers and military boots I put the vest on. It came down to my knees, making me look not unlike a medieval soldier. I put my belt on over it and began to ape Lohengrin. Paco and José María roared with laughter. Suddenly the Father came in, and I stopped in my tracks. He asked us what we were up to, and Paco explained candidly that I was doing Sigfried. From then on the vest was called 'Sigfried's vest'. The other garments that we used in rotation also had proper names: 'the chauffeur's pyjamas', 'the convict's pyjamas', and so on.

Sigfried's vest was the cause of my overstepping the mark in my desire to take care of the Father. He did not want to wear the famous vest, arguing that he had a particular aversion to such garments. That was true. But basically he did not want to wear it out of a spirit of mortification and so that we could have it. That was until one day when it was particularly cold and the Father was still hoarse and had a terrible cough. Paco and I forced him, almost physically, to put it on. We did it out of affection but without much respect. After a few minutes he had already taken it off, and then we realised how inappropriate our behaviour had been. We apologised and agreed to look for other ways of caring for his health.

You are Peter!

In the midst of those straits Paco and I tried to get the Father to rest and we did our best to entertain him by telling him amusing stories. I remember telling him about one particular event from my recent stay in Pamplona which he enjoyed a lot. The bishop had organised a special fiesta around the celebrations for the Pope's feastday: Holy Mass with a reception afterwards, a chance to kiss his ring and a sermon in St Nicholas' Church in the afternoon. As I knew him personally I went to the church. I sat in one of the front pews, facing the pulpit. At the appointed hour Don Marcelino entered and began the sermon. He paused, and then suddenly exclaimed in thundering tones: *"Tu... eres... Pedro! –* You are Peter!"

I thought he was addressing me and was taken aback. I jumped in my seat. Then I realised that he was quoting from the well-known verse in the Gospel: 'You are Peter and on this rock I will build my Church.'

With anecdotes of that sort we tried to ease the Father's suffering for those left behind in Madrid: Alvaro, Isidoro, Vicenton, his mother, his sister Carmen and his brother Santiago... He used to talk about them very often. He worried about the ones at the front, at Madrid and Teruel, where there were a lot of casualties. He also suffered because of the difficulties he was encountering once again, after ten years of continuous work, in getting the apostolate off the ground.

Sabadell Hotel

During the weeks we spent in the St Clara pension, the Father spoke several times about getting a flat so that we would be able to attend to the apostolate better. At the time renting a flat in Burgos was almost impossible if you did not occupy a high military office – not the case with any of us. Neither could these problems be solved with money, for we had none.

Some members of the Work sent us money sporadically. Ricardo, Juan and a few others went to extraordinary lengths to skimp and save, so that they could send us part of their modest salaries. José María did not earn very much either. As for Paco and me, we got two pesetas a day from the army. Moreover, as I said before, the Father had decided not to accept Mass stipends or stole fees for preaching, for the sake of the virtue of poverty.

That explains why I tried to get Captain Martos not to appoint Pedro Ybarra and me Honorary Officers, as he had planned.

According to the rules only army officers could belong to the Cipher Section. If I were to be made an Honorary Officer the only distinction I would gain would be losing my two pesetas daily, with no other form of compensation in exchange. I would also forfeit the right to use the mess allocated to the soldiers at the headquarters where I normally ate.

When we shelved the idea of getting a flat in Burgos because of its sheer impossibility, we thought we were taking a great step by vacating the St Clara pension to move into the Sabadell Hotel. We moved in there on 29 March. It was a third-class boarding-house, on the banks of the River Arlanzon, at 32 Merced Street.

The building could be seen until quite recently, although differently numbered – eleven – and being used for other purposes. It had an attractive facade in a flowery provincial style so characteristic of the time it was built. There was a high porch, made of iron and glass, above the entrance which was bright and airy. It gave almost direct access to the staircase. There were three storeys above the ground floor, with three bedrooms facing on to the street. Our room was number 9, and was on the first floor, with a glass covered balcony on the left hand side immediately above the front porch.

To understand what follows properly, a fairly accurate conception of the material circumstances in which we lived is needed; that is why I am going to give a detailed description of the room. All four of us, the Father, José María, Paco and I shared that room. The entire floor space measured 28.35 square metres. In that reduced space we prayed, worked and slept, we washed and shaved and received visitors – lots of visitors. Though it sounds incredible, our apostolate extended to more than a hundred people of different ages and life-styles. As a modern decorator would say, our room had three district 'areas'. The biggest one, the room properly speaking (4.63 by 3.92 metres) was furnished with three beds; mine, Paco's and José María's. There was just enough space left for a small wardrobe, big enough nevertheless for the few clothes we had, a rectangular table and a couple of chairs. Opposite the door there was another 'area': a covered balcony with two small arm-chairs, a small cane table, and some blinds made from green painted wooden laths which protected it from the sun and the curiosity of passers-by, giving it a certain privacy.

Opposite the balcony, beside the door of the room, was the third 'area': a small Venetian-type room which was the Father's bedroom. There was no direct light, but it had a bed, a bedside table, a wash basin with running water and a clothes hanger (fastened by a nail above a small door which opened straight into the corridor but which was always kept shut). The 'partition' between the room and the Father's bedroom consisted simply of a whitish, almost transparent curtain, of poor quality cloth.

The room was uncomfortable and small. Above the door there was a ground-glass panel, so every hotel guest who came back late at night would invariably wake us up by switching the light on in the corridor.

But gradually the room took on a family feel. The Father suggested the idea of making some little flags, in the style of university sports clubs. We bought some scraps of blue, yellow, and white coloured felt. The Father had started doing apostolate with some girls, thanks to the help of Vicente Rodriguez Casado's mother. I made the pattern for the flags and the girls cut them out and sewed them together. One of the flags bore the name RIALP, the woods we were in while crossing the Pyrenees; the other DYA. Those flags livened the room up considerably. We also stuck up some maps of the different regions of Spain.

The Father received lots of visitors in the balcony. It was a tiny place (1.78 metres long by 0.80 cm wide). The visitors were mostly students who had frequented the DYA Residence in Madrid and who in their turn were bringing new friends along. Some of them died later at the war front.

I have to acknowledge that, outside that young milieu, neither Paco nor I were over-enthusiastic about the other older people, equally numerous, that the Father received. When young people came we would have a get-together; and if it were Sunday, we would go for a walk to Las Huelgas or somewhere else outside Burgos. The Father would often take advantage of those outings to speak to each person in private. We would walk along the banks of the Arlanzon no matter how hot or cold it was or whether it was raining. But the older visitors were another story altogether. Paco and I called them the VIPs. They arrived. They greeted the Father who would invite them to sit down in the balcony. They closed the shutters – and we were plunged into darkness. We had to turn the light on even though it might be mid-day. Every time that happened Paco would whisper to me: "Good night!"

Many of those visitors were priests. Some of them later became bishops or archbishops. I remember Don Antonio Rodilla, Don

Angel Sagarminaga, Don Daniel Llorente (later Bishop of Segovia), and Don Casimiro Morcillo, the future Archbishop of Madrid, among many others. Don Casimiro was the one who came most frequently. They all thought the Father an exceptionally holy priest and they used to tell Paco and me so in asides. I must acknowledge that my interior reaction was not very humble, as I could see that for myself day and night. When they said so I would think, "You're telling me!"

It happened that our room in the Sabadell Hotel was frequently plunged into darkness. We did not understand too well why the Father received all those older people and priests. We thought they were wasting his time. Only years later with the growth of the apostolate and when married men and diocesan priests joined Opus Dei, did I finally comprehend the Father's priestly zeal in that little balcony in the Sabadell Hotel.

A fine Havana cigar

There is an amusing tale which points to the precariousness of our household economy in Burgos, though at first sight it might appear to be quite insignificant. One day the Father told us he had been given a fine Havana cigar as a present. He was thinking of giving it to Don Francisco Navarro Borras, our erstwhile professor, who often came to visit him. Don Francisco was very partial to Havana cigars, which were in short supply in war time. Thinking how pleased he would be when he gave it to him, the Father wrapped up the cigar carefully and put it away in the drawer of the small writing desk in our room.

However, Paco and I were also partial to cigars... and our reasoning went like this. Some cigars are longer than others; some are pointed at both ends, others not; and, as this one was very long and pointed at both ends, it would never be noticed if we cut off one of the ends very carefully with a razor blade. So without more ado we trimmed off two bits. We crumbled the tobacco and made two very slim cigarettes.

The trouble was that the following week we still had no money and no cigarettes, so we repeated the operation. That happened several times until the impressive cigar was reduced to a pitiful stub. One fine day Navarro Borras appeared, and you can imagine how ashamed Paco and I were when the Father said, *I've got a surprise for you, a fine Havana cigar as long as this...* He opened the desk drawer and when he saw the stub to which it had been reduced, he pretended he could not find it and changed the subject. As soon as Don Francisco had left he said: *When we have a cigar and you want a smoke, have it by all means. But please don't put me in those embarrassing situations!*

Years later the Father enjoyed telling that story which, above all, comments eloquently on our penury.

Vectorial accounting

The little money we did have, went into a common cash box, the content of which was as poor as was the container itself. It was a square wooden box which had once contained a Burgos Cheese which someone had given us as a present. The lid swivelled round on one of the four nails which held it down. Paco saw to the accounts in a very rudimentary fashion. He would write down the amount on a sheet of paper, with an arrow pointing inwards or outwards depending whether it was a credit or a debit. Come the end of the month, he would add up the amounts with arrows pointing inwards, then the ones with arrows pointing outwards, subtract one from the other, and the difference was the balance. The Father had not realised how we were keeping the books, until at one stage Paco had to go away and gave the box to José María. The latter remarked frankly that Paco kept the accounts in vectors.

The Father wondered what that meant and when José María explained, praising it as a very ingenious method, he said: *You ought to be ashamed of yourselves. Two mathematicians and a research scientist, and you keep the books worse than my mother's cook.*

So we bought a proper little book and began to book-keep respectably. No more arrows or vectors of any kind!

Whenever I remember those little incidents, I realise that had it not been for the clarity, serenity and lightness of touch with which the Father communicated things to us, he would not have been able to form us with the necessary fortitude and constancy. God gave him the gift of knowing how to make demands on us and he certainly did just that, and yet at the same time he managed to leave us with a good feeling after every correction.

That was not just on account of the advice itself, but also because of the love he showed us whenever he rebuked us. We had a wonderful knack of saying things well.

His words would really sink in and we listened with great respect. But he had such talent and such a keen sense of humour that even though he spoke in earnest, sometimes we would have really to contain ourselves so as not to laugh. The charity and wit he used taught us not to forget the correction. But he never left us feeling hurt or resentful.

Living as we did, right on top of each other, we noticed even the smallest details. I realised, then, just how well the Father lived the virtue of order, even in details which might seen tiny and insignificant. He achieved something besides, more difficult still: maintaining order in the midst of our disorder. I can still remember a small tin box where we kept needles, thread and buttons of every kind. Any time any of us used the box we would leave it all topsy turvy. Then the Father would tidy it up again, very patiently, at the same time dropping a hint.

He sewed the buttons back on his cassock himself, whenever they came off. It was not only then that he kept that custom up, in the special circumstances we were living through. Years later, when he lived in Diego de Leon Street in Madrid, he still kept a similar box in a chest of drawers in his room. Although he was not particularly good with his hands and often pricked himself with the needle, I often saw him sewing on the buttons on his cassock.

Day after day I witnessed his constant acts of kindness with every one. He always spoke well of everybody. I can remember one particularly telling event. He had invited a boy to breakfast, and we had chocolate 'con churros'. When he had gone we complained to the Father that his guest had really had a good appetite, for he had guzzled several cups of hot chocolate one after the other, and several lots of doughnuts. The Father charitably and cheerfully made excuse for him as he always did. The problem, he said, was that the boy had not managed to get his calculations right. He had finished a doughnut while he still had some chocolate left, and the hot chocolate was downed while he still had some doughnuts left... That comment is an excellent example of the warmth of his charity. He always knew how to put a sympathetic slant on any comment which might be, or seem to be, critical even through it was only meant as a joke or referred to something quite unimportant, as in this case.

As regards myself, in spite of my unfortunate blunders, he was always very patient with me. Year later when I had already acquired more formation. I heard him sighing: *Poor man! Poor man!* One day I was intrigued and I asked him, "Who are you referring to, Father?" *Your father, my son, who else?*, he replied, with that loving sense of humour so particularly his own. *Your father must have been a saint to put up with you! And he's left me the job of taming you!*

The Father's penance

There is no help for it now, but to tackle a chapter of our stay in Burgos which is really hard to write about: the mortification and penance the Father practised. It still makes me shiver to think of it.

We can best understand a phenomenon when we see it in context; that is to say, when we see it in the place in which it belongs within the whole, considering it and evaluating it within the framework of its own surroundings. It is for this reason that I have taken pains to describe the place we lived in, and I have also tried to relate what he was like to those of us who lived with him. It is only within that context that some of the Father's attitudes at that time can be understood. The same goes for aspects of our behaviour which were motivated by our desire to take care of his health.

We paid four pesetas daily per bed in the Sabadell Hotel, that is, sixteen pesetas altogether. I cannot remember how much we were charged for each meal, but the normal price in any modest restaurant in Burgos was never less than eight pesetas. When José María Albareda was in Burgos, the Father had lunch with him in the hotel. When he was not there, he had no lunch at all or just a bite of something so he would be able to say he had had lunch. Paco and I had lunch in the barracks. When we got back we used to ask him where he had lunched and he would avoid answering the question. He used to fast just as he has written in *The Way*: *A strict fast is a penance most pleasing to God. But with one thing and another, we've all grown lax. There is no objection – on the contrary! – if, with your director's approval, you fast frequently.*

During the time we lived in Burgos the Father had no habitual spiritual director. Normally he went to Fr Lopez Perez CMF or to Don Saturnino Martinez, a secular priest, for confession. I do not know how much those good priests knew or what they thought about the matter. What was clear was that Paco and I were in total disagreement with the Father concerning his fasts. And we let him see our dissent according to our characters and our human and spiritual maturity. As book-keeper, Paco was able to gather how little the Father ate from what he spent. He must have gone to such a cheap place and eaten so little that he only spent two and a half pesetas. At night, when we got back from the barracks, Paco would tell me that the Father must have gone without lunch once again, and I would go into action often in an unduly cavalier fashion.

"Father," I would ask, "did you have lunch today or not?"

The Father would get round the question by replying that he had had something to eat. But we had got wise to that as we had discovered that 'something' was a few cents worth of peanuts. He had had 'something' so that when we asked him he would be able to say he had eaten.

"Father," we would insist day after day, "why not have dinner to night? Look we could go to..."

No, but thank you all the same, he would answer. *I am not hungry.*

Some nights we were successful, and after making a nuisance of ourselves with our persuasion, we managed to get him to have a small potato omelette, sold at a canteen in the railway station, for just one peseta. However, although the Father tried to hide it from us, we suspected that some days his fasting was total.

His mortification did not stop at fasting. Sometimes it would be time for thirst to take its turn – so he would not have any water. There is a very expressive point in *The Way*: *I'm going to tell you which are man's treasures on earth so you won't slight them: hunger, thirst, heat, cold, pain, dishonour, poverty, loneliness, betrayal, slander, prison...* Paco continued giving me a report every night: "I don't think he has had any water today either."

We could even notice it, because when he spoke his mouth and throat would be dry. Days passed in the same manner until one night I could control myself no longer, and I decided to act and put an end to all this. I filled a glass with water and I gave it to him commanding, "Drink it!" The Father refused, and said I was overstepping my bounds. Then, only barely keeping my temper, I snapped back: "Either you drink it or I drop it."

When I saw he would not give in, I dropped the glass on the floor and it smashed into smithereens. Amused and mimicking my tone, the Father said patiently: *Temper!*

The upshot of it all was that I apologised, and Paco and I picked up the glass from the floor. A little while later, when I was on the point of getting into bed and was kneeling down to say three Hail Mary's, he said affectionately: *Be careful, don't walk around barefoot, there might be some splinters of glass on the floor.*

Added to not eating and drinking, there was the discipline. He could not use it in the bathroom because it was at the end of the passage, and everybody on that floor would have heard it. Normally he used his discipline when we were out, but when that was not possible he would use it in his room, separated from ours by only the thin curtain which gave only relative seclusion. And when I dared to interfere even in that, trying to get him to moderate his mortification, his answer was in a similar vein to what we read in *The Way*: *If they have witnessed your weaknesses and faults, does it matter if they witness your penance?*

As well as not eating, not drinking, and using the discipline, there were also the nights he slept on the floor. He did that quite often, lying in the narrow gap between his bed and the wall. One day I wryly suggested to him that since he did not use his bed it was actually rather superfluous.

The Father did his best to behave in such a way that his mortification would not be noticed. Nevertheless, it was not difficult for us to guess what he was about, no matter how hard he tried to disguise it. We would know from the very slight noise he made that he was not lying down on his bed - or if he did do so, when he thought we were asleep, he would get up and stretch out on the floor. He slept with his head resting on his breviary, a very useful tome in a single volume, which Don Eliodoro Gil Rivera had given him. I class it as a 'very useful' book as the Father used it twice over. By day it served to pray the Office with, and by night it served as a pillow.

On top of not eating, not drinking, the discipline, and sleeping on the floor, we have to add the Father's poor health. He was still weak, and two or three months after moving to the Sabadell Hotel he was having high temperatures again. We worried a lot, so much so that it occurred to me to ask God to take away the temperature from him and give it to me instead. Maybe I made my petition without much faith that the Lord would hear me. So I got a big fright when that same afternoon I went down with a really, high temperature and the Father got better.

They called the doctor. He diagnosed typhoid or paratyphoid and ordered some tests. The result of the test was negative but my temperature still did not abate. Deeply embarrassed and ashamed, I ended up telling the Father about my request to the Lord.

Don't you dare do anything like that again, he said. *But now, stop worrying.*

Shortly afterwards the fever left me just as suddenly as it had come.

As the reader can appreciate, we did not know which way to turn to take care of the Father; so we wrote to Juan and Ricardo about it. A long time afterwards I found out about the existence of a letter the Father wrote to Juan in the same period, subsequent to ours. In it he explained the reason for his behaviour and asked Juan *to snap them out of it*, that is, snap us, with one of his clear and precise instructions. The Father's opinion was that, in spite of our good intentions, the devil could be using us to sap his spirit of mortification. He referred to Paco and me affectionately as 'these children'. He felt that God was asking him for the mortifications he did, in order to move the Work forward.

The letter, which I am quoting in full, is a demonstration of the heroic degree of his virtue, his desire for sanctity and his deep humility. Speaking about himself, he said he needed 'knocking into shape'.

Dear Juanito,

I thought, and still think, that it would be a good idea to see you, for many reasons. Nevertheless, if our Lord does not arrange it, he always knows what is best.

First of all I am aware that these children have sent you a famous letter telling you about my plan of life. I want to tell you that they have the best intentions, but that they don't realise they are playing into the hands of the devil.

Owing to their intervention, sometimes a bit rough, even though well-meant, instead of reasoning with them orally I wrote these boys a sharp note. I believe they have written to both Ricardo and you.

I want to state clearly that, although I do not have a director in Burgos, I do not do anything that would directly endanger my health. However, I must not lose sight of the fact that we are not merely playing at doing something good..., rather, to fulfil God's will, I have to be a saint whatever the cost, even if it were at the expense of my health, which it won't be.

I am so utterly convinced of this – I see it so clearly – that no human consideration can be allowed to prevent me from putting it into practice.

I am telling you this in all simplicity. I have my reasons. You have lived with me longer than anyone else and you surely understand that I need to be knocked into shape.

So please calm these children down and snap them out of it.

Mariano
Burgos, 30-IV-938

Noticias – News

The Father continued keeping in contact with the members of the Work and young men he knew in Madrid though the pages of *Noticias*, as he had done before the war. We put the newsletter together with the scanty means we had at our disposal. We would have been grateful then to have had the jellygraph we had had in Ferraz St.

Not having a jellygraph, we had to make do with a portable typewriter. We had bought it for a song in a shop under the arcade, round the Great Plaza which was then called the José Antonio Plaza. It was a very old Corona model and you could only do an original and two copies at a time. That meant we had to bang out the Newsletter on the curious old contraption time after time, until we had the number of copies we needed.

I call it a curious contraption advisedly, for it was a very peculiar apparatus. Each key had three characters on it. One was a small letter, another a capital, and the third, brackets, an exclamation mark, numbers, a semi-colon and so on. When you wanted to type one of the third sort the whole carriage rose two or three inches. To put the contraption away in its case, you had to unhook the carriage which turned on a hinge over the keys.

We wrote the first wartime issue of *Noticias* on that museum-piece in the St Clara pension; the others followed later from the Sabadell Hotel.

I can remember some words the Father addressed to that old friend of mine, Ignacio de Landecho, in the first number. We had already managed to get in touch with him: *LANDECHO, Ignacio. We know a lot about this great man. But we do not wish to publicise it until he writes us another six-page letter.*

In the first issue, the Father also referred to Carlos Aresti who had been a resident at Ferraz. He had been seriously injured and the Father travelled to Bilbao to attend to him. He arrived in time to give him spiritual comfort, but the boy died almost immediately. *Aresti has died*, the Father wrote with great sorrow. He went on to say how Aresti had recognised him in spite of being on his deathbed, and *he made the effort to smile. How much he is going to help us from heaven!*

The April issue of 1938 was headed with these words from the Father: *I'm very pleased with you, all of you, for the family warmth you put into your work. Your letters come in from all over the place, from towns, big and small, from the fronts in Jaca, Huesca, Teruel,*

*Albarracin, Guadalajara, Madrid, Avila and Andalucia, and from
ships of the fleet. They have the same vibrancy, common concerns
and the same supernatural and joyful optimism. God bless you!*

Following that was a long account of the news we had from
different people, interspersed with spiritual advice and apostolic
encouragement, witty yet serious. One of them read, referring to
Juan's style of writing: "Doctor JIMENEZ VARGAS's tone is
intimate, clear, no nonsense. His letters to his friends are like
injections of determination and effectiveness... It is such a long time
since we have had any news of LAHUERTA! And we're so keen to
hear from him!"

In that issue we again referred to my friend Ignacio de
Landecho and the letter he had written to us previously, and tried to
buck him up. "He tells us about the sufferings his family have been
through and is still suffering. We're right behind him, so that he can
rise above all that, higher even than the heights we already know
LANDECHO to have scaled. Up! Up!" (That 'up!' alluded to
Ignacio's well-known ability to climb up buildings on the outside.)
Poor Ignacio! Perhaps if our Lord had not taken him so young, he
would have given him a vocation to the Work.

*We carry on working – as is both natural and supernatural –
with the same effort as always,* the Father wrote around that time.
*Ten years of hard work! Within the eleventh, which will be
beginning soon, Jesus and I expect a lot from you. The impetus of
our work depends so much on you right now, wherever you happen
to be, in the barracks, in the trenches, at the barricades, in your
forced confinement to a hospital bed. It depends on your prayer,
your upright living, your difficulties and successes. We have our
own special communion of saints, so each one of you will feel the
joy and strength of not being alone at the moment of interior battle
as well as at the hour of armed conflict.*

The spiritual impact of those copies of *Noticias* was immense.
The Father always wrote a few lines personally, varying in length
depending on who he was writing to, but, as he once said, *a little
something for everyone.*

Paco and I also wrote to people, and put the newsletter in the
envelopes too. José María felt great satisfaction every time he took
a stack of letters to the post office. After passing the obligatory
wartime censorship (though they were hardly ever opened), the
letters were swallowed up by a post box in the form of a lion's
month in the outside wall of the post office.

In *The Way* the Father quoted verbatim the words of one young man who received *Noticias*. *'Before their letter arrived I had been feeling in low spirits – for no particular reason – and I was immensely cheered as I read it and saw what the others are doing.'* And another: *'Your letter and the news of my brothers helped me like a happy dream in the midst of the reality around us!...'* And another: *'It's so wonderful to receive these letters and to realise that I am a friend of such friends!'* And another, and a thousand others: *'I had a letter from X and was ashamed to think of my lack of spirit compared with his.'* Now, don't you agree that the *'letter-apostolate'* is effective?

A sombrero at the front

Although this is a totally different subject and is only of minor importance, I will never be able to forget it. It shows how patient the Father was with us. As I have already said, in Pamplona Don Marcelino had given the Father one of his sombreros, an already well-worn hat, as a stop-gap. However the gap-filler had become permanent. The hat was quite old at the outset. It had deteriorated even further due to the rain and snow of the Castillian winter, as well as the summer sun. It had lost all shape and had taken on a greenish hue. We tried to insist that the Father buy a new one, but he always got off the hook with the excuse that we had no money.

"But that one's green", we would say.

Fine, launched the Father. *That is what the bishops wore last century – green sombreros.*

One day Paco and I were alone in our room in the Sabadell, and we began discussing the green hat again. We came to the conclusion that the time had come for action. This time it would be irreversible action. The Father had gone out with someone by car. It was our chance, now or never! It might never come round again, for the coincidence of the Father's being out and the sombrero being there, on its peg, was rare indeed. Moreover, we had almost finished our task of getting an issue of *Noticias* ready to send out. The envelopes were done; all we had left to do was to put into each one a copy of *Noticias* together with the Father's letter and our own. We had what we thought was a very bright idea. Why not cut up the sombrero into little bits and send them to the members of the Work as souvenirs? They would undoubtedly be delighted. And not having the old one to wear, the Father would have no choice but to buy a new one...

No sooner said than done! Without further deliberation we set to work. I cut off a first scrap of felt. Once the damage was done there was no going back, and we continued cutting. Paco co-operated enthusiastically. The pieces of felt were small enough for the envelopes not to require additional stamps, as those had already been stuck on. We posted the lot forthwith. It was all so easy...

It was not so easy explaining to the Father when he returned what had happened to his sombrero. He began searching for it until we told him.

"It is already at the front."

What do you mean "it's at the front"?

We explained our deed. He could not understand our thoughtlessness, and even less so when we mentioned the word 'relics'. Relics! He did not understand. Relics! We listened to his reprimand in silence.

Despite the storm-clouds we felt that it had been worth it. The Father, however unwillingly, had to buy a new hat. And years later he would gratefully tell the story himself, moved and amused by the event.

Emboldened by our achievement we decided that the hour had come for his cassock too. It really was ancient; so much so that the Father had to darn the collars and cuffs. As with the hat, we had insisted he have a new one made – to little effect. One day, the Father lowered his guard for a moment and left it in the room while he was in his bedroom. On a pre-arranged signal, Paco and I ripped the cassock down the back, where it was already very worn. We did not foresee the outcome. When he realised what we had alone he did not say a word. When we got back from the barracks we were ashamed to find the Father still patiently engaged in sewing the cassock together again. We had failed completely. The Father continued wearing the cassock without ordering a new one. Our failure was aggravated by the fact that the mend had not turned out very well, and the Father now had to wear his cloak every time he went out. This was during the hottest part of the Burgos summer.

In spite of everything, I am sure that deep down the Father was grateful for our actions. He really understood the mentality and the way of being of young people; and Paco and I were very young. When he saw us laughing at something nonsensical he would say: *How fortunate you are!*

It was a loving way of saying: 'How simple-hearted these boys are!'

A tragic event

One day towards the end of July 1938, as José María Albareda and I were walking along the street in Burgos, we met Don Jorge B's wife. By the time we finish this chapter I hope the reader will understand my reasons for not giving his surname.

When she saw me she looked surprised and displeased. We did not say hello. It was not a pleasant meeting for either of us. That was the beginning of a particularly painful episode. It was, without doubt, the incident which made the deepest impression on me in all the time I lived in Burgos with the Father. To be able to understand what happened we need to go back quite a few years and to explain some things.

I knew the lady, though not very well. Her husband was an employee at the Treasury in Albacete. According to popular opinion he was right-wing; my father, as we have already seen, was left-wing. Nevertheless, there had never been any conflict or personal enmity between them as far as I remember.

Later I found out that he was from La Union, a place in Murcia where my great grandfather had developed several mines many years ago. Did something happen then between his family and mine? There is no way of knowing. What I do know is that I never heard anything about the family in my parents' or grandparents' houses.

Don Jorge had a high social standing and a comfortable economic position in Albacete. He lived with his children and sister-in-law in Cresifonte Gallegos Street, almost opposite my parents. The two families were not on particularly friendly terms, except that one of the boys, the youngest one, was my age and we were together in sea scouts from 1929 or thereabouts.

In 1934 or 1935 it was said in Albacete that the man had run up a lot of debts. We was selling off whatever possessions he had left and had asked to be transferred to some other provincial capital. I should think that around that time it was also being rumoured that my parents had increased their wealth a lot, thanks to the political situation. However that was not entirely true. The reason for our sudden financial gain was that we had given up the house we had in Murcia. Up till then my parents had had houses is both Murcia and Albacete. That move, combined with a certain generosity on my grandfather's part, and the fact that my father was earning two salaries, having also been nominated Director of the Training School, was obviously evident to people.

There was just one significant incident concerning these people. I used to like antiques and almost independently of my parents, I went to a private auction they held to sell some of their furniture and household effects before moving to Burgos. After a lot of bargaining at the auction I bought several things from Mrs B. – a multi-arm chandelier, calamine and glass wall-lights, Philippine swords and armour, and probably a few other things. That was the sum total of our relationship until they moved to Burgos shortly before the outbreak of the civil war.

Some things I did not understand began to happen after my chance meeting with Don Jorge's wife. The first was that the Father or José María, I cannot remember with certainty which of the two it was, asked me that same might when I got back from the barracks who the lady we had met in the street was, and what her husband's job was. I told him the story of events in Albacete. Later we found out he was the Housing and Territorial Contribution Administrator, one of the highest posts in the Treasury in Burgos.

Then the Father told me as a matter of urgency to go and visit Mrs. B. at home at a time when her husband was at the office. I would go with Miguel who was in Burgos for a few days on leave. We were to try to convince her that though my father had been a known left-winger, I had nothing at all to do with his political position, that my conduct in Burgos was loyal and on the level. In short, we were to endeavour to get her to persuade her husband not to accuse me or if he had already made a statement against me, to withdraw it.

A denunciation? I could not see why. Why should the man want to accuse me? Then the Father was more explicit. He told me that Mr. B. had already made an accusation against me or was on the point of doing so, containing various allegations. I heard afterwards that the Father had found out about it through Monsignor Lauzurica. The denunciation stated, no less, than:

(a) My father was a mason and a communist;

(b) That he had caused great damage in Albacete besides, by persecuting and killing a lot of people on the political right.

(c) That I was also a Communist as I had distributed propaganda of that nature in Albacete at the time of the elections in 1936 when the Popular Front won.

(d) That I had crossed over to the nationalist zone in order to act as a spy within Franco's Army, and I was doing my espionage at General Orgaz's Barracks.

In times of war accusations of that calibre were extremely serious. They could mean the death penalty. And I had little chance of proving the truth amidst so much falsehood.

At most, and that only with luck, I might have been able to demonstrate that from Christmas 1935 until the beginning of July 1936 I had not set foot in Albacete. So I could hardly have been distributing any type of propaganda, right-wing or left-wing, in that city. It was precisely during those elections that I had been doing a retreat with the Father in Madrid.

However, to demonstrate conclusively that and above all to refute the other accusations which were utterly false, I had no proof other than the testimony of the Father, some members of the Work and, at best, perhaps of my uncle Diego Ramirez Pastor. The latter knew nothing of my travels or my activities. These testimonies would not have carried much weight as the people had not been in Albacete at the time. On the other hand, Don Jorge's accusation could be dangerously decisive. He was a man of fifty-one and a high-ranking official in the Inland Revenue, publicly known for his right-wing opinions, and well up in the provincial politics of Albacete. He had two sons in the Army, both lieutenants, and one of them was at the front.

To complicate matters still more, my post in Burgos was particularly sensitive. My job was, of all places, in the Cipher Section through which secret military commands passed, even those which were received or sent by Headquarters.

On the morning of 1 August, Miguel and I went to call upon Don Jorge's wife in her house on the third floor of 5 Primo de Rivera Square. The visit was counterproductive. She was very rude to us. Among other things, she said it was unjust that while her son was risking his life at the front, I was peacefully in the rearguard, spying for the reds! Ignoring our arguments, she refused to listen, and said she did not intend to intervene in what her husband was doing. Miguel defended me warmly and entered the fray with her, so that I was hardly able to get a word in edgeways. I remember coming down the stairs, both of us feeling thoroughly thwarted by the failure of our mission.

That same morning the Father and José María went to the Revenue Office, in an old building at 2 St John Street, to speak to Don Jorge who had his official office there. It was a highly unpleasant interview. Don Jorge was cold and insolent. Defending me with fatherly affection, the Father preserved a serene composure throughout. At first the Father was gentle, but then he strove very forcefully to make Don Jorge see the injustice he was committing. He told him that he was going to deprive my mother of both her husband and her son, and should think what that would be like for his own wife.

It seems that Don Jorge reasoned that as he could not at that time get my father punished or even arrested, I should pay the price on his behalf, innocent or not, and that there were many innocent people dying at the front and in secret police cells in the red zone. José María was impressed by the Father's strength of character, trying to get Don Jorge to understand that his attitude was not that of a Christian who knows he has to give an account of himself to God. The Father went on to say that he would not like to be in his shoes, with such resentment in his soul, when he had to present himself for God's judgement. He advised him to think that that very day our Lord could ask him to render an account of what he intended to do.

But neither the Father's charitable pleas nor his strong words were able at that moment to soften the poor man's heart, who repeated stubbornly, "Both the father and the son have to pay for this!"

The Father left the office saddened and in silence. I have spoken to José María several times over the years about this episode; both the Father's defence of me and the callousness and stinging tone Don Jorge had maintained during the whole incident had left a deep impression on him. The Father went down the stairs in a very withdrawn, absent state, his eyes nearly closed and said, almost as if thinking aloud:

Tomorrow or the next day, a funeral.

That same morning, after visiting Don Jorge's wife, I went straight on to the barracks. If I am not mistaken there was a lot of work to do in the office. It was an important moment in the development of the war in Catalonia; may be it was the crossing of the Ebro at Lerida. The captain seemed to be reacting strangely, and Pedro Ybarra too, I thought. It might have been because of the work itself or because I arrived late or for some other reason, but I jumped to the conclusion that it was because of the accusation against me. I was all thumbs, almost sure that they knew something already. If so, I had no idea how they had found out, as I had told them nothing about my critical situation nor had I commented on the visit I had just made.

Neither did I know anything about the Father's visit to Don Jorge. I only knew they intended that morning to try and do something about my predicament.

The Father wanted me to do my best to come home for lunch (to the Sabadell Hotel). Normally I used to have lunch in the barracks with the soldiers. However that day we were very busy and I got home pretty late. Only then did I hear the outcome of that tragic affair. The Father told me what had happened in the most gentle way imaginable. He said he had been to see Don Jorge that morning with José María, and that soon after they left, Don Jorge had suddenly died.

The Father had found out about his death quite accidentally. When he went out he had seen a notification of his death stuck on a wall next to the Merced Church. It was customary to do that in Burgos when someone died.

The sad news had a great impact on me. I fell ill and had to lie down on the Father's bed. I lay down there as it was in the most secluded corner of the room. Meanwhile the Father helped me to regain my composure and quietly told me to be at peace concerning Don Jorge. The Father was morally sure that God our Lord would have mercy on his soul and had given him the grace of final repentance. He added that since leaving his office he had not ceased praying for him and for his children. He also said that I should be grateful to God for the care He had taken of me and of my father, even though the death in itself was so sad and painful.

On returning to the barracks after lunch I passed by the Merced Church. That was the only way I could go. I saw Don Jorge's death notice. A couple of hours earlier I had passed by and not caught sight of it at all.

Later I heard how he had died between eleven and twelve noon, in his own office. We had received a visitor before becoming ill. Someone had warned, 'Don Jorge is ill'. His colleagues went in to him immediately. Don Jorge raised his hand to his head and died a few minutes later.

From that day forward, all my life I have prayed for his soul and for his whole family. I am sure he enjoys the glory of God thanks to divine mercy and the Father's prayers. God will have rewarded him for all his good works and will no doubt have forgiven him for those moments of darkness so understandable in the chaotic climate of war.

When the Father saw I was so affected, he advised me to ask for a short period of leave to pull myself together. I was given it and went to Bilbao where my uncle was. I came back calmer, although the episode will be engraved on my heart for the rest of my life. Since then I have hardly spoken of those events, partly out of respect and partly also because I have never wanted to pry into those things outside ordinary Providence which happened in the Father's life, though I knew only too well that God's providence had shown itself many times in ways which were beyond the ordinary.

A few weeks after Don Jorge's death I learned that one of his sons, an airman, had died too. He must have been my age. He was a flight lieutenant. Once again I was knocked sideways by the news. I told the Father and he said, *Pray for him. I will too.* Some days later I came across Don Jorge's widow in the Jesuit church. When I realised it was her, I slipped out of the church as unobtrusively as possible. But she saw me and it seemed to me that she looked kindly at me.

Working non-stop

During that period José María Albareda went to Vitoria very often, and even on the days he did spend in Burgos his work occupied most of his time. Paco and I spent an average of eight hours a day in the barracks. So, the normal thing was for the Father to be alone most of the day. What did he do in that time? The best answer must be a point in *The Way*: *to work without resting*.

To sum up those months: They were full of constant, arduous work. He spent a lot of time keeping in touch with the members of Opus Dei who were at the different fronts, and ministering to their spiritual needs. To do that he had to make frequent trips around the Peninsula, in terrible conditions of poor health, uncomfortable journeys, and economic hardship. He even managed to get permission to visit the front-line to take spiritual care of people there. However, the permit did not include a free pass for the train. So he had to pay for that with money we did not have. That was the cause of all kinds of suffering.

I do not remember all the trips he made, but I know that there were a great many of them. He travelled on a shoestring budget. For instance, he went to Cordoba by train in April. The train went through Extremadura and passed through Seville first. On the way back, on that long journey, he had nothing whatsoever to eat.

In June he went to the Madrid front, passing through Avila to see Ricardo Fernandez Vallespin who had been wounded. And there were many other such journeys. They were very long and exhausting, in typical, crowded, wartime trains. They made only slow progress along their tracks, jerking and jolting along, enveloped in dense clouds of dust and soot-laden smoke.

On the other hand, many of the young men he went to see and to whom he gave spiritual care would, in their turn, use up the best part of their leave coming to Burgos, even if only to spend a few hours with the Father. That was a great consolation to him.

Many of those boys were not members of the Work. They had no other connection with Opus Dei than that of having taken part in the means of formation in Ferraz Residence. I can remember, for instance, José Felix de Elejabarrieta who had been wounded at the front. When he left hospital, he got leave of only a few days to visit his parents in Vizcaya. On the way he stopped off in Burgos to see the Father. The Father was away; so he decided to wait more than twenty-four hours for him to return. He spent a whole day with him, even though that meant he would have only one day with his family before joining his unit. His was not an isolated case. That was why, when those lads came to Burgos, the Father would bend over backwards to give them warmth and affection, whether they were members of the Work or not. He would compensate generously with his personal attention for the inevitable irregularity of spiritual direction caused by the war.

During his short journeys, he would write to those of us left behind in Burgos. They were intimate letters, as a father writes to his children, showing his concern about all kinds of matters, from the most sublime to the most material. For instance, during his stay in Avila from 8 to 14 August, he wrote to Paco, José María and me with the following message: *When you write to Juanito,* (he meant Juan Jimenez Vargas), *tell him to buy some new glasses. And as soon as he gets paid, he should get a pen too. Although it might be better for you to buy one there, whenever you can manage it, and send it to him.*

He was very solicitous about our health. To Paco, who was naturally very thin, he wrote, *Pacorro, when you write you must tell me if you are having afternoon tea or not. It is a disgrace that there are still some tins of jam in the cupboard. The others should buy you some small pots of marmalade; then have one of those with a roll.* He then told me to buy the jam for Paco and some cheese portions as well. And he finished off the letter reminding us: *And you both – you, who are getting to be more skin and bone, though elegantly so – must encourage each other and have tea every single day. Is that clear?*

When he got back from Avila I remember he told us a funny story which very well illustrates the kind of wartime atmosphere we were living in. Normally he would lodge in the bishop's house. But he had arrived is the city very late at night and had decided not to bother anyone. So he lodged in a very basic pension; he inquired as to the whereabouts of the shower (ducha), but the person misheared him and replied, "Oh, don't you worry about that. The *lucha* (warfront) is a long way off."

In a letter of 13 August, the Father told Ricardo his schedule. It speaks for itself: *Tomorrow, the 14th, to Burgos until the 16th. The 16th in Vitoria, preaching a retreat until the 26th. On the 27th, in Logrono with José Ramon, who is ill; 28th, Burgos again until 3rd September. 3rd to Vitoria; 4th, at the Seminary in Vegara – to give another retreat for priests, until the 10th; 11th, Burgos.*

Besides his journeys to the different fronts, the days of recollection and retreats he preached, apostolic activities which qualify as formal, we also have to reckon on his extensive priestly work in Burgos which we can denominate as informal. I refer to the numerous apostolic conversations with different people, walking along the banks of the Arlanzon, on the way to Las Huelgas, the Carthusian Monastery of Miraflores or Fuentes Blancas. One of the people to whom he used to talk was my companion, Pedro Ybarra. He prepared him for his marriage to Adela Guell Ricart, which took place around that time.

On top of all those journeys, retreats, and spiritual guidance, we have to add his huge amount of apostolic letter-writing. He spent a lot of time at that. The result was that every time we sent *Noticias* out, the number had grown; so too our rudimentary file of addresses was enriched with new ones from the fronts at Andalucia, Madrid, Jaca, Teruel, Albarracin, and so on. The Father always added a few words in his own hand, normally very short and to-the-point. The members of the Work usually wrote every week, but sometimes they would be late. Yet, the Father never failed to write a letter every week.

I recall those letters perfectly. He would write on both sides of the sheet of paper, in his characteristic bold handwriting. I think that a point in *The Way* probably refers to himself: *I don't always find words when it comes to putting down things that might be useful to the friend I am writing to. But when I begin, I tell my guardian angel that all I hope from my letter is that it may do some good ... no one can take from me or from my friend the time I have spent praying for what I know he needs most.*

This point reflects his habit of always praying to the guardian angel of the person he was addressing.

The Way

As though all that were not enough, we have to add another project: the re-working of *Consideraciones espirituales* which was published soon afterwards under a new title, *The Way*. Years later other books followed, such as *Holy Rosary*, and posthumously *Furrow*, *The Way of the Cross* and *The Forge*. These books were born of a desire which he had nurtured for years, ever since God has granted him a divine locution on 7 August 1931. He wrote: *In spite of feeling myself devoid of all virtue and knowledge (humility is the truth – this is no sham), I would like to write books of fire, which would run like wild-fire throughout the world, giving light and warmth to men, turning their poor hearts into burning coals, that can be offered to Jesus as rubies for his kingly crown.*

He wrote *The Way* with those young people who came to see him particularly in mind. Many of them were at the front, exposed not just to the danger of bullets and shells, but also to that of 'the dead hours'. There were many hours 'to kill' in the barracks, and even in the trenches. Especially so when there was no movement on the front for weeks on end. That aspect – the idleness – worried him a lot. He could envisage the future and was afraid that by the time the war ended, those boys might have lost the habit of studying. He mentions this in the March *Noticias*: *Why not make the most of all the free time you have on your hands to brush up on a language? A dictionary and a book to translate can fit into anything.*

He insisted over and over again that they did not give up. He busied himself sending them books in different languages and mini-dictionaries which would fit snugly in their pockets. He wrote to one of them: *Ah. English grammars are not to be found in Burgos. Let's see if there are any in Bilbao. An English newspaper is coming your way.* He approached several intellectual friends of his to that end. He asked them to procure some textbooks, preferably, foreign ones for him. But he suffered a number of disappointments. He wrote in *The Way*: *Books... I put out my hand, like one of*

Christ's beggars, and I put my hand out, like one of christ's baggars, and each time and again I was disappointed.

Why, Jesus, can't people understand the profound Christian charity of this almsgiving, more effective than a gift of the finest bread?

At first we wondered where we would store all those books when we got them. But we never did get them. We only got a few in Italian, published by the Universita Cattolica del Sacro Cuore in Milan.

How did he write *The Way*? Since I met him, I had noticed how every now and again he would jot down one or two words in a diary or small notebook which he used to carry in the left hand pocket of his cassock. He would pull it out of his pocket quite frequently, even during a get-together or when he was talking tete-a tete with someone informally. It was a very rapid motion, all without interrupting the conversation. Those words, sometimes just one word, served to remind him of an idea he had had or a happy turn of phrase he had heard. Later, in his working hours, he would expand on the idea on an index card. They were not even real index cards but just bits of paper which, out of poverty, he cut from bigger pieces already used on one side, rather than throwing them away. He called them his little bagpipes. He explained that it was not enough to read the points but rather one had to tease out their contents and apply them to the circumstances of the moment. *They are 'little bagpipes' because they make no sound unless you blow*, he said. Every day when we got back from the barracks he would show us a pile of index cards and ask: *Well, what do you think of these 'little bagpipes'?*

As a result of this work, the Father had published *Consideraciones espirituales* in 1934 in Cuenca, with the approval of Don Cruz Laplana, the bishop of that diocese. In Burgos he decided to fill out the book and get it reprinted. When it was all set for going back to the press he decided to call it *Camino (The Way)*. He did all the preparation in our room in the Sabadell Hotel. He typed out the whistles on proper sheets of paper. It was not all plain sailing, for the typewriter (the Corona I described before) was very tedious and the Father never was much good at typing. He often struck the wrong key and the machine itself was very primitive. Then he would scratch away at the paper with a razor blade, because if he used an eraser he would invariably rub a hole right through the paper. On one occasion I pulled his leg on the subject, affectionately but without disrespect: "Father, you are very abrasive!"

But his misfortunes did not stop there. Besides wearing through the paper with the eraser, when he wielded the razor blade he would often cut himself. Something similar would happen when he used a pencil. He would break the lead. I would offer my services but he did not want to usurp our time. Yet, if having offered in vain to help him, I saw that he continued to have mishaps, I would not hide my glee. Then the Father would be the first to laugh. Years later, he got used to dictating into a tape-recorder and correcting the typed text later. One day he wrote to me saying, *You won't call me very abrasive now!*

Despite his wishes he was prevented from publishing *The Way* in those early months by the lack of resources, as all the printers in Burgos were concentrating exclusively on work for the government or the army. He had to wait until April 1939. I must admit that I did not then foresee that that little book, fruit of the Father's daily battle with a rudimentary old typewriter, would do such spiritual good or that millions upon millions of copies would come off printing presses throughout the world.

The Father's work did not stop there. To the trips he made to the different fronts, to the visitors be received in Burgos, to the retreats and days of recollection which he gave in different cities, to his intense personal apostolate, to his letter writing and the preparation of *The Way*, to all that we have to add yet another occupation, which helps imagine the intensity of his work without rest during the months spent in Burgos. This was the writing of his doctoral thesis in civil law on the Abbess of Las Huelgas. Before the conflict he had begun a thesis on a different subject, but had lost all his research material in the reverses of war.

He spent many mornings at work in the Accounts office in the royal monastery of Las Huelgas, located some distance from Burgos. He had to come and go on foot. The Abbess was Doña Esperanza de Mallagaray. She gave him access to plenty of material and the nuns would bring the documents he needed down to the Accounts office. The thesis was published in 1944 after he had revised it.

Scientific research

This leads me to mention another facet of the Father which was a real discovery for me during those months in Burgos – his extremely deep learning. In Burgos his mastery of Sacred Scripture became more obvious as we did not have any books and he had to quote texts from memory when he was writing his notes.

Besides his theological knowledge, I was amazed at his familiarity with the Spanish classics and many contemporary authors. He did not quote them to show off his erudition, but his wide culture showed through from occasional comments he would make. Quotations from the classics would slip out even though he might not remember the exact chapters or would express doubt about the source.

He had an eye to style when writing, and tried to help me improve mine. On one occasion he read something I had written. He pointed out that my sentences were too long and complex. There were too many subordinate clauses and the punctuation needed tidying up, especially when and where not to start new paragraphs. He suggested I read the tales of Azorin. One day I made a spelling mistake using a 'j' instead of a 'g'. *You wouldn't get away with that even if you were Juan Ramon Jimenez*, he said, laughing.

He did not deify culture; nor did he despise it. He had wide intellectual horizons, and he encouraged us not to be mediocre or run of the mill. *There is no excuse for those who could be scholars and are not*, he had written in *The Way*. He considered human intelligence as a spark which our father God had granted from his own divine intelligence, and he said we had an obligation to cultivate it for His glory. In *The Way* he had also written: *Culture, culture! Good? Don't let anyone get ahead of us in striving for it and possessing it.*

But remember that culture is a means, not an end.

During that time he often spoke to us about scientific research. In particular, he talked to José María Albareda on the subject, then a young teacher. In time José María would become Secretary of the Superior Council for Scientific Research, the first Vice-Chancellor of the University of Navarre and an outstanding figure in the scientific world. The Father's thinking on this subject is condensed into this point of *The Way*: *Formerly, since human knowledge – science – was very limited, it seemed quite feasible for a single learned individual to undertake the defence and vindication of our holy Faith... Today, with the extension and the intensity of modern science, the apologists have to divide the work among themselves, if they want to defend the Church scientifically in all fields. You... cannot shirk this responsibility.*

He always had a very positive approach to the intellectual world. *I am not anti-anything*, he used to say. But that did not stop him suffering when he saw the unchristian practice of some intellectuals and certain organised groups who, under the guise of professionalism or laicism, had corroded cultural life and the university atmosphere.

He firmly maintained that the world of culture and scientific research ought not to be built around cliques, that is exclusive groups which put only their friends on pedestals or create mutual praise societies. He reminded us that university professorships should not be conceived of as a source of power.

He also recalled that people with the necessary talent for teaching others, be it in the spiritual, professional, intellectual or scientific fields, should give of themselves in such a way that their younger colleagues would be able to start working not from the bottom upwards, but already *from up here*, pointing to his head. He underlined the moral duty they had not to make themselves indispensable. One ought not to act like the cook who made a pudding and kept the recipe secret by keeping the kitchen door closed to the others.

Being a priest one hundred percent

Deep piety, constant work and a thirst for souls filled the Father's life. Day by day I witnessed that at first hand: he was a priest one hundred per cent, all the time, whatever the circumstances, in pre-war Madrid, during the persecutions on our difficult journey across the Pyrenees, and in the volatile, bellicose atmosphere of Burgos which was more surprising still. Not once did I hear him talk about politics in any one of those situations. He would explain, *My mission as a priest is exclusively spiritual*. His attitude was particularly eloquent in the havoc of war, so given to extremism and to partisan bias. The Father's arms were open to everyone, because he wanted to save everyone, without leaving out anybody.

During those months I witnessed his great love for freedom and personal responsibility. This led him never in all his life to make any particular directive to members of the Work in financial, political or cultural areas. Years later he expressed this way of behaving of Opus Dei members in plain terms: *Each member*, he wrote emphatically, *is absolutely free to think and to act as he thinks fit in those fields. In all temporal matters he enjoys the greatest possible freedom. Opus Dei is open to people of every political, cultural, social and economic persuasion that a Christian conscience can accept.*

He gave the necessary instructions to Directors in the Work

never to impose political or even professional criteria on other members. He made it clear that if a member of the Work were to attempt to do that or to use other members of the Work for human motives, that person would be expelled forthwith *because the others would quite rightly object.* In conversation, he always zealously defended the freedom of conscience, *which is not the same as autonomy of conscience,* he would state. He was also a keen advocate of human dignity, always respecting other people's opinions. However, be was never inhibited when the opportunity arose to profess his own faith, *a faith so palpable that I could cut it with a knife,* as he used to say.

He was broad-minded, unusually so for that time, and not just in theory. In those days there was a certain confusion in many people's minds concerning the religious and the political spheres – any objective person could see that.

The Father was saddened, therefore, every time the radio or the press reported official occasions or ceremonies which were open to interpretation as using the Church to further political ends.

I recall a relevant story someone told me about that period which will help the reader understand this. Some Francoist authorities had organised a solemn ceremony in the Monastery of Las Huelgas. They had arranged everything but had forgotten one small 'detail': to ask Archbishop Manuel de Castro's permission, for the monastery was his responsibility. When they did ask for permission, rather late in the day, he refused to give it saying he paid the piper and on that day the Monastery was closed. Several people had to intervene at the last minute to get him to give way.

At that time the Father also dealt with lots of people who were not Catholic, or at least had lapsed, or were 'persona non grata' in the prevailing political climate. Later he intervened to mitigate more than a few injustices, no matter what the political affiliation of the person concerned. For instance, it was common that some exiles who returned to Spain felt lost or at least uneasy. I remember well, some time later, at the Father's suggestion, inviting Gregorio Marañon to give a lecture, at the Moncloa Residence, a corporate work of Opus Dei. At the end of the lecture, Maranon told me privately, (later he said so publicly), that it was the first lecture he had given since being ousted from his professorship at the Central University.

One of the subjects that frequently came up in our conversations in Burgos was the Father's desire for Catholics in every nation to be informed about the sufferings of their fellow Catholics in other countries where the Church was being persecuted or had no freedom. He wished intellectual Catholics in every country to be aware of the efforts and achievements of Catholics the world over, so they would all be united, not blinkered by favouritism or sectarianism.

I recall a very significant story on this subject which came up at one of the retreats which he gave in Burgos, in the chapel of the Handmaids of the Sacred Heart near the River Arlanzon, just outside the parish of Our Lady of Mount Carmel. The retreat had been organised by the National Association of Catholic Propagandists. The chapel was fairly large and was full of professional people and academics. Some of them were very well known in the cultural milieu of the time. I remember the retreat very well. It was one of the few occasions Paco and I had in those days to hear the Father preach to people other than ourselves.

The Father spoke with the same fervour as always, perhaps even more vehemently than on other occasions. He did not mince his words. His preaching was based on the Gospel, and employed simple but clear and memorable imagery. He sat at a small table beside the lectern, as was his wont. He began by saying that in front of such a select audience, he felt like a watchmaker in his workshop, contemplating an extensive array of finely crafted parts. He could see the little platinum cogs, the sapphire jewels; but, he pointed out, the danger lay beyond. It might be that, when it come to trying to put those pieces together to make the clock, the size of each piece might not be in proportion to the next, and so they would not fit together properly. Then perhaps the friction between them would stop the clock from working or make it run slow or stop altogether, often ticking for a few minutes only. *If my clock does not work, if it does not tell me the time, it is of no use to me*, the Father stated forcefully. *I would prefer a five peseta alarm clock of the kind sold in Sepu! (Sepu was a well-known warehouse in Madrid, where you could buy all manner of items cheaply).*

With the sensitivity of someone who is praying on his own account, rather than as someone who is addressing an audience, he went on to develop the theme of the clock, and finally concluded that understanding, charity and unity were indispensable virtues if the professional work of Christians was to be of service to God and to other people for His sake.

He clearly differentiated between two things that day. It is one thing for a person to have a noble desire to progress upwards when exercising his profession, as a result of his personal effort (involving study, scientific research, order, method and persever- ance) and of God's grace too, which helps him to make the talents he has bear fruit. Another thing altogether is that avidity for promotion which arises from ambition, from a thirst for power, from selfish motives.

In a word, he condemned the habit of climbing the ladder by means of mutual praise, sabotage or trampling on others. I call that kind of moving up, status seeking, social climbing, and you must not do that. He affirmed that being at the top or the bottom is not what counts: the most important thing is being close to God serving him and serving others for Him. What mattered was trying put God at the top, right up there on high, not oneself.

Everyday heroism

As has invariably been the case in the lives of people of God, the Father was not always understood. The wartime climate drove many people to put off any form of lifelong commitment until 'afterwards'. Contrary to what one might think, the patriotic fervour of the moment prompted many young people to reduce the ideal of serving God to no more than a temporal dimension. In those circumstances many devout young men had only one goal in the ascetical struggle: to live in the grace of God so as to be prepared in case they should die on the battle-field. Every one of them thought he was doing all he needed for his faith by risking his life at the front, in the struggle for an ideal which did, in fact, lead many to the peak of heroism.

The Father spoke a lot about another kind of heroism: the hidden heroism of everyday life: heroism at work, heroism in perfectly ordinary things. For although it may seem strange, the danger of death as an abstract thought, 'going to war' as a second lieutenant or a lieutenant, even managed to have its appeal for some people. It was the attraction of activism, and even of the risk involved, the attraction of being 'a man of action' at the centre of an adventure very different from that sometimes tedious one of everyday life – the hours of study, the corridors and the lecture halls, the examinations of university or college. In short, the war had the deceptive and fleeting attraction of the extraordinary.

I do not wish to under-rate or detract from the young people who risked their lives in those years and so often died for their principles. I only want to point out that danger which is common to all wars and which was given vivid expression by a writer of the time: "We will rue the day that peace breaks out!"

So it was not easy to do apostolate or to enkindle deeper longings in people then. Conversations would become polarised around subjects related to the war. Even in an atmosphere of undoubted religious faith, the crudeness of language in some military establishments left no room for conversations of a spiritual nature or for a certain widening of horizons.

On the other hand, although the Father loved his country very much, his heart was open to every country, race and culture. There was no sign of narrow mindedness or personal bias in his preaching. So if someone referred to a defect of a particular nation, he would always turn things around so as to stress some positive aspect. He declared that his motherland was the world; and he was happy to know that the blood of various countries, especially Italy, ran in my veins. I remember telling him that some of my forebearers were called Carrara and Ferrara, and it was very likely that I had Jewish blood, as Italian Jews used to take the names of cities as their surnames. That pleased him, though actually for the Father there was only one race: *the race of the children of God.*

Meanwhile the conflict was scaling down. The total number of the members of the Work at the end of the war was, in spite of the Father's apostolic zeal, disappointing from a merely human point of view. There had been only one new vocation to Opus Dei, José María Albareda, and some had fallen at the fronts. To make up for this, by the time the war ended, we members of Opus Dei had reached a maturity which we would never have achieved had it not been for the hardships of those three years. That was thanks to the Father's example and the formation he had given us. In that sense the Father would say to us that the war had brought about a great spiritual good in us, even in the midst of so much suffering, calamity and persecution.

On the feast of Our Lady of the Pillar

The Father was still worried about the people who had stayed in Madrid. Isidoro kept us posted about those who were still in refuge in the Honduran Legation and in the Norwegian Embassy. He also told us how the Grandmother, Carmen and Santiago were getting on. His letters came by quite a complicated route. First, they went from Madrid to France, and from France they were sent on to us in Burgos. With all that the letters were not as frequent as the Father would have wished, and the post was slow. One day, God showed the Father that some of those who were in Madrid, Alvaro del Portillo and Vicente Rodriguez Casado among them, would cross over to our zone on 12 October 1938, feast of Our Lady of the Pillar. The Father told us this some days in advance.

I interpreted his words as an ardent desire for that to happen, like a petition to our Lady. Nevertheless, the Father was so sure that it was going to happen that he went to see Alvaro del Portillo's mother, Doña Clementina Diaz de Sollano, who was in Burgos. He assured her: *On the 12th your son is going to cross over.* Through a special inspiration from our Lord, Isidoro Zorzano also learned about it while he was praying before a crucifix in his room in Madrid. Till then he had always advised them to wait, as many people had died in the attempt. During his prayer he also 'knew' that on the 12th they would reach the other side.

Soon afterwards, Alvaro del Portillo, Vicente Rodriguez Casado and Eduardo Alastrue joined the Republican Army; after a series of providential incidents in which our Lord's help was clear to all, they crossed over to Cantalojas, a town 'on the other side', while the church bells were joyfully pealing in honour of Our Lady of the Pillar.

I awaited the 12th eagerly; when I got back to the Sabadell Hotel in the evening, I saw that no one had arrived. I was sorry for the Father's sake; he would be frustrated and worried, I thought. But he was not. Although it seemed unlikely to me, the Father was sure they had achieved their objective. On the 13th he was peaceful and contented and told us to be ready to welcome them when they arrived. Paco recalls that the following day he said to us: *I will call you at the Barracks as soon as they get here.*

That same day, 14 October, the Father called Paco on the phone: *They have arrived. Come home.*

In Calatayud

Soon afterwards, for different reasons, the Father was left almost alone in Burgos. The first one to leave was José María. He lived in Vitoria during that academic year 1938-9 as he was a teacher at the Institute. Alvaro del Portillo arrived in Burgos on 14 October and left on 10 November to join the Engineering Academy of Acting Lieutenants in Fuentes Blancas, which was a few kilometres outside the city. Vicenton went to a military posting in Saragossa. And in December I left for the Levant Army

Headquarters in Calatayud, where Pedro Ybarra and I had been posted. We would continue to work in the Cipher Section.

The upshot was that in mid-December only Paco was left to keep the Father company in Burgos. So they moved soon afterwards, just before Christmas, to a pension at 9 Conception Street, on the third floor.

When I set off for Calatayud the Father gave me his blessing. He encouraged me to keep up my plan of Christian life and he gave me pieces of advice. *Write often. Be cheerful. Use your time well and remember you can do a lot of good to that lad.* He was referring to Pedro Ybarra who had become a good friend of mine and was making a lot of progress in his spiritual life.

I arrived in Calatayud, and spent Christmas there with Paco who had come to accompany me at the Father's express wish. Later we went on to Saragossa together to be with Vicenton. The war had reached a critical juncture. The Republican Army was crumbling and the end of the conflict was in sight. Towards the beginning of January I got a letter from the Father from Burgos asking me to make inquiries about getting *The Way* published. *Are there any printers there who could do it?* he asked, and went on: *I only have 80 considerations still to do. It will only take a few days.* In fact he finished that job on 22 January and immediately set to work to type it up. He finished it around 2 February, and put that data on it as the nearest feastday of our Lady.

In Calatayud the ferment of activity at the Levant Army Headquarters gradually subsided and the military environment lost its rhythm. I got permission to teach mathematics in the Institute. Thanks to that job I got to know quite a few people who were temporarily residing in Calatayud because of the war, as well as others who had always lived there. I set exams for, among others, students from the Marist Brothers school in Calatayud. Meantime our Cipher Section office was turning into a social club. It was a cubicle in a corner of the offices, which in fact were situated in the big library of the Provincial Casino. The cipher office had been a highly classified place, but now it was a hut for informal meetings among lieutenants and captains. I was none too pleased as I could not get on with my work, and I was not at all interested in the latest news about promotions and military appointments. On 1 April 1939 Headquarters buzzed with enthusiasm over the latest official news: the war was over.

CHAPTER 11

Beginning again

Back in Madrid

In the Provincial General Headquarters of Valencia, my last posting, I anxiously awaited the definitive demobilization. I was released at last, thanks to a simple document signed and sealed by the chief of staff, and was able to pick up civilian life again. I headed for Madrid in search of the Father.

Where would I find him? 16 Ferraz Street had been totally destroyed. I learned later that the Father had arrived in Madrid on 28 March and had visited the ruins of the residence that day. There he had found a Latin text on parchment among the ruins. It had hung in the study in the residence to show people the value of fraternity in a visual manner: 'Mandatum novum do vobis. A new commandment I give unto you, that you love one another as I have loved you, that you also love one another. By this shall all men know that you are my disciples, if you have love one for another' (John 13:34,35).

At last I discovered that the Father had been living in the old building of the Rector's house in St Elizabeth Street since the 29th. The church had been destroyed in a deliberate arson attack in July 1936. Among other works of art, a picture by Ribera which had served as a reredos for the altar had been consumed in the flames. However, the Rector's and chaplain's house, although requiring major repairs, had not been damaged by artillery or bombs. The Rector's house had been used by a Revolutionary Committee. When the Father and those with him arrived, they found the white flag of surrender still hanging from the balcony.

Paco described the state of the kitchen. They found a meal ready and waiting: the soldiers obviously had had to abandon the building at a moment's notice. "We ladled food on to the soldiers' plates and we took them across to the Rector's flat in the Real Patronato. It was stew. Someone said it might be poisoned, but that hypothesis did not prevail. We were hungry."

I met up with the Father again and he suggested I go immediately to Albacete. Ever since I had joined the group crossing the Pyrenees, my parents had not had much news of me because of the war (although any news was good news in the midst of that terrible situation). I had written to them from Barcelona. So as not to arouse suspicion I wrote very succinctly: 'Concerning the sorrow that afflicts you, you can rest easy.' Later I wrote another letter from Andorra, addressed to my brother Josemaria (Pepe). I wrote in childish language as if I were a friend of his of similar age. They had received a few other letters from me written in Burgos and sent to London to a friend of Pepe. He had sent them on to my parents.

Although my mother had the comfort of knowing I was alive in the last months of the war she had had a very bad time. When I reached Albacete she was alone with my brother Pepe, as my father had just taken the last boat out of Alicante before the National Army entered the city. At the time we did not know where he going to.

With things as they were, my mother and I agreed that the most prudent thing to do was for her to move to Los Hoyos and to clear the house in Albacete as soon as possible, storing the furniture and household effects in the premises of some trustworthy friends. That was what we did. As far as my brother was concerned, we realized he would have to resit his baccalaureate to legalize his wartime studies. Following the Father's advice he went to boarding school with the Marist Brothers in Calatayud. Although it was holiday time, they accepted him.

My mother gave me a lot of furniture from the house in Albacete with which to furnish the new residence. Isidoro Zorzano was very efficient at helping me get the furniture to Madrid in a couple of railway carriages. During all the travelling that supposed, I was able to talk to my mother on various occasions about Opus Dei and she began to admire it and feel affection for it. I also talked to Pepe about Opus Dei.

At the end of the summer my mother decided to go to Barcelona to live with Pepe. My uncle Diego lived there and Pepe was able to carry on with his studies there. My mother stayed in Barcelona until we learnt that my father was in Oran in Algeria. So she went there to join him.

Jenner

After attending to the family affairs I returned to Madrid. I headed for the Rector's house where we had set ourselves up in poverty-stricken fashion. Our household effects consisted of a strange collection of the kind of objects which are left lying around after wars: soldiers' camp-beds, army blankets and so forth. We spent just four months there. The Father wanted to give the house over to the enclosed Augustinian nuns as soon as possible, as their convent had been destroyed. The Father spoke to the Assumption nuns about provisionally lending part of the school they did not need in the summer months to the Augustinian nuns. Thanks to that the Augustinians were able to renew their community life in Saint Elizabeth.

Meanwhile we hunted all over Madrid for a house to rent where we could open the residence. On 6 July the contract was signed for the house which was to be the future students Hall of Residence. The residence combined three large flats on the first and third floors of 6 Jenner Street, very near the Paseo de la Castellana. There were two apartments on the third floor. These were joined together and the oratory, sitting room, library, a small reception room and the students bedrooms were put there. On the first floor we set up the students' dining-room, another smaller one for guests, a reception room, the Father's room, a second room for the Grandmother and his sister Carmen, and a third room for his brother Santiago, then a student at university.

During that period bishops from many Spanish dioceses, who were attracted by the Father's apostolic zeal and his reputation for holiness, called on him to ask him to give retreats for priests. He directed a great number of courses of spiritual exercises in Madrid, Avila, Segovia, Vitoria, Pamplona, Lerida, Valencia and Leon.

I recall going for walks with the Father during that time. We would go to the second-hand shops and the flea-markets in Madrid, looking for cheap furniture with which to furnish the new residence in Jenner. In the entrance hall he had us put up a planisphere with the motto, 'A solis ortu usque ad occasum', by which he reminded us that people and countries from the whole world ardently awaited their meeting with Christ in their ordinary everyday lives, according to the spirit of the Work.

At last, on 15 July, the move began. On 6 August the Father blessed the new Centre in Jenner Street. A new chapter was opening in the history of the Work.

My brother, Pepe

Two months previously around mid-May 1939, Pepe had come to Madrid to spend a few days with an uncle and aunt of ours, and

the Father had invited him to lunch. I had told the Father various
things about Pepe and as soon as the Father saw him he said, *I have
prayed to our Lord a lot for you.*

As Pepe's memoirs recount, that brief fleeting meeting with the
Father impressed him very deeply and was the beginning of his
vocation. From that moment on, his vocation to the Work started
taking root in his soul. Six months later, over Christmas, I spoke to
him at length about Opus Dei, and he told me he had decided to
give himself to God.

We agreed to talk again on the subject a month later when I
would have to travel to Barcelona, but he reported that he was
adamant. Pepe recalls, "It seemed unnecessary to me to wait
another month as I was totally convinced I had a vocation, that God
was calling me to Opus Dei, the same as Pedro. Pedro's example
influenced me as did the example of some other people in the Work
I had met in the last few months. This coincided with a remark my
mother once made to me: 'One of your brother's friends, called
Alvaro del Portillo, has been here. I don't know what it is about
your brother's friends, but I would like you to be like them." Still,
my brother had to wait, and not only one month but three. I talked
to him again in Barcelona where he was studying. He was living
with Uncle Diego, the editor of El Correo Catalan, still thoroughly
determined. I told him he would have to wait another month, until
the Father came to Barcelona. The reason for making Pepe wait lay
in the fact that the Father wanted to be sure that he was not acting
on a passing whim.

"On 12 May 1940," Pepe recollects, "I had a phone call at
lunchtime. I was told that the Father had come to Barcelona and I
could go and see him that same afternoon at the Urbis Hotel. I
hurried round there straight after lunch. The Father received me
immediately. One of his first questions was if any one had put any
pressure of any kind on me to come to that decision. I do not
remember his exact words but they were more or less as I have said.
His manner of speaking was serious and abrupt, so much so that I
was taken aback for a few seconds. I recovered quickly answered:
'Father, no one has tried to influence or persuade me. Pedro
explained the Work to me but he had never tried to put any pressure
on me or sway me. It's I who want to belong to Opus Dei.'

The Father asked me the same again, this time in a less severe
tone and suggested I think again, to see if I had not allowed myself
to be influenced in some way. I said no again, because that really

was the truth.

A third time the Father asked me, wanting to know if I were acting freely and whether I had considered my vocation slowly in God's presence. I replied that I had done that, I had thought about it for months, and had no doubt whatsoever.

At last he let me ask for admission. He told me to go and talk to Alvaro del Portillo who would tell me a few things about the plan of Christian life proper to a person in Opus Dei. Then, in a cheerful tone, he told me I had made him very happy.

Bringing this conversation to mind has reminded me of how very careful the Father was that our self-giving should be totally free, ensuring that we were sincere and our motives were exclusively supernatural. The Father's love for freedom surprised me from the first. Freedom was not a value people talked about much in those days. Other values were much more fashionable: serving one's country, discipline, rebuilding the nation. The Father, on the other hand, always talked to me a lot about freedom and responsibility, that Christian freedom which comes from a profound sense of being God's children."

Pepe's case was not an isolated one. Other members of Opus Dei had brothers or sisters who also asked for admission to the Work at that time. For instance, God granted vocations to Paco's two sisters, Enrica and Fina, who had made a good recovery from her illness. Enrica asked for admission to the Work on 7 April 1941.

The Grandmother and Aunt Carmen

We return now to Madrid where we were living with the Father in the Residence in Jenner Street. In September 1939 I took the exams I should have taken in 1936. So I graduated in Maths/ Physics and now I was working on a doctorate. It was during this period that I was really able to get to know the founder's mother and his sister, Carmen. They lived in Jenner and I saw them daily; and, I would dare to say that we became very close. We all called them affectionately 'Grandmother' and 'Aunt Carmen'.

Carmen took care that the hired help did a good job looking after the whole Residence. The grandmother spent many hours in her room; she was not at all keen on going out. But every time I saw her, she was always occupied with something useful. She was never just sitting there doing nothing.

When one is young there are a lot of things that pass one by, and perhaps it was the same with me. With hindsight I realize how hard the situation must have been for them. There were more than fifty of us young students, living in the Residence. Many more used to come to the house. Yet everything to do with the running of the house, which depended upon them, never went other than admirably smoothly and we never had to give it a second thought. They knew how to put the finishing touches to things as only an educated and refined woman knows how.

Those members of the Work who lived in the Residence would depend on the Grandmother and Carmen for every material need, from sewing on a button to mending a tear. They welcomed us warmly and would solve the hundred and one little material problems we all had. They were always approachable. From the material point of view, they were not exactly in an enviable position. They shared a bedroom, which was furnished only with the absolute necessities, and another small room looking onto an interior patio. The room was hot in summer and cold in winter. They spent many hours in there; it was by turns, their sitting room, a sewing room and very often, too, the dining room for both of them as well as the Father and Santiago.

I recall so many little, intimate, family events from that time! I remember when Paco and I arrived home from our Ph. D. classes (our lives continued as parallel as Plutarch's characters), we would always go to the Grandmother's room. We would tell her the day's incidents, the peculiarities of the different professors, exams results and so forth. At first we thought about doing theses on aspects of astronomy. That gave rise to a lot of witticisms. She realized we were exaggerating in order to amuse her and make her laugh, and she would say good naturedly: "You make my head spin. When you go, I can't even think straight." But the truth is that she enjoyed our being there a lot and she was very fond of us.

Actually Doña Dolores' situation was not at all easy, as the mother of the founder of Opus Dei and living with him in the only Centre the Work had then. I never thought about it, precisely because I never heard her complain and she made the whole thing seem totally natural. She behaved as though she were our real grandmother, giving up anything she needed to help us. The Father said on one occasion: *I see it very much as God's providence that my mother and my sister Carmen gave us so much help in achieving the family atmosphere we have in the Work. God wanted it that way.*

The Grandmother's affection for us was highly ordered. She treated us all differently, just right according to each person's circumstances. She treated the older ones, who helped the Father, in a special way. Those were Alvaro del Portillo, Ricardo Fernandez Vallespin, Juan Jimenez Vargas and Isidoro Zorzano. She treated Paco, Vicente Rodriguez Casado and me, differently, and Pepe my brother, the youngest of us all, differently again in a very special way. He came to live in Jenner in July 1940. Pepe brought out a special tenderness in her because he was young and because our parents were in exile. She worried the minute he lost any weight and would say: "He is at a bad age. He does not have much appetite and he is not strong." She would justify all the exceptions and special treats she gave him, with remarks like those.

When the Father preached about the relationship between justice and charity, he more than once referred to the justice practised by grandmothers who treat their different children differently; that is just what the Grandmother did.

In Diego de Leon Street

From that year on, the apostolate grew steadily in Madrid and in other Spanish cities such as Valencia, Valladolid, Saragossa and Barcelona. We would often travel to those cities especially at weekends. Like that, we did not neglect our professional work or miss lectures at university. After each trip we would recount stories of the apostolate there, and new names cropped up as well as old ones. The Father himself made many trips and personally took the Work's first steps in many cities. For instance, in September 1939 he went to Valencia and blessed a small flat we had acquired there, which we called 'El Cubil' ('The Den') because of its tiny dimensions.

In November he went to 'El Rincon' ('The Nook'), the first Centre in Valladolid. It also was so named on account of its size! Then there were other journeys to Salamanca, Barcelona, Valencia.

Apart from the apostolate in the provincial cities, the Father was also doing a lot in Madrid, where he ministered to people from all walks of life and of very varying ages. There were doctors, lawyers, white-collar workers, priests. He attended to women's spiritual needs from a confessional in a parish church, devoting special attention to apostolate with women during that period.

God blessed our efforts with abundant fruit. Within a short time we literally no longer fitted in Jenner. It became impossible to attend to the organization of all our work from there; so we set about seeking an appropriate place to establish the headquarters and the first Centre of Studies, where the more recent vocations could receive formation. The Father had had that plan in mind for some time. Not long afterwards his plan became a reality. In the summer of 1940 we acquired a house on the corner of Lagasca Street and Diego de Leon Street. The Father moved in with some members, which included me. We also rented a flat in Martinez Campos Street.

I lived in the Centre at Diego de Leon for some months. The Father, Grandmother, Carmen and Santiago were all living there. On the first floor, the Grandmother and Carmen had a room overlooking both streets, with a covered balcony in the corner. We hoped she should have more space there. However God took her to himself soon afterwards.

Later the Father would tell how he went to take leave of his mother who was ill in bed, *to go to Lerida to preach a retreat to diocesan priests... "Offer your discomfort for the work I am going to do,"* I asked my mother as I said good-bye. She agreed, even *though she could not help saying in a low voice: "This son of mine!..."*

He went to Lerida to preach, preoccupied about his mother's state of health. The doctors had reassured him it was nothing serious. He abandoned himself in God's hands, pleading, *Lord, take care of my mother, for I am looking after your priests.*

Later he related how, in the course of a talk he gave on that retreat, he spoke to those priests about the lofty supernatural calling of priests' mothers, together with their sons. When he finished the talk he stayed on in the chapel to pray. In a little while the bishop of the diocese came in with a sombre expression to say that Alvaro del Portillo was on the line from Madrid. He heard him say, "Father, the Grandmother has died."

The Father went back into the oratory, and with a lacerated heart made an act of total devoted acceptance of God's will in front of the Tabernacle: *'Fiat, adimpleatur, laudetur... iustissima atque amabilissima voluntas Dei super omnia. Amen. Amen.'*

It was 22 April 1941. He discovered a friend who was going to Madrid by car and who offered to take him quickly. However, the car broke down and they did not get to Madrid until two o'clock in the morning on 23 April. When he entered the oratory in Diego de Leon and saw his mother's body there, he broke down in silent tears. When he came out they told him how her death had come about so unexpectedly. He whispered: *My God, my God, what have you done? You are taking everything from me, everything you're taking away. I thought my mother was essential for these daughters of mine, and you leave me without anything, without anything?*

My brother Pepe recalls, "It was the first time I saw the Father cry. It was also the first time the Father gave me a prolonged, long hug almost hanging round my shoulders, his head against mine. For some moments he was almost wordless. He only said *Pepe!*. I understood then just how great were the love and the heart of the Father. His self-giving to the will of God knew no bounds."

Some days later, during a meditation, he said aloud: *Lord, I am pleased you have had such trust in me. Though we try make sure my children are at their parents' side when they die, it won't always be possible, because of the needs of the apostolate. And you have wished me, Lord, to lead the way in this too.*

Much later he commented: *I have always thought that our Lord wished me to make that sacrifice as an external sign of my love for diocesan priests. I am sure my mother is still interceding for them specially.*

I felt the Grandmother's death very deeply. I was then in Valencia as the Director of Samaniego, a new students' residence, which had just begun.

When they phoned us from Madrid to tell us of her death they stressed that we should offer many suffrages for her soul. We were also asked not to go to Madrid for the funeral; this instruction I found very hard to fulfil because I loved her a lot.

Universal outlook

We must refer, if only briefly briefly, to the priests of the Priestly Society of the Holy Cross. For the last few years Alvaro del Portillo, Josemaria Hernandez Garnica and José Luis Muzquiz had been preparing for Holy Orders, following a plan approved by the bishop of Madrid. This, despite the fact that the Father still did not know when or how their ordination could take place. He was praying and asking the Lord for light to find a solution which would combine both the secular and lay character proper to Opus Dei, with the incorporation of the priests needed to attend to the universal apostolate.

The uncertainty was resolved after a few years, *after searching for and not finding the juridical solution*, as he would say later. On the morning of 14 February 1943, God gave him the *precise and clear* solution while he was celebrating Mass in a Centre for women members of Opus Dei in Jorge Manrique Street. The first tabernacle in a Centre for women of Opus Dei was there. When he finished saying Mass he drew the seal of the Work on a page of his dairy, the Cross of Christ reaching around the world from within its very heart. From then on he was able to speak of the Priestly Society of the Holy Cross.

After Mass he went to the Villanueva Centre where I was then living. The Father asked Ricardo Fernandez Vallespin to draw properly the seal of the Work, which he had just sketched in his diary, with a compass and in Indian ink. Next day he went by car to a small hotel in the Guadarrama mountains where the three first ordinands were working hard at their studies. He wished to speak to Alvaro del Portillo, who was Secretary-General of Opus Dei, as soon as possible.

The Priestly Society of the Holy Cross was the solution the Father had been looking for, in vain, for a long time. It was clearly the answer to the light he had received on 2 October 1928 in which he had seen Opus Dei with priests and laity in intimate cooperation.

The new priests of Opus Dei were ordained under the title of the Priestly Society of the Holy Cross and would form an integral and inseparable part of the Work. It was now possible to ordain some laymen of Opus Dei who would thus be able to assist all the other members spiritually and attend to the apostolic activities promoted by them.

The ordination of the first three priests took place on 25 June 1944. The ceremony was performed by the bishop of Madrid, Bishop Eijo y Garay, who loved and appreciated our founder very much. The Father was very moved, as we all were, by this transcendental step in the development of the Work. Bishop Eijo knew that out of humility the Father would not be present at the ordination Mass. He then decided to invite himself and go for lunch with the Father and the three new priests in Diego de Leon.

During the ordination ceremony the Father stayed at home in the Diego de Leon Centre. He celebrated Mass and prayed for the ordinands, true to his motto: *I must hide and pass unnoticed that Jesus only may shine forth.* Much later the Father told us that the next day he wished Don Alvaro del Portillo to hear his confession. It was to be the first confession Don Alvaro was to hear. From then on he was the Father's regular confessor for the rest of his days.

Isidoro

One year earlier, on 15 July 1943, the eve of the feast of Our Lady of Carmel, Isidoro Zorzano had died, after a painful illness. He had borne it with great fortitude, offering his sufferings for the future priests of Opus Dei.

Isidoro was a pillar of the Work, especially during the period of the Civil War. I lived with him on several occasions. We had been together in the last weeks of the Ferraz Residence, after his transfer from Malaga to Madrid. Later I lived with him for a whole year, first in the Centre at Jenner Street, then in Diego de Leon for the first few months it was open. Later still, I coincided with him again in another Centre when he was in the final stages of his illness.

He was an exemplary person. He was the first Administrator General of Opus Dei, and had to face many financial difficulties. When he fell ill he went to a clinic run by nuns. The nearest Centre was in Nunez de Balboa Street; and so those of us who lived there spent the most time with him, as it was easier for us to take it in turns visiting him than for those living farther away. We were uplifted by his example both beforehand, when he was in good health, and later, when he had to stand up to the pain of his illness and his agony. We saw how a member of Opus Dei could live, work and die as a saint. The Father lavished attention and affection on this son of his and had the joy of seeing the Church open the Cause of beatification of this good and faithful man.

New horizons

Some months later, on 6 January 1944, I went to live at La Moncloa Hall of Residence. It was the continuation of Jenner Residence which we had vacated the previous summer. The reason for my change was that the Director of the new Residence was unexpectedly called up, and what was more, he got a bad bout of typhoid. The Father indicated that I should replace him.

In spite of living in La Moncloa, I often used to go to Diego de Leon. There something unusual once happened to me. One particular day the Father had invited for lunch various bishops whose names I am not sure of. That was nothing unusual. He habitually received Spanish bishops; he would frequently also welcome foreign cardinals and bishops who were passing through Madrid on their way to Rome. That day the luncheon invitation had taken Carmen by surprise and she called me to help her sort out a few details.

The morning was exhausting both for Carmen and for me. At last everything was ready and the visitors and some members of the Work, may be Alvaro del Portillo, I do not remember exactly, went in to lunch. During the meal I had to do several jobs which meant running down stairs from the third floor and then back up again several times. The last time I ran up, I felt rather ill. I could not get my breath and I noticed my heart was racing. I thought that if I were to lie down I would be all right in a few minutes. So I did. But instead my heartbeat grew even more irregular; I came to think I was going to die. I tried to call out to somebody but I could not make myself heard because I was short of breath.

At last one of the residents, who was passing by, noticed my predicament and, very frightened, he called the Father and a doctor immediately. When the Father came into the room he found me stretched out on the bed, propped up with lots of pillows so I could breathe, surrounded by several alarmed residents who were trying to hold back their tears. The Father was perfectly calm. He gave me absolution and said: *Don't worry, this cannot be anything serious. You have to be a priest and go to a faraway country to begin the work there.*

Then Dr Serrano de Pablo arrived and diagnosed a temporary tachicardia. It was not a case of heart disease. In a couple of days I was quite well again, although a bit ashamed of the fuss I had caused, and particularly struck by what the Father had said to me.

His words had cured not just my momentary fright, but also the short-sightedness which often afflicts us when surrounded by our daily cares. They illumined for me once more the Work's universal horizon, the essential catholicity of Opus Dei.

Anyway, I would like to re-emphasize how normally those events which bordered on the extraordinary came up. The Father had warned us against seeking extraordinary or dramatic things; he constantly insisted on the *extraordinary sanctifying value of the ordinary*, of everyday work done for God's sake. But it is an undeniable fact that God bestowed many extraordinary graces on him to sustain and confirm him in the fulfillment of his mission; he rarely spoke of them and when he did, it was only with the older members.

Don José Luis Muzquiz points out in his recollections: "If on the odd occasion he spoke to us about more special graces, he would always do so very humbly. One day I heard him mention how, in the early days of the Work, when he had been going through a very bad patch, an image of our Lady smiled at him. The figure is on the facade of a house in a street in Madrid. But what most impressed me", Don José Luis stresses, "was the simplicity and humility with which he said: *It's what I needed then.*"

The Father's humility

I said earlier that humility presided over all the Father's activity. I could detail many events to illustrate this point. He avoided everything that could be a motive for personal pride. Nevertheless, those of us who were by his side could not help marvelling at the great supernatural gifts which God granted him. It was because of that, that when the Father noticed the admiration and affection he caused in people, he would do his best to make sure that souls should not cling to him. For instance, he did not want people to get used to going to confession only to him. And when people who admired him very much came to see him and I asked him later who they were or what they wanted, he would answer. *Nothing, my son. They only wanted to have a look at a 'specimen'.*

Far from being roused to vanity, he used to joke about the interest and admiration he caused. He would avoid the slightest sign of what people call 'personality cult', no matter how insignificant or innocent it was. I could give lots of examples but one will do. It happened years later.

It was a specific occurrence and, although small, in my opinion it was particularly telling. To make this clear, I must first of all explain that I have always been interested, naturally so, in getting to know the places where the Father had lived before founding Opus Dei. I was also curious about other personal circumstances. But the Father fended off all queries. He wished to keep everything personal in the background. He used his skill and good humour to great effect to parry my persistent curiosity.

Well, some years later I thought I was going to achieve my objective. In 1946, Victoria, the eldest daughter of my friend Pedro Ybarra and Adela Guell made her First Communion in Barcelona. The whole family had begged the Father to be the one to give Victoria her First Communion. He agreed. So Manolo Barturen and I went to Barcelona with the Father.

The Mass was on 31 May. On the way back to Madrid, on 1 June, I pestered the Father to let us drive through Barbastro, his home town, even if we did not stop there. I told him I would love to

see the city where he had been born and the house he had lived in
when he was small. But the Father did not want to. Because of my
incessant pleading he at last agreed that we could drive through –
without stopping. However, after hours of driving under the mid-
summer sun I fell fast asleep, and when we were near the city the
Father said to the others in the car: *We are nearing Barbastro. If
you wake Pedro up I'll murder you?* A while later when I woke up
the Father had a good laugh and said, to my great annoyance,
Perico, we passed through Barbastro several kilometres ago!

When he saw the disappointment on my face he added merrily:
*It seemed such a pity to wake you, seeing that you were sleeping so
contentedly... In the next city we will stop so you can have
something to drink. Besides you'll have other opportunities of
visiting these cities in north Aragon.*

Two priest sons

When the Father left for Rome in 1946, we, the second group of
Opus Dei priests, had already been ordained deacons. I have only
very vague memories of all the ordination ceremonies. For the
tonsure I had to shave off my moustache, wear a cassock, a cape
and a shovel hat.

It was not easy to embark on clerical life or get accustomed to
specific usages. One day, when I had just received Minor Orders, I
was walking past outside the Colegio del Pilar in Madrid. Suddenly
I saw a multitude of children, at school there, launching themselves
towards me to kiss my hand, as was customary then. It made a
novel impression on me, and at that particular moment it was very
disconcerting.

Don Leopoldo Eijo y Garay, the Bishop of Madrid, adminis-
tered the tonsure, Minor Orders and the priesthood. He loved the
Father and the Work a lot. During the ceremonies the Bishop was
very fatherly towards us. At the tonsure he joked with me and cut
off a lock of my hair very close to my head. That meant that I then
had to get my hair cropped short.

I do not remember much about the foregoing ceremonies of
ordination to the sub-diaconate or to the diaconate, except that they
were very long. At the sub-diaconate ceremony Friar José Lopez
Ortiz, the bishop of Tuy, officiated. It took place in the Centre in
Diego de Leon. We received the diaconate from Don Casimiro
Morcillo, Auxiliary Bishop of Madrid at the time, in the Parish
Church of his home-town, Soto del Real, which was then called

Chozas de la Sierra. We processed through the town: I remember that we ordinands paraded through the streets under a blazing sun with dalmatics over our shoulders.

I suppose the reader can already imagine who one of the other ordinands was. Yes, he was there, by my side. Leaning on my shoulder, as he felt a little faint, was the inseparable Paco – from then on he was to be called Don Francisco Botella.

We remained deacons for several months, waiting for the Father's return to Madrid. He had gone to Rome to sort out the business of getting the first Pontifical approval of Opus Dei. We received the priesthood in the chapel in the Episcopal Palace of Madrid on 29 September 1946. Just as he had done with the first three priests of Opus Dei, the Father did not attend any of the ceremonies. He stayed in Diego de Leon praying for us, and during the ceremony of the ordination to the priesthood he was in the Centre we had at the time in Espanoleto Street.

My parents could not attend my ordination as they were still in exile, in the city of Oran in Algeria, which was then under the French flag. I celebrated my first Mass in Bilbao at the Shrine of Our Lady of Begona. The Father wished Don Alvaro del Portillo to go to Bilbao with me. Many very close friends also came.

From June of that year a new chapter had begun in the Father's life. He had moved to Rome. On 16 July he had the joy of being received in a private audience by Pope Pius XII.

Soon after my priestly ordination he returned to Rome where he settled for good. That is why from now on this narrative will skip years and dates. I will limit myself to recounting the more significant meetings I had with our founder during his long period in Rome. I will also touch on some other events which I consider of particular interest.

CHAPTER 12

Expanding the apostolate

America

One morning in 1946, soon after being ordained a deacon, I was walking with the Father along Lagasca Street in Madrid. He was telling me about some aspects of priestly work which I would be carrying out once I was ordained. He said in passing, without giving it further importance, that after working for some time in Spain as a priest I might be able to begin the apostolic work in an American country, because *we've got to cross the pond.*

Again his words took me by surprise. As had happened before, they plucked me out of my own little world of specific problems and faced me with a much wider geographic and spiritual dimension. It was no longer a matter of going to another city but to another continent. I consoled myself by thinking that the inter-continental leap would only occur after quite some years had passed. At that time Opus Dei had just begun in Italy and Portugal, and I guessed that quite a while would pass before beginning in farther countries.

However, about a year and a half later, at the end of March 1948, I had a letter from the Father in Rome. He asked me to get ready as a matter of urgency for a long trip around America. He wanted me to visit the archbishops and bishops who had expressed a wish that Opus Dei be established their dioceses. He wanted me to weigh up *in situ* the different circumstances of each place so that the preliminary steps could be taken to organise a stable apostolate in those countries. Once again I realised that the Father was marching *at God's pace* whereas my pace tended to a much slower rate.

So it was that I set off with two other members of Opus Dei on a long peregrination which lasted for six months. It began with a flight from Madrid to New York. We had large numbers of very varied interviews. We never omitted to visit the local bishops and the university authorities so that we would be able to inform the Father about the circumstances and apostolic possibilities of each country.

In April I visited Cardinal Stritch, the Archbishop of Chicago. José María Gonzalez Barredo, who knew the cardinal, came with me.

The Prelate welcomed us warmly and said jokingly;

"There is something about Opus Dei that I don't understand. How did it come to be born in Spain which is such a traditional country, when the spirit of Opus Dei is so open, and so in tune with the needs of the Church of our time? To what do you attribute the fact that Opus Dei was born in Spain and not in some other country like the United States?"

"Your Eminence," I responded, in more or less these words, "the Lord chose a Spanish priest to found Opus Dei. When our founder received that light from God he was living and working in his country. However, he has transmitted a universal spirit to his children which is neither Spanish, nor French nor European nor American. It is a catholic spirit, that is, universal."

"That's very clear," the cardinal agreed.

After visiting Chicago we went on to Toronto, Montreal, Ottawa and Quebec. After that we travelled to Mexico, Peru and Chile; and from there, to Buenos Aires and Rosario in the Argentine. We received an excellent impression from all those countries and we saw great possibilities for beginning Opus Dei in all of them as soon as we could. For the most part we stayed from one to three weeks in each country, except for Mexico where we spent two months and it was still just a taste.

We wrote to the Father from each city, at least a postcard, to let him know how we were getting on. When we finished the trip we spent some time with him in September at the Molinoviejo Conference Centre near Segovia in Spain. We told him our impressions of all we had seen in America. In view of what we said he decided to take the first steps to establish the apostolic work of Opus Dei in the United States and Mexico.

Beginning in Mexico

And in this last-mentioned and beloved country I arrived in January 1949 to begin the work of Opus Dei. I had travelled a long voyage aboard the transatlantic liner, the 'Marquis de Comillas'. After giving us his blessing and while we were saying our good-byes in Molinoviejo, the Father said to Bishop Morcillo who was there: *This blessing and statue of our Lady are all that I can give them for beginning in Mexico.* The figure of our Lady was a simple ceramic one of Our Lady of Rocio. She was 'the foundation stone' of the apostolic work in my new country. Today she is kept in Montefalco with all affection and gratitude.

A detailed report of the beginnings would deflect me from my main aim in these pages, which is to write about the years I lived with the Father. Suffice it to say that, in general, the beginning of the apostolic work of Opus Dei in Mexico included the difficulties characteristic of all beginnings. We had to come to grips with the financial problem; we did not know if we would get residence permits, and a host of other hurdles. We had been able to spend some time in Mexico during our earlier exploratory trip thanks to a tourist visa we had obtained in New York. Now we needed immigration visas and work permits. That was why we had decided to travel by boat, not because we had wanted to go on a cruise. Thanks be to God, some good friends helped us to get the documents as immigrants for an indefinite period at the Mexican Consulate in Havana.

The financial problem remained; with the little money we had on us we did not even have enough to pay the consular expenses. Thanks be to God again, a generous person trusted us enough to lend us what we needed in Havana. So by the time we disembarked at Veracruz, our initial accounts were already in the red.

When we reached Mexico City, we rented an apartment in 33, London Street and we began work. However, our monthly earnings from our work contracts just covered the rent, water, light and telephone bills. We had only 250 pesos left for food and the other expenditure necessary for simple survival. Thanks to God, as always, we scraped by.

The Father was continually writing to us from Rome and encouraging us. From the start we relied on the affection of the then Primate of Mexico, Archbishop Luis María Martinez, who was pleased to celebrate Mass and reserve the Blessed Sacrament in the Oratory on 19 March of the same year. The oratory was the best room in our tiny apartment.

The earliest people to begin frequenting our first Centre in London Street were some law students and some cadets I had become friends with. God blessed our apostolic work abundantly. In a short time the flat was too small, so we decided to move to a two storey house at 70, Naples Street.

God's help also came to us through Opus Dei's first Mexican co-operators. Those generous folk helped us tremendously at that time, and they reminded me of the people who helped the Father at the very beginning. I cannot forget either the parish priest at the Church of the Sacred Heart of Jesus, Monsignor Vallejo Macouzet. We struck up a friendship very quickly and had a good working relationship. I helped him with confessions in the parish and with preaching. Some Lenten sermons had been organised for domestic workers and that was the first time I preached to a large congregation in Mexico. So the work grew and spread among people of all social classes, which were much more marked then than they are now.

During that first period I was the only priest of Opus Dei in Mexico. However, despite the distance from Rome, I felt the constant company of the Father, thanks to his frequent letters. They were brief and encouraging, written in his characteristic firm handwriting. In July 1949 he wrote, *The Archbishop of Mexico and the bishops of Veracruz and Tacambaro came to lunch with us in May.* In the same letter he said: *I would like to send you another priest soon. Let us see if it can be early in 1950. I would like to send women as well. Why don't you think about a house where you could have them look after the housework?*

In August the same year, after bringing me up to date with the amount of work the buildings of Villa Tevere meant, he finished off: *I am dying to see you in this beloved Mexico! A big hug and your Father's blessing.* He still signed himself Mariano, as he used to do during the Spanish civil war.

On 25 November 1949 he wrote to us from Milan, saying, *We are organising the refurbishment of the house here on our way to Austria and Germany. We are going to have a look round with the intention of opening a couple of houses there as soon as possible, with God's help.* Around then he begged us to pray *for the things I have in hand, as they are very important for the whole Work.* He would often say, *I very much want your sisters to join you. And even more to send you a couple of priests.*

The first women of Opus Dei set foot in Mexico in March 1950. A year later, in 1951, a priest, Don Emilio Palafox arrived. Until the arrival of Don Emilio I used to go to confession with Bishop Gastone Mojaisky-Perrelli, Chancellor of the Apostolic Delegation in Mexico, who was very fond of our founder and admired the apostolic zeal of Opus Dei.

Following in our founder's footsteps, we began a student residence at 70, Naples Street.

Our first resident was from Yucatan. Later he became a member of Opus Dei. The second one was from Michoacan. It was a pleasant house, but it did not meet the requirements necessary for the women of Opus Dei to be able to take on its domestic administration. So when the first women of the Work arrived in Mexico they did not do that; instead they set up the first Residence for women university students in Copenhagen Street.

Soon afterwards the three adjacent houses to 70, Naples Street become vacant. Our penury conjured up memories of DYA Residence. But again we followed our Father's footsteps, made an act of faith and left 70, Naples Street for the three identical neighbouring ones: 64, 66 and 68.

The Juarez district, where these Centres were situated, was in the old residential area that had been built in the times of General Porfirio Diaz. Our three identical houses had a basement and three floors. They had attic rooms in the French Renaissance style, with a faintly Versailles look about them, but only a very faint one. Thus was the architectural fashion which had been so popular in Mexico during the long presidential reign of Don Porfirio, at the end of the nineteenth century and the beginning of the twentieth. Some people thought they were not exactly pretty; but once communications doors had been made to link them, it permitted the women of Opus Dei to organise the domestic administration completely independently of us. The residence had an Oratory, a study, a second study for architecture students, a dining-hall and so on. In one of the offices a chemistry laboratory took shape where Ramon's friends would come and do their experiments. Ramon was one of the first members of the Work in Mexico. He was studying chemistry at the time.

The Residence had lots of space. Many students come from the different schools in the Autonomous University, from the Free School of Law and from the military schools of medicine and agriculture. It was the first students' hall of residence of Opus Dei on the American continent. We recorded this reality joyfully on its shield, *Prima Americae.*

Very often we would have get-togethers on the flat roof of the Residence to the sound of Mexican folk music. I would recall old times in DYA and I would dream an almost impossible dream of how the Father would love to know first-hand these lands and these people. The work was growing apace, fruitful, from the hand of Our Lady of Guadalupe whose image we venerated in the Oratory of that house.

I know how much the Father longed to come to Mexico. One of the many times he expressed his desire to me was on 24 January 1950. *I pray for every one of my children whom I am longing to meet and spend time with. I will be overjoyed to spend a good long while in Mexico. It will be a happy day for me when I can celebrate Mass before our Blessed Mother of Guadalupe.*

The Father had been keeping Mexico close to his heart for many years past. In a conversation with him in the mid-fifties, he told me how during the persecution suffered by the Church in Mexico, in the second decade of this century, he had prayed a lot for Mexico, commending her specially to Christ the King and to Our Lady of Guadalupe. He was not yet twenty at that time. He felt deeply sorry about the sufferings of the Church in this country, and prayed and offered sacrifices particularly for her during his years in the seminary in Saragossa, at the beginning of his work as a priest and later on, in Madrid too. Those were the most virulent times in Mexico in what relates to religious persecution and the prohibition of public worship.

An article attacking Opus Dei

Around the year 1955 or 1956, when the Father related the above, was just the time when an article about Opus Dei was published in 'Atisbos'. 'Atisbos' was a unique newspaper. It was not exactly a daily paper, nor was it a weekly one. I seem to recall it came out every three days. It was characterised more by its polemical style than for its informative rigour. The editor, the proprietor, and the author of the article in question were all one and the same person, a journalist called Rene Capistran Garza.

That article was the first of a series about Opus Dei in which numerous errors were propagated. For instance, it stated that the Work had political aims. I did not know much about Mr Capistran, except for what I had heard people say about his talent for controversy. So I reckoned the most prudent thing to do would be for me to go to visit him personally to clear up his mistaken points of view. Since I knew very few people in the press world, it occurred to me to seek help from María Teresa Muro, who was the widow of Martinez Pando. She had worked for years in the Inland Revenue and Public Credit offices; so she was well acquainted with that sphere. Coincidentally, she had met Capistran Garza in Havana around 1947 on the occasion of a meeting of counsellors and Inland

Revenue Ministers in the Cuban capital. She introduced me to Capistran. My first meeting with him was not exactly easy. He was prejudiced against Opus Dei on many counts, as a result of pressure and biased reporting from Spain. Yet, in spite of everything, he came to understand just sufficient about the aims and apostolates of the Work.

Shortly afterwards I had to make a trip to Rome. During a conversation with the Father I told him about the articles in 'Atisbos' and my interview with Capistran. The Father said: *He must be a good man. When you get back to Mexico you ought to treat him with affection and understanding. You can do him a lot of good. There is probably some bitterness in him because he has suffered a lot and he needs to unburden himself.* He continued in more or less these words: *You have peace there now, even though the laws have not been repealed. But I remember how the faith was put to the test in Mexico, and the faith with which people turned to Christ the King and Our Lady of Guadalupe. I also prayed, to Christ the King and to the Blessed Virgin, that the faith of those people would not be destroyed. I remember that in the years 26 to 29 no public worship was allowed.*

The Father recalled the monument to Christ the King which had been put up in 1923, in the Cerro del Cubilete as a sign of the Mexican nation's great devotion. He pointed out the extraordinary eucharistic piety of the Mexicans, who were capable of celebrating a Eucharistic Congress just one year after these events, in 1924, in circumstances which called for true heroism.

The Father went on: *And I remember that I often followed those sad incidents precisely in the reports of Rene Capistran Garza which were published in a Madrid newspaper.* The Father concluded by telling me that a man who was capable of writing those reports must definitely have had a strong faith and a big heart. A man like that was worthy of respect and affection even though he was once blinded by somebody else's influence.

Those words of the Father cheered me up, and when I returned to Mexico I met Capistran again. Everything the Father had said was fulfilled to the letter. I remember him with great affection; he unburdened himself to me; he told me his sufferings, the calumnies and falsehoods which had been levelled against him, the poverty and loneliness he had suffered in his years of exile in Havana. It was the beginning of a deep friendship while lasted for many years, until his death at an advanced old age.

'As tradition requires'

As the apostolate grew and grew, we had to open new Centres in Mexico City. In 1953 we rented a house in Georgia Street. Like the others, the name of this street harped back to Europe. But we did not stay there for long – just long enough while we refurbished the definitive Centre in Nuevo Leon Street.

Mexican vocations started coming, and we began to pass on the spirit our Father had taught us to them. We would take advantage of the school holidays, which started then at the beginning of December, to give them more intensive formation. To begin with, since we did not have a suitable locale, we would go to different places lent to us by Co-operators and friends. I recall going with the other members of Opus Dei to the La Gavia ranch at the foot of Nevado de Toluca in a short convoy of cars. We intended to spend several days there giving spiritual formation to the recent vocations.

But we had not foreseen what we would find there. As soon as we arrived, word spread like wildfire, from one ranch to another, that a priest had arrived at La Gavia and there must therefore be 'a mission' on. Men and women and children began to arrive in great numbers for me to preach to them, administer the sacraments and say Mass. I was moved to see so many people thirsting for God.

Those were delightful and wearying days at one and the same time. Besides giving necessary formation to the members of the Work, I spent several hours each day hearing these country-peoples' confessions. They would struggle in at dusk, after hours of walking, to attend 'the mission'. I had to say the Rosary at five because, they explained to me, 'that's what tradition requires', although it had been interrupted for many years from lack of clergy. We also organised some catechism classes. When the school holidays were over and my companions went back to Mexico City I stayed on a few more days, hearing people's confessions and attending to various sick people 'over the hillock' as they say in those parts...

The apostolic work developed along God's lines, so different at times from ours. For example we meant to stay in Mexico City, one of the most densely populated cities in the world, set up the Work there and, only after that was done, travel to other areas in the Republic. For the time being we had no plans to start in other cities. But God knows best. In 1949 the engineering company which had taken on the two men who had come to Mexico with me, was transferred to Culiacan in the north-east of the Republic. That was why we began in different places in Mexico very early on.

Without forming cysts

When I had already been in Mexico for eight years, the Father and the General Council in Rome assigned some apostolic work to me for which I had to go to Central America, Colombia and Ecuador... After such trips I would generally go to Rome to tell the Father my impressions and experiences. I could relate lots of tales from those trips and, in particular, the Father's comments. However because of the limitations of space, I will restrict myself to those which testify to his universal vision. In point of fact I will just relate what he said on my return from Panama.

For various reasons I met a group of coloured Panamanian students in the cities of Panama and Colon. Some of them conserved their African ascendancy to a marked degree in their features. Others were children or grandchildren of orientals... The Father was keenly interested in the apostolate which could be done with them. They, in their turn, could eventually do the same in their countries of origin. Once again I witnessed how his universal spirit traversed all frontiers and all kinds of ethnic or cultural barriers, the latter often more difficult to cross than national borders.

The members of the Work, no matter what their original nationality, who have gone to begin the Work in Africa or in the far East know very well how much our Father prayed and how much love he put into the first steps they took on those continents. How he longed for the first vocations from the new countries to come to the Roman College of the Holy Cross! The College had been opened in 1948 on the feastday of St Peter.

Since the time of its foundation, thousands of members of Opus Dei from different countries in the world have studied there. Some of them would be ordained. Others, on finishing their course of formation, would contribute to giving the Work in their respective countries a universal spirit, or they would reinforce the apostolic work in other nations. He was delighted to see that the universality of Opus Dei had been re-affirmed in Rome and from Rome. That is, it bore the stamp of Rome which, for the Father, was synonymous with universality.

For this reason the Father vehemently insisted that no matter where we were, we should avoid the appearance of being an isolated cell, like a foreign body which is not integrated into the life of the country. That explains why he never wanted a large group of foreigners to go to the same country; still less, foreigners of the same nationality. To avoid non-assimilation, he expressly indicated that we should not centre our work on colonies formed by our own compatriots in new countries.

That was not easy to do. We, who started the work in Mexico where there was a high proportion of Spanish immigrants, were Spanish ourselves. Very often we had to be quite quick-witted, making amicable excuses to dodge the numerous invitations we received from the Spanish colony. Sticking to our guns caused occasional bother but thanks to our holding closely to that policy in Mexico and everywhere else, Opus Dei took firm root from the word 'go'.

Kenya

In the meantime, Opus Dei's apostolate was spreading all over the world. Throughout those years the Father kept sending out members of the Work to break ground in a great many countries on all five continents.

They started in whatever way they could. It was nothing new for us to begin with no material resources. We began in Portugal in 1945, a year later in England, and the following year in Ireland and in France. Two years later, in 1949, as well as in Mexico the Work commenced in the United States; in 1950, in Chile and the Argentine. In 1951 the first members went to Venezuela and Colombia. In 1952, we started in Germany. In 1953 it was the turn of Peru and Guatemala. 1954 saw the beginning of our apostolate in Ecuador; 1956, in Switzerland and Uruguay. In 1957 the first steps were taken in Austria, Brazil and Canada. In 1958 we went to El Salvador, Kenya and Japan; in 1959 to Costa Rica, and in 1960 to Holland...

The consequence of this expansion, fruit of our personal apostolate, was that corporate apostolic initiatives sprouted up: universities, schools, dispensaries for poor people, agricultural schools, cultural and community centres. God blessed with abundant vocations the seed we had sown. We received frequent letters from the Father, guiding and encouraging us from Rome. Meanwhile he gave thanks to God for the fruits of sanctity which the spirit of the Work was ripening the world over.

Recounting all that would fill another book. I will cite just one example of the Father's concern for a specific apostolic initiative in which I myself was directly involved. At the beginning of October 1958 I received, in Mexico, a letter from the Father telling me he needed me permanently in Rome. That meant leaving Mexico. As the Father knew, I had many close affective ties with the country. Once I got to Rome the first thing the Father asked me to do was to go to Kenya for a few weeks to talk to Monsignor Mojaisky-Perrelli who was now the Apostolic Delegate for the various British Dominions in East Africa.

When Monsignor Mojaisky arrived in Kenya he had found a terrible problem as far as education went. African students and the children of the numerous Asian immigrants had little chance of getting into university. On finishing secondary school they came to a bottleneck. The English educational system required two years' intermediate study between secondary school and the university. That two year course could only be taken in special, officially-recognised schools of which, in fact, there were very few in East Africa.

Europeans could send their children back to the mother country to study, but that solution was beyond the reach of the local population for many reasons. It was impossible too for the Goans, Pakistanis and other Asians who lived in Kenya. When Monsignor Mojaisky became aware of the situation the first thing that came to his mind was to write a letter to the Father, asking him to get Opus Dei to found a school to solve the problem.

Monsignor Mojaisky's petition found a ready response. The Father sent out various members of Opus Dei who knew the English educational system and British laws. In fact Monsignor Mojaisky had asked the Work to start a university in Kenya, but after careful research on the ground it seemed that a college would be better suited to the country's urgent needs. And that was how Strathmore College in Nairobi came into being.

For one of the journeys I made to Kenya around then, the Father laid down the principles on which this important institution should be based:

Firstly, the College had to be multi-racial. That is, we were to make sure, right from the start, that the Centre was not exclusive to any one ethnic group. Rather, the different races should intermingle and get to know and love one another. That was quite revolutionary at the time, for some 200,000 Asians and more than 50,000 Europeans then lived in Kenya.

Secondly, the College must be open to non-Catholic and non-Christian students. There must be no selection criteria other than the purely academic.

Thirdly, we must point out and explain to the authorities, right from the start, the secular nature of members of Opus Dei and that this was not a mission school, nor were the teachers missionaries but secular, professional people with the appropriate academic qualifications, who were practising their respective professions in full freedom.

Fourthly and lastly, the students should be fee-paying, even if they only paid a symbolic amount because, according to the Father, *people don't appreciate or take seriously what they receive gratis, and besides, it might humiliate them and give rise to complexes.*

This is not the moment to relate the vicissitudes of Strathmore's early days, nor the difficulties Kianda had to overcome. Kianda was set up by women of Opus Dei as a corporate venture for young African women. The Father prayed a lot for these projects, offering up many sacrifices and spending many hours studying them – long before teaching began in Strathmore. I only wish to record that, if Strathmore very soon became the first multi-racial educational Centre in East Africa, with no discrimination in any form, it was directly due to the Father's concern.

As the years passed, I was able to meet various past pupils from Strathmore College who had read Medicine, Engineering, Architecture and other subjects in the universities of Rome, Padua, Palermo and Navarre. Many of them told me of their surprise that at times of acute racial tension in the country, in Strathmore there had been only *the one race of the children of God.*

Mother of two priests

I must now bring the reader up to date again on my brother Pepe. At the very beginning of these recollections I said I did not know if the parish priest of Torrevieja was able to gauge the exact significance of his prophecy. (He was the one who had told my grandfather that the children from the marriage – of my parents – which so worried him, would give themselves to God.)

But the fact is that his words were fulfilled beyond his wildest dreams: a few years later on 1 July 1951, my brother José María was also ordained a priest, together with nineteen other members of Opus Dei, in the Irish Church in Madrid.

My mother was overjoyed at our ordinations and she said that from then on we would have to pray very specially for her, so that just as God had given us both a vocation to the priesthood, He would also give her the vocation to be the mother of two sons who were priests.

When I told the Father my mother's singular petition, he said, *She is absolutely right and she has a great deal of supernatural sense. There are many ways of living out the Christian vocation, and she too has a very great vocation as a good, generous mother. You have to pray for her perseverance, and pray also that many priests' mothers and sisters see things that clearly and know how to support their sons or brothers, praying for them and looking after them generously. That way they carry out a great service to God and his Church. What would I have done, especially at the beginning of the Work, without my mother and my sister?*

Thank God, my father was able to attend Pepe's ordination. He had returned from exile a year after my ordination and had the consolation of being rehabilitated and restored to his position as a Professor. He had taken up a post in Aranda de Duero this time round. He went to Madrid frequently during those years and met the Father whom he admired very much. The Father received him several times very affectionately.

The Father had won the grace he had asked of Our Lady in Lourdes. My father had come back from exile a changed man from the spiritual point of view. He had suffered a lot of material deprivation, but the Lord had gradually granted him faith, and together with faith, a life of sincere piety. During the last eleven years of his life he was a man of prayer, who went to Mass and received Holy Communion every day. He would read a spiritual book for a while and pray the Rosary every day too.

I remember his growing enthusiasm for St Teresa and St Augustine, (who had gone through a conversion as he had too), for St John of the Cross and of course, *The Way*. Seeing all that, I could not but give thanks to God and remember the Father's words at the foot of the altar in Lourdes...

After being a co-operator of Opus Dei for several years, he bore his final illness with great conformity to God's will, and having received the last rites, he died very much at peace, on 10 February 1960, the day before the feast of Our Lady of Lourdes.

In Italy

From October 1958 until May 1966 I worked with the Father on Opus Dei's General Council and in the Italian Region. I made several trips to different countries but my normal work was in Italy.

My mind throngs with memories of the many apostolic initiatives the Father promoted during those years in the land of my ancestors. He was the driving force behind them, although, as always, other people were at the forefront.

In the autumn of 1958 the building and furnishing of the

Residenza Universitaria Internazionale (R.U.I.) was being completed. At the same time some Italian members of Opus Dei launched the Fondazione RUI. It was set up to raise donations from leading Italian companies and businesses to establish a scholarship fund which would make it possible for Italian, African and Asian students with little or no finances to read for degrees in Italian universities.

It was then that I began to be in contact with the Prefect of the Sacred Congregation for the Propagation of the Faith (later called the Evangelisation of Peoples), Cardinal Agagianian, and also with His Excellency Pietro Sigismondi and His Excellency Monsignor Nigirs. They all held the Father in high esteem. Monsignor Sigismondi understood the Work very well. He took a lot of interest in the professional and Christian formation of the laity in new countries, those which had just attained independence or were on the point of doing so. A very significant percentage of the RUI scholarship students were Afro-Asian.

I used to go to RUI almost every day and I was the Father's channel, as it were, for his apostolic zeal for those African and Asian students. The Father liked me to follow RUI's apostolic work closely. He was delighted to hear the stories I would tell him about the students from those exotic lands and he prayed a lot for that work. In many cases it was the first step in Opus Dei's apostolate in African and Asian countries, far from Rome.

A few months before the death of Pope John XXIII, the Italian bishops hadgathered in RUI. The Patriarch of Venice, Cardinal Urbani and the Archbishop of Milan, Cardinal Montini stayed in the Residence. When the election of Paul VI took place, the residents began to call Cardinal Montini's room 'the room of Paul VI'.

I cannot conclude these brief memories without referring to the Centro ELIS. I will summarise its history. During the Conciliar years there were some areas on the outskirts of Rome where social unrest was prevalent; but few were like the Tiburtino district, rightly considered one of the worst. It was a working-class, predominantly communist area, which had witnessed frequent crime and social disturbances. It was afflicted by a combination of poverty, delinquency, cultural neglect, religious ignorance and rabid anti-clericalism.

Those were some of the reasons which moved John XXIII to invest the money collected from Catholics world-wide to honour Pope Pius XII's eightieth birthday, in the promotion of a social enterprise in the area. He decided to entrust it to members of Opus Dei.

It was a formidable task and the first people to go there had to overcome hundreds of difficulties. Nevertheless, a few years later, with the Father's constant encouragement, the ELIS Centre was built in the middle of the Tiburtino area, beside the Parish Church of St Juan Bautista al Collatino. ELIS stands for Educazione, Lavoro, Istruzione, Sport. In time there would be a secondary school and a centre for technical training for young workers as well as a catering school for women... The ELIS Centre was inaugurated at a solemn ceremony on 21 November 1965. Paul VI wished to attend personally.

The following morning the Father said, *I wanted to wait for him on my knees, as a priest who is fired with love for the Pope and the Catholic Church.*

However, as soon as the Pope saw him, he went to meet him, raised him to his feet and, breaking completely with the protocol of the time, gave him a moving embrace.

Referring to the ELIS Centre, the Pope declared : "This is a work of the heart, it is the work of Christ, it is an evangelical task, wholly oriented towards the benefit of those who use it. It is not simply a hostel. It is not simply an office or a school. It is not any old sports field. It is a centre where friendship, trust and joy permeate the atmosphere. Here life finds its inherent dignity, its real meaning, its true hope. Here Christian life is affirmed and developed. Here many things which are of great significance for our times are demonstrated in practice."

During the ceremony the Father said that Opus Dei had welcomed the apostolic request from the Holy See with particular gratitude, *not only because as I so often say, Opus Dei wishes to serve the Church in the way the Church wishes to be served, but also because the task entrusted to us corresponds perfectly to the spiritual and apostolic characteristics of our work.*

He explained the reason why. In the ELIS Centre, children from poor backgrounds, children of that working class area, were being taught to become saints in the midst of their work, sanctifying it and doing it with human and supernatural perfection. Later students would also come from other very poor regions of Italy.

At the end of the ceremony the Pope, resting his arms affectionately on the Father's shoulders, said to him: "Tutto, tutto qui e Opus Dei – Everything, everything here is Opus Dei."

CHAPTER 13

The Father in Mexico

The Second Vatican Council

The Pope's visit to the ELIS Centre took place a few weeks before the close of the Second Vatican Council on 8 December 1965. I recall how, when the news of its convocation by John XXIII on 25 January 1959 came through, the Father started to pray and to get us to pray *for the happy outcome of this great initiative: the Ecumenical Council.*

Some members of Opus Dei took a very active part in the Council projects. Don Alvaro del Portillo, then Secretary General of Opus Dei, was appointed President of the ante-preparatory Commission *De laicis* (on the laity), member of another preparatory commission, and finally Secretary of the Conciliar Commission *De disciplina cleri et populi Christiani,* and consultant on other Conciliar commissions.

I would like to draw attention to one particular point about this era – the Father's delight when he heard the Council's many teachings concerning the universal call to holiness. The Council solemnly proclaimed to the whole wide world what had been fundamental aspects of the Father's preaching since 1928.

However, as everyone knows, after the Council there were some people, who shielding themselves behind a false Conciliar spirit, began to stir up doctrinal and practical deviations within the Church. Some of the media threw themselves into proclaiming to the four winds certain specific disagreements; and this caused great confusion among the People of God.

Learning about those things hurt the Father very much; yet, as always, his reaction was profoundly supernatural. He prayed and encouraged other people to pray a lot for the Council. He turned to Our Lady, Mother of the Church, with heartfelt aspirations. During those years he had his mind and his heart centred in a very special way on the Council's projects.

It is difficult to reflect in writing what intense suffering the Father, in close union with the Pope, endured during those years on account of this situation. It was an acute grieving, motivated by his deep love for the Church and for Christ.

He wrote at that time: *I suffer a lot my children. We are going through a moment of madness. Souls by the million are experiencing confusion. There is a great danger that, in practice, the sacraments will be emptied of meaning, all of them, even Baptism, and even the Commandments of God's Law will lose their meaning in people's consciences.*

As always, he turned with all his heart to the maternal protection of the Blessed Virgin. And among other Marian pilgrimages, he decided to come to Mexico to pray before the image of Our Lady of Guadalupe.

At the feet of Our Lady of Guadalupe

In the meantime, in May 1966, I had returned to Mexico as the Counsellor of Opus Dei there. That allowed me to live out our final years at the old house at 66 Naples Street. Soon we moved to Rodin Street in the Mixcoac district, to our first purpose-built house.

In this, my second sojourn in Mexico, God granted me one of the greatest joys of my life. In Rome, just before I flew to Mexico, when the Father gave me the blessing for the journey, he had said: *This time I really do promise to go to Mexico.* And he fulfilled his promise.

The Father set foot on Mexican soil on 15 May 1970 at about three o'clock in the morning. I had gone to meet him at the airport. The main reason for his journey was to pray to our Lady. He was so longing to prostrate himself at her feet and pour out his heart to her that very night, that shortly after I picked him up at the airport, while on our way to the Regional Commission of Opus Dei in Mexico, he asked if we might pass by the Villa. In Mexico, the Basilica of Our Lady of Guadalupe is known as the Villa. We told him the Villa was in the opposite direction and besides, it was closed at that time of night.

I have come to see Our Lady of Guadalupe, he explained to us, *and, incidentally, to see you. You don't mind being in second place, do you?* Soon afterwards he humbly added: *I haven't come to teach, but to learn.*

Travellers from Europe generally rest for two or three days after arriving in Mexico to become acclimatised to the time change and the difference in altitude; yet the Father wished to visit the Basilica straight away, the day after he arrived. It was a Saturday. First he went to see the Archbishop Primate of Mexico, Cardinal Miguel

Dario Miranda, who was delighted to welcome his long-awaited visitor. 'At last we've managed it, at last!', the Cardinal repeated exitedly, as he embraced the Father for the first time in Mexico.

After that the Father proceeded to the shrine. He entered through the sacristy and knelt in the chancel for a long time, utterly absorbed and without moving a muscle. He was pleading for the Church, the Pope, the salvation of souls...

I find it hard to describe my emotion during those minutes. Time was passing and the Father did not move. With his eyes fixed on our Lady, he was praying intensely. Members of the Work started to arrive at the Basilica. After a long while I went up to the Father to tell him that the church was full of sons and daughters of his in Opus Dei, men and women who had come to pray at his side. The Father stayed there praying for an hour and a half: an hour and a half of love, of intense supplication and fervent petition.

I have come to Mexico, he explained to a group of members of Opus Dei from the United States who had come from their country to see him, *to do a novena to our Blessed Mother. I'd have come on my knees, as the Indians here do, but they wouldn't let me. I have come to Mexico for this, to love our Blessed Mother more. I think I can say that I love her as much as the Indians do.*

The next day, 17 May, he returned to the Villa to pray there again. Seeing the mass of people who habitually come to the door of the Basilica on their knees along the esplanade, moved him. Many of them are country people who come barefoot, walking long distances, or Indian women bringing their babies or toddlers in bundles on their backs, or sick people who come accompanied by relatives... From that day, the 17th, he was able to pray more discreetly because we were granted access, using a spiral staircase with uneven steps, to a gallery situated above the chancel. So the Father was able to pray without attracting people's attention. Don Alvaro del Portillo, Don Javier Echevarria, Alberto Pacheco, Adrian Galvan and I were with him.

The Father's fervent supplication to our Lady set the tone for the remaining days of the novena which we did more or less like this. To begin with the Father would pray aloud. Now and again he was silent and we would pray a mystery of the Rosary. After that he would continue praying aloud, and then we would say the other decades. We continued like that until we had finished all three parts of the Rosary.

From the top of the gallery the figure of the Blessed Virgin was very near the Father, who addressed her with in trusting prayer.

During his prayer on the fifth day of the Novena, while gazing upon the figure of 'La Guadalupana', he said: *It makes me so happy to be able to contemplate the Mother of God and our Mother physically with my eyes, and with my understanding and my heart too. She is always attentive to her children. She lived, and she lives!, to give peace, happiness and fortitude to others. We have come here with the utmost confidence to beg, to beg and to feel how much we are God's children, because she is God's Mother.*

Have you seen how people run after a celebrity, a queen for instance? They get all excited because they have seen her pass by, and if she so much as glances at them they're filled with a joy they wouldn't exchange for anything in the world. And they tell the whole story, over and over again. People run after earthly celebrities – and you, my Mother, you are the Queen of Heaven and Earth!

We come here full of love, although, on occasions, it seems we can't think of anything to say to you. And you are, I repeat, our Mother, the Queen, who can do everything. I recommend that all of us, at this moment especially, relive our childhood, and to recall, as I do quite clearly – try your hardest, if you need to, to remember - the first time you turned to our Lady knowing what you were doing and wanting to do just that. Pray now with the selfsame trust using, if necessary, the childlike devout prayers you learnt from your mother's lips.

In Spain some time ago, probably now as well, they used to say 'Pray to Mary'. When the month of May came around, everybody took her flowers. I did too, just like these wonderful Mexicans. Our Lady, now I bring you thorns, for I have nothing else, the thorns that are in my heart. But I am sure that through you they can be changed into roses.

How many children of mine from all over the world will be bringing you flowers today! And they will join me with this petition of mine which I present to you with such sorrow. Please answer us soon. Hurry! Here, in this Mexico so blessed by you, where such splendid roses grow all year round, that physical detail gives us yet another motive to talk to you and to beg you to make it happen that, in us too, in our hearts, little roses should be in bloom all year round, the blooms of our ordinary everyday life, but rich with the scent of sacrifice and love. I said 'little roses' on purpose, because they suit me better, as all my life I have only known how to busy myself with normal ordinary things, and often I have not managed to finish even those off properly. But I am certain that it is in this everyday, normal behaviour that your Son and you are waiting for me.

Recalling now that first time in my childhood when I knowingly rendered you homage, it is easier for me, my Mother, to take your hand boldly and trustingly. I am doing the same now as I did then, although in the gallery of this church I am physically higher than you – you know what I mean, because I know very well that I am made of poor quality tin and what happens is that the dross always floats, it comes up to the surface easily, while the good stuff, the gold, is hidden underneath, serving as the base and the foundation – I'm sorry, Mother: I'm only talking like this because I want to beg you to see me, to look upon me. Here I am, because 'You can!' because 'You love!'

He continued making endearing expressions of love to our Lady and pleading for the Church. Presently he said: *We love you in every representation of you. All your likenesses make us fall in love. But we have come here where you deigned to imprint your features, reflecting your love for those of us who are your children. I want to put up the date of this novena in Torreciudad – because I am sure you are going to hear us – with a splendid mosaic of your image, there beside the confessionals, where you will work so many wonderful miracles to convert souls to the love of your Son...*

If you listen to me, I will give your mosaic its first kiss, with all the love of a grateful son. All five of us who are praying here now will be present as a way of saying thank you. If I cannot be there, because I am no longer alive, it will be the most senior person of us in the Work. I would like it to be me, although I do not feel any attachment whatsoever to life: the only thing that interests me is God's love and yours too. I work esteeming my life because that way I can bring you souls. If my self-giving is only for your Son and for you, how can I possibly cling to life? Although, if our Lord does not wish otherwise, I think it is better for me to stay here on earth, to love you more and to bring more souls to you.

But now I realize what I am saying. It was a first impulse caused by the fire of my love. Mother, I place no conditions, how could I dare to? Your image will be there; there are five witnesses here, so they all know we will put you there. Besides, how am I going to lay down conditions if you will grant 'sooner, more and better,' what we hope and ask you for?

The get-togethers

The Father's stay in Mexico lasted for more than a month, from 15 May until 22 June 1970. Many people of all kinds came from different parts of the country to listen to him : professional people from the capital, mothers and housewives, craftsmen, agricultural workers, domestic workers, business men and women, intellectuals, priests, Indian women in local multicoloured costumes.

The Lord had given the Father, right from the beginning of his apostolate, a tremendous 'gift of tongues' – he spoke very simply and was easily understood by everyone. Whatever their mentality, idiosyncrasies, nationality or race, he had a charm and a warmth which captivated his listeners. He know how to convert those great gatherings into delightful intimate conversations reminiscent of early Christianity, where anyone could ask questions and talk with complete spontaneity and freedom. We used to call them 'get-togethers', because that is what they really were, in spite of the fact that at times there would be hundreds, sometimes thousands, of people of different nationalities present.

My astonishment grew from one day to the next. The groups to which he talked of God were so different, so distinct one from another. People in business, people in the professions, members of the Pan-American Institute of Advanced Business Management, peasants from the Agricultural and Fisheries Centre of El Peñon in Montefalco; young university students from the R.U.P. (Pan-American University Residence); mothers; domestic staff; poor people from villages in the interior; priests; intellectuals... Often the get-togethers happened one after the other, and the Father would not have time to reflect or to find out who would be going to listen to him next.

He explained an aspect of Christian living; he gave doctrine on another; he suggested solutions or remedies; he encouraged people in their struggle... and always in a cheerful, optimistic tone punctuated by jokes and stories. I realized then that, like good wine, his virtues had been enhanced with the passing of the years; they were in crescendo. Over the years the Father had become brim-full of God. His preaching was imbued with sanctity: the spirit of the Gospel and spiritual profundity.

He was able to get through the everybody. I recall, for instance that on 15 June he extolled the apostolic work with domestic staff. *Dealings between the lady of the house and staff have often been unjust on both sides. We have to try to eradicate this injustice, and, by making it more professional, get people to understand what the supernatural meaning of this kind of work is: in other words, knowing how to serve, now that no one wants to.*

I am very happy to serve God. I am nothing more than a servant of God and I pray that I may have a deeper desire to serve him every day. We have to practise Christian justice; there must be neither exploiters nor the exploited. One of those girls, living within a family, can be an angel of light or a devil... That's how important she is...

On that occasion a large group of young women in Opus Dei were listening to him. Some were university students, others domestic staff. He went on: *Remember that we are a family. We are all equal in the Work: there are no classes. Those of you who are undergraduates have specialized in learning because you have had more chance to study. Other daughters of mine have not had those opportunities and have not acquired the same degree of learning, but because of their interior life, they do have the gift of wisdom which is worth more than all knowledge.*

Then he said something which reminded me of old times in Ferraz. *I too have swept floors, and tried to sweep them well. I did not sweep the dirt under the carpet because I was doing it in God's presence. If it wasn't perfectly done that's because sweeping floors is not a speciality of mine... although I would like it to be. When you are doing the cleaning, do it as though you were in the house in Nazareth; to please Jesus, Mary and Joseph. You are domestic staff in the Holy Family's home in Nazareth. If you work with the right intentions with love for God, you are sanctifying yourselves.*

Mexico really touched his heart. Why not say so, outright? In short: he absolutely fell in love with it. He lavished praise on our country. *What wonderful fruit you have in Mexico! The only fruit which is better where I come from are the peaches,* he said laughing. *Everything else is better here. It tastes so good – it smells so nice...*

He understood the Mexican soul very well and when people asked him things, both human and divine, he tried to soften the sharp edges of his Aragonese accent to adjust to the smoothness of our way of speaking.

"Father", he was asked during a get-together with a lot of mothers present, "say something to us about big families."

My daughter, when I see a big family I feel I want to get down on my knees there before you. How good you are!

Sometimes his answers were long and he took some time in order to explain a point of Christian doctrine. However, he normally gave a supernatural angle to each question with a single, brief and simple, but very clear and expressive, brush-stroke. Like that he would make fundamental points of doctrine accessible to everyone. It was a real catechesis in which the wealth of Christian life was revealed.

"Father", a young girl asked him on another occasion, "why do you say you bless the pure love of our parents with two hands?"

My daughter, because I haven't got four... the Father answered charmingly and good naturedly.

Thousands of people came to listen to him and they asked him very diverse questions on bringing up children, married life, freedom in education, the sanctification of work, the sacraments... One woman asked him if women ought to work.

Do you think they don't work? Those who are engaged in a job or a profession do very well. Others already have plenty of work running the home, taking care of the children, preparing a loving welcome for their husbands. Don't you think that is enough? I think that is wonderful professional work... Then he remarked humorously: *And for the record, I am not against women being Mayors and Governors.*

Another lady asked him about childless couples. *If they have no children it is because God wants more from them... Be grateful, too, to the Lord who has not given you children, because he will give you a lot of love to bestow on those around you. If you don't know what to do, tell me, and I will give you work. And you must love each other exactly the same, with all your heart, do you understand? Husbands and wives who have no children: you are not miserable creatures, or people who have been cheated out of something: you are people to whom the Lord has providentially denied that consolation, but has given you such a great capacity to love...*

From childless couples he would go on to talk about sacramental confession, or he reminded them about the Church's doctrine on infant Baptism or on helping the needy. *You have to intensify your apostolate among workers and country people. We have to help them, with human warmth and supernatural affection, to acquire the necessary learning to be able to reap more material benefits from their work, so they can support their families more easily and with greater dignity. To achieve that you don't have to bring down the people at the top; but neither is it right that some families should always be the underdogs.*

From peasants he went on to intellectuals, from intellectuals to businessmen, from businessmen to mothers and then on again... But before proceeding, I would like to pause and talk about the Work's apostolic efforts among the country people in Mexico. One such is summarised in the name 'Montefalco'.

Montefalco was not a dream

At the beginning of the fifties we made a car journey from Mexico City to Monterrey by way of the Huaxteca. We stopped to buy petrol in a place in the mountains near Tamanzunchale. I was alone in the car when a young Indian lad of about fourteen, a nice-looking boy, poked his head in through the window and said point-blank:

"Father, take me with you."

"Where do you want to go?"

"Wherever. I want to serve God."

As you can imagine I was not able to offer the lad any solution, but he gave much food for thought for the remainder of the trip. That fresh encounter with the Indian population was added to earlier experiences in other parts of the Republic. For yearly retreats and study courses we had been to people's ranches or old haciendas which had been lent us by their owners in La Gavia, Huixcoloco, San Carlos, Mimiahuapam... For the rest of the journey I wondered how and where we could begin a stable apostolic initiative among the country people.

When we reached Monterrey, the Director of the Centre there told me how they had started catechism classes in a small town a few kilometres from Monterrey. A woman cooperator of Opus Dei had lent them 'El Molino', a small ranch, and the apostolate was growing tremendously. Those coincidences seemed to indicate that the Lord was asking us to begin working in rural, indigenous Mexico. We wrote to the Father and told him all about it. Montefalco began soon afterwards.

Montefalco was an old colonial estate, a sugar plantation in the Amilpas Valley which, in its time, had encompassed thousands and thousands of hectares of sugarcane plantation. Popular songs still recall how, during the Revolution, Emiliano Zapata sacked and burned many estates in the present-day state of Morelos.

'...Anenecuilco in Morelos, oh happy town
boasts a son of great reknown.
For there on her native earth
Emiliano Zapata had his birth.

Nineteen eleven was the date
Emiliano Zapata sealed his fate.
Forth from the mountains he did sally
Mounted men and arms did rally.

On a spirited horse he was sat
Keen as a wolf, lithe as a cat,
His steed he was of goodly height
With silver horse-shoes shining bright...'

The only thing Zapata left unburnt in Montefalco was the church. Then, under General Cardenas, there was the agrarian reform and the huge old estate was reduced to little more than thirty hectares. And that was how it stayed, long-abandoned, a charred empty shell until 1952, when the owners donated it so that Opus Dei could use it as a base from which to work among the local community.

To describe the condition the old estate was in, one observation will suffice: when we went to look it over, the only way we found to do so was by climbing up one of the church towers to get a rough idea of the heap of ruins which had become ambushed in the midst of the tropical undergrowth. Only from that height could one locate a huge square surrounded by the incendiarized walls of the old building. We could also see that not a single roof was left to shelter under during the storms, except for the windowless naves of the Church.

So derelict was Montefalco, in fact, that when Ignacio Canals went to see it, he had to hack his way through the undergrowth with a machete. (Ignacio was one of the first members of Opus Dei who came to Mexico. At the time of writing he is a Professor at the Autonomous Metropolitan University.) As he advanced he discovered things which were half-buried under the plants and the debris: the square, a courtyard, another courtyard, a fountain... He unearthed, for instance, a kiln for bricks; with it they were able to bake bricks similar to the ones used last century. Later we repaired the little aqueduct which carried water to the 'trapiche' (the Mexican term for a sugar-cane mill). Other elements also came to light, certainly less useful and rather more dangerous – like snakes, scorpions and vipers.

Practically the whole place had to be rebuilt. To this end we took along an architect friend of ours to see the broken-down walls and carbonized stones. When he saw them he inquired: 'But how can you possibly want to accept this? It is a complete ruin.'

We replied in consonance with what we had heard the Father say so many times: *Dream and your dreams will fall short.* We dispensed with the architect.

With the help of two young aspiring architects, I began the first, basic reconstruction of the building. Providentially, in Chalcanzingo, we came across a bricklayer called Florentino. We soon discovered it was better to explain the works to him orally, rather than give him the plans. That way he and his little team were able to carry out our ideas better, and the parts rebuilt looked more genuine because the materials and workmanship were local.

It was providential, too, that we found Bernardo, who was very young then, to be the caretaker at Montefalco right from the start. Florentino and Bernardo have become a real institution in the rebuilding of Montefalco: they have given over a great part of their lives to working there and God has given both of them a vocation to Opus Dei.

The first person to stay in Montefalco at night was Manuel Alfonso Calderon, another of the first group to come to Mexico. Manuel was brave enough to stay in Montefalco for a period with a dog, Palomo, to supervise the work.

The beginnings were hard; but with time the difficulties were ironed out and after a few years there was a school for the local people, a Conference Centre and various social projects organized by members of Opus Dei, all up and running. The Father fostered the development of these initiatives from Rome and it is easy to picture his joy the day he saw the buildings with his own eyes. He spent three days in Montefalco and experienced the difference between reality and mere reports. He had not imagined just how big the whole ensemble was.

What a lot there is still left to rebuild, he exclaimed, when he saw the ruins that were still untouched, *even though you've already achieved a lot.*

We explained each one of the activities which we run from Montefalco with the rural poor from the surrounding areas. He was over the moon. *I am here. It isn't a dream. I really am here in Montefalco.*

When he saw the old hacienda, the church with its great dome and two high towers, the new buildings and the whole conglomerate of ruins and blackened stones still awaiting rebuilding, he was very moved and said: *Montefalco is an act of madness for the love of God. I usually say that Opus Dei's teaching comes down to two points: act with common sense and act with supernatural sense. In this Centre, Don Pedro and my Mexican daughters and sons have acted with supernatural sense only. Happily taking on a pile of ruins... is absurd from the human point of view... But you have thought of souls and you have brought into reality a marvel of love. May God bless you.*

I am ready to stretch out my hand to beg for money to finish Montefalco. And finish it we will, with your sacrifice and with the help, as ever, of so many people who are willing to help in an enterprise which will benefit the whole of Mexico. It is a foolhardy venture but also a venture born of the love of God.

I think Montefalco appealed to him in a very special way. He remarked: *I would love to stay here! You do not really realize what you have done. All of this has come out of heap of ruins, without a penny, from the work of so many children of mine who have had to struggle and suffer, and from the warmth and generosity of so many other people.*

Today, this is a marvel!, he said to a group of rural women. *The people who worked on this enterprise now have the happiness of seeing how your souls wish to be better, how your lives will be more noble and more dignified, and how you will be ready to make sacrifices so as to be good Christians, good mothers, good wives... This is something very beautiful!*

Nowadays, Montefalco comprises a Conference Centre which was opened in 1952, a Domestic Science School running two-year courses, an Agricultural School opened in 1958, the Montefalco School for women and a Teacher Training Centre.

While the Father was in Montefalco, he asked us to think about how we could help more academically able children so that they would be able to further their studies. To a group of Opus Dei women who were responsible for this kind of apostolate he said: *Teach them to live as good Christians. Tell them they are God's children and they ought not to obstruct the sources of life. Teach them, not by complicated theories which would be of little help to them, but in a practical way to improve their economic and social situation... Anything else is a waste of time for them.*

For instance, think about how to help the cleverer ones so they can carry on with their studies. Some of them could become teachers and later on they would be able to teach others. My daughters, I am not talking about philanthropy or being charitable. We have charity in our hearts. Giving people material means is an obligation for those who have received these from God to administer them.

The people of Montefalco are strong and tough, rugged as the three mountain peaks which dominate the valley; but on the inside these souls are tender and their hearts are big. Indian blood runs in their veins, their origin can be divined from their faces, their dark complexion, and sharp features and from their lilting speech. When the Father met them he said, *No one is better than anyone else, no one! We are all equal! Each one of us is worth the same, each person is worth Christ's blood. Think what a wonder that is.* Referring to the image of Our Lady of Guadalupe, he went on: *Look at the beautiful, magnificent face which our Lady left on the cloth in Juan Diego's hands. You can see she has Indian and Spanish features. Because the only race there is is the race of the children of God.*

Nowadays there are a lot of enterprises similar to Montefalco scattered throughout Mexico. Toshi for instance, which means 'Grandmother's house' in the Mazahua language, carries out far-reaching work with the local rural population. This hacienda is situated in western Mexico, beyond Toluca. The people are mostly members of the Otomi and Mazahua indigenous tribes.

There are also many Centres, run by women members of Opus Dei, dedicated to educating girls from economically deprived backgrounds. The names of their centres have a strong local flavour: Nogalar in Monterrey; Jazlim in Hermosillo; Palmares, Los Altos or Cecaho, in Guadalajara; Yalbi in Mimiahuapam; Yaxkin, Oxtopulco and Yaocalli in the Federal District of Mexico. Many of them have a dispensary providing free medical assistance to poor families in their area. Others are primary schools, residences for domestic workers or girls from rural areas. They are the living expression of the apostolic dreams the Father talked of in the little room in the Sabadell Hotel.

With the Indians of 'El Penon'

A year after we had been given Montefalco, a group of Mexican professional men, many of them members of Opus Dei, formed a trust called "Countryside and Sport" to promote social projects aimed at people living in large concentrations in rural areas. That was how El Penon began, an agricultural and fisheries centre in the Amilpas Valley. It covers nine towns and a population of 80,000. During the fifties the Valley was a typical example of the problems of the Mexican countryside, with long periods of drought, no irrigation of any kind, almost a total dearth of farming technology and the division of the land into allotments which were too small to be viable. On top of this was a climate of general discouragement among the people; their only way out was to migrate to the cities, where they frequently became marginalized and fell into even greater poverty.

During his stay in El Penon, the Father said: *You are all anxious to improve, to get out of this situation, so that you'll no longer be crushed by financial pressures. And we, too, are anxious for you to do so... We are going to make an effort as well to get your children some schooling. You'll see how, between us all, we'll manage it, so that those of your children with aptitude for study and who want to, will be able to go far. To begin with there'll only be a few but later on... And how will we do all this? Like someone doing you a favour? ... No my children, not like that. Haven't I said we are all equal?*

Beside Lake Chapala

Lake Chapala is the biggest lake in the Mexican Republic. It appears as the Chapalico Sea on old maps of New Galicia. Near its shores stands Jaltepec, a Conference Centre, fifty kilometres from Guadalajara, the provincial capital of Jalisco. From the balconies of Jaltepec one has a wide panoramic view of the lake bordered by hills, dotted with red-roofed houses. The lake inspired the famous song which runs like this :

> *Over Otoclan the sun gets up*
> *Over you, Chapala, ascends the moon,*
> *Gently the tide rises in the lagoon...*

and reaches its moving finale:

> *Chapala, place of love,*
> *Where souls speak intimately to God above...*

The Father lived there, beside Lake Chapala, from 9 to 17 June. There were get-togethers with all kinds of people and the Father taught them to 'speak intimately' to God as the song says.

There was a large number of married couples at one of those get-togethers. Some were members of Opus Dei, others co-operators or friends.

If you have patience enough, I want to talk to you about three sacraments in particular. Will you be patient?, he asked them.

With one voice they replied, 'Yes, of course, Father.'

Well then, let's begin with the sacrament of Matrimony. It is a blessed sacrament with which God wanted his children to attain a marvellous holiness. Marriage demands a lot of sacrifice but what a lot of well-being, peace and consolation it brings. If it doesn't then it's because they are bad spouses. The sacrament of Matrimony confers spiritual grace, supernatural help, so that husband and wife can be happy and bring children into the world. Obstructing the sources of life is a terrible crime, and here it's a betrayal of your country too, because Mexico needs lots of Mexicans.

It is right and holy that you love each other. I bless you and I bless your love for one another, as I bless the love my parents had for each other, with these two hands of mine, priestly hands. Try to be happy in your married life. If you are not, it is because you don't want to be. Our Lord gives you the means... Turn over a new leaf if you need to. Love your wives, and respect them. With your children, spend the time they need.

The Father paused and then went on: *I am going to talk to you now about the Blessed Eucharist... I will say to you what I have already said maybe a hundred times already in Mexico, and thousands of times since I became a priest because I love Jesus our Saviour, perfect God and perfect man, with all my heart.*

After explaining our Lord's reasons for instituting this sacrament he exhorted them: *Let's be grateful. What would we not do for a person who had done for us the tiniest fraction of what Jesus did for love of us? Love our Lord in the Blessed Sacrament. When you go into a Church, go first of all to the Tabernacle and say to Him: I believe, even though there are whole heaps of people who say they don't believe. More still: I believe on their behalf.*

Then he moved on to penance. *The sacrament of Penance cleanses us, makes us less proud, and brings happiness back into our lives if we have lost it. By going to confess our faults, keeping to the conditions we know from the catechism we studied when we were children, the priest absolves us from our sins and even from the greatest of crimes. But, I recommend you go to confession regularly, even if you don't have any grevious sins to be forgiven. The sacrament of Penance strengthens the soul, gives it new stamina, makes it capable of things which are more Christian and more heroic.*

My children, I am sure that if I spoke to each one of you I would find you have done heroic things in your life, even though it seems otherwise to you. At least I would find the heroism of the ordinary everyday life lived honourably. Let us love the sacrament of Penance.

He spoke frequently during his stay in Mexico on this last point – the sanctification of ordinary life. He inquired: *Which kind of work is more beautiful, a peasant woman's or a member of Parliament's? I don't know. Whichever is done with more love for God and with a purer intention. Is that clear? All human work is holy; at least, it can be made holy. God our Lord asked me when I was very young to tell the people of the world not to look for excuses. I call people who look for excuses, 'eyewashers': I wish I hadn't married, I wish I weren't a doctor, I wish I weren't... I wish I didn't have this mother-in-law: 'eyewash-ers' every last one of them!*

No sir! With the mother-in-law, married, single, whatever; in a workshop, factory, field, university, in parliament, everyone can be a saint if he wants to be. All you need is really to want to and to act appropriately as a good Christian ought.

The Father's words really sank in with everyone: with intellectuals, with the simplest of people. I recall a farmworker from San Juan Cosala, a little hamlet of a few houses and huts near the lagoon, so small it does not even appear on the map. He composed a delicate poem of gratitude for the Father's words. I treasure it as a particularly touching souvenir of those days. The poem is written according to the rules of the heart and of gratitude (although not so much in conformity with those of grammar or spelling) and goes like this:

> *The 'Virgencita morena' of our town*
> *With smileing eyes on you, looked down,*
> *For you she had waited many years*
> *Before your greeting reeched her ears.*
> *En Jaltepec, Jalisco*
> *There you did sew*
> *Your wizdom's pearls among*
> *the gathered people old and young.*

> *We ask, you senor, whose so close to God*
> *That our faults He forgive us*
> *And may your blessings on us be pored."*

The Father also met a large group of diocesan priests. They had a long and lively get-together in the sweltering heat. At the end of it he was exhausted. He retired for a while to have a rest. On the wall facing his bed he noticed that the picture was one of Our Lady of Guadalupe giving a rose to Juan Diego the Indian.

That is how I would like to die, he mused, *looking at the Blessed Virgin, and she gives me a flower.*

A song of farewell

On 22 June, when his stay in Mexico was coming to an end, he had a get-together with a group of young university students. One of them took up a guitar and told the Father he wanted him to listen to a song which is normally sung when people go to serenade the Virgen of Guadalupe at the Villa early in the mornings.

The Father nodded his agreement and the lad began to strum the guitar, singing softly at first:

> *Lady, to you I wish to sing,*
> *The finest of my songs.*

Then, in full voice, he continued:

> *My heart is yours*
> *Oh sun of my desiring*
> *All my love is for you,*
> *And my very being too.*
> *A heavenly hope casts its rays*
> *Lighting up my darkened days...*

Suddenly the Father jumped to his feet. *Why don't we go to the Villa, all of us*, he suggested, *and sing that to Our Lady, to serenade her?*

*   *   *

At eight o'clock that evening, the agreed time, we were all together in the Villa, beside the Father, at the feet of Our Lady of Guadalupe. As soon as he arrived the Father went directly to the sanctuary and, standing in front of the main altar under the image of our Lady, he began to intone the *Salve Regina*. The shrine was absolutely packed. Hundreds of people, of all ages and backgrounds, had come to serenade our Lady with the Father, to honour her and to demonstrate their love.

After the *Salve Regina* the Father moved to the right hand side and stationed himself beside a kneeler. The guitars began to sound:

> *Lady, to you I wish to sing,*
> *The finest of my songs.*

The Father remained standing, his eyes fixed on our Lady. He was very moved. At a certain moment he knelt down and covered his face with his hands, leaning on the back of the kneeler, holding back his tears. A second song began:

> *I told her my heart on her was set*
> *She alone's the one that I desire,*
> *That never can I e'er forget*
> *Her eyes of heavenly fire.*
> *The more I think about her*
> *More and more do I love her...*

The introductory chords of the third song began.

> *Thanks for having known you...*

When he heard those words, the Father rose, visibly moved, and left the church. A few of us went out with him, while nearly everyone else stayed on in the Basilica singing their song of love and gratitude to the Virgin.

We went through the sacristy, full of votive offerings, and along the gallery of miracles. We came to the car and set off home. We had already driven some distance in an embarrassing silence, which none of us dared to break, when the Father exclaimed quietly: *This Mexico of yours takes some beating!*

CHAPTER 14

In Torreciudad

Doing the Father's bidding

We kept the Father's promise to put up mosaic of Our Lady of Guadalupe in Torreciudad. On 28 June 1977 we went to this Marian sanctuary set in a breath-taking spot in Upper Aragon in Spain, very near the Pyrenees. It overlooks a peaceful reservoir formed by damming the waters of the River Cinca.

We were delighted to go there, although at the same time with deep grief. The Father was no longer with us to keep his promise on earth, although we were sure he was accompanying us from heaven.

God had called him to be by His side two years previously on 26 June 1975 at about noon. He had died *without being a nuisance*, as he had often asked our Lord to allow him to do. He died with all the simplicity with which he had lived, in his office at the central headquarters of Opus Dei in Rome. His heart failed suddenly just after his eyes had alighted – something he had also asked for – on a picture of Our Lady of Guadalupe...

The next day he was buried in the crypt of the present Prelatic Church, then the Oratory of Our Lady of Peace, in Opus Dei's headquarters. And from that moment on, his reputation for sanctity spread all over the world. A few weeks after his death some prayer-cards for private devotion were printed in Italian and subsequently in over forty languages.

All of us who had accompanied the Father during his novena in the Basilica of Guadalupe in Mexico were there in Torreciudad to keep his promise: Don Alvaro del Portillo, Don Javier Echevarria, Alberto Pacheco, Adrian Galvan and I.

Don Alvaro del Portillo was our Founder's first successor. He had been elected nearly three months after the Father's death, on 15 September 1975, by representative members of Opus Dei. They met in Rome for an elective congress and Don Alvaro was elected unanimously at the first ballot.

The fulfilment of our founder's promise to the Blessed Virgin Mary was a very simple, intimate, family occasion. There were very few of us. Don Javier Echevarria started to read the words our founder had addressed to Our Lady of Guadalupe on 20 May 1970, which I have transcribed above. However, after a little while, emotion prevented him from continuing, so Don Alvaro finished reading and then went on praying out aloud, following our Father's example. He recalled his holy death and the benefits gained through his intercession all over the world and he encouraged us to be faithful to his spirit. He reminded us that "when the Father spoke to his children in Mexico he pointed out right from the beginning that he had *crossed the pond* to see the Blessed Virgin, Our Lady of Guadalupe. Those were times of mental anguish on account of the many sorrows which weighed so heavily on the priestly soul of our beloved Father. They were hard times, now past, thanks to God's help and that of His Blessed Mother, who heard the prayer of the faithful son our founder was."

He concluded: "During those days, before the image of the Virgin Mary and on many other occasions, the Father made this invocation: *Domina nostra de Guadalupe, ora pro nobis.* Our mother, listen to us! We ask you this now with the faith, with the hope – with the conviction! – and the love with which our founder, your most faithful son, spoke to you."

When we had finished our prayer, we kissed the mosaic and said the Glorious Mysteries of the Rosary. Soon afterwards we went to the shrine which has drawn popular devotion from people in all the villages of Upper Aragon since the eleventh century. Our founder's parents took him there at the beginning of the century in gratitude to the Virgin. When he was just two years old he had become so ill that the doctor despaired of his life. "He won't last the night", they had told his father.

Then his mother, Doña Dolores – the Grandmother to members of Opus Dei – appealed to Our Lady and told her, "If you cure him for me I will take him to Torreciudad." Before daybreak he was cured, and soon afterwards they kept their promise and travelled to the shrine in gratitude for such a great favour.

While the Father was alive, whenever he told the story of the new sanctuary he retired humbly into the background, not wanting to hold the limelight. *It's an act of devotion my children have made,* he explained. *Torreciudad is one of an infinite number of spots world-wide where figures of the Virgin Mary can be found which the faithful have respected, loved and venerated for centuries. She has been there since the eleventh century. There is also something of my own which is circumstantial and quite irrelevant...*

From the hermitage I contemplated the buildings surrounding the shrine. They sprang from the Marian devotion of our Father who never wanted to set himself up as an example of anything except in just one thing – *the love I bear for the Blessed Virgin.* With the splendid frame of the Pyrenees in the background I recalled so many manifestations, big and small, I had witnessed of his love for the Virgin Mary: that *Salve* when we crossed the border into Andorra after crossing the Pyrenees; our first visit to Lourdes, frozen with the cold; his prayer in my pension in Pamplona; the novena to Our Lady of Guadalupe.

I heard how the Father had been to Torreciudad twice as a pilgrim, while it was still being built. On the first occasion, 7 April 1970, he took his shoes off one kilometre before arriving and, though the weather was inclement, he walked barefoot over the stones and gravel until he arrived at the hermitage.

Forgive me, Mother! he exclaimed when he arrived. Recalling his first visit as an infant: *From two years old to sixty eight. What nothingness I am! But I love you very much, with all my soul. It makes me very happy to think of the thousands of souls who have honoured you and have come to tell you they love you and of the thousands of souls who will come in the future.*

He said he expected from Torreciudad *an outpouring of spiritual graces... which the Lord will want to concede to those who come before this tiny statue of His Blessed Mother, which has been venerated for centuries. That is why I want there to be lots of confessionals, so that people can be purified in the holy sacrament of Penance. Then, renewed in spirit, they will confirm or begin their Christian lives again. They will learn to sanctify and love their work, bringing the peace and joy of Jesus Christ to their homes: 'I leave you peace, my peace I give you.' Thus they will gratefully accept the children heaven sends them, using in a noble way their married love which allows them to participate in God's creative power. God will not fail in those homes. He himself honours them by choosing those souls to dedicate themselves to Him with a personal and free dedication at the service of his Divine Will.*

When I left Torreciudad a few days later, I understood that the novena we had done at the Villa seven years previously had remained unfinished, and that we had just completed it on the 28th in that intimate simple ceremony.

I went to confession in the same confessional our Father had used; and that day and the next one too, the feast of Saints Peter and

Paul, I meditated a lot on the accidental glory of our founder in heaven, for I saw how his desire, that many souls should honour the Blessed Virgin there and be purified in the sacrament of Penance, had become a reality. What joy he would have in heaven seeing Don Alvaro, his successor, Don Javier and his three Mexican sons, fulfil his promise to the Virgin Mary.

CHAPTER 15

17 May 1992

That morning in Rome

"What were you thinking about that morning?", people asked me when I got back to Mexico after my stay in Rome for the solemn Beatification of the Father on 17 May 1992. I did not know what to reply. Normally I am very slow to react. Besides the memories and emotions came flooding back in such a way that I found it difficult to explain my feelings. Like water caught by a tumultuous current, I needed a backwater of peace, space to step back from things, time to think, silence.

Now, from a certain distance, I can weigh up my feelings and memories better. That 17 May was a splendid Sunday, bright, in radiant sunlight which reminded me of this wonderful land of Mexico. St Peter's Square was full of members of Opus Dei and of people who love the Work and have devotion to our founder. They had come from the furthest corners of the earth. Races and cultures were mingled: Africans with Asians with people of Andean features... It was a multi-coloured joyous crowd of 300,000 people, according to L'Osservatore Romano, where different age-groups and social conditions all came together, a relaxed crowd which completely filled St Peter's Square and overflowed from the perimeter of Bernini's monumental columns and extended past Pius XII Square, right down the Via della Conciliazione like a peaceful flood.

On Maderno's magnificent facade there were two tapestries still covered over, one depicting the Father and the other a Canosian nun from Africa, Josephine Bakhita. I remembered then how very often I had crossed this same square with the Father, heading for the Basilica where now the tapestry was hanging with his portrait.

I could not avoid the indescribable emotion – nor did I want to – which I experienced when the Pope from the East, John Paul II proclaimed in Latin: "With our Apostolic Authority, we concede to the Venerable Servants of God Josemaria Escriva de Balaguer, priest, founder of Opus Dei, and Josephine Bakhita, virgin, daughter of charity, Canosian, that from now on they may be called Blessed."

Following this proclamation there was an explosion of peaceful joy among the thousands of people present. The cloth which covered the tapestries of the two new Blessed ones was raised. From that moment on, our Father became the happy patrimony of the universal Church. I thanked our Lord for having granted me the great gift of having known him, of having lived through so many unforgettable times by his side, of following in his steps and of loving so deeply this man of God whom the Church had just raised to the honour of the altars.

So many memories came into my mind! In my imagination I flew back to those Sunday get-togethers in the Ferraz Residence where Juan, Ricardo, José María, Paco, Alvaro and so many others had been gathered round him... In a certain way we were still together on that Sunday in May. Some of us on earth, and others in heaven gathered round the Father and very united to the Pope.

Juan Jimenez Vargas, as decisive and sparing with his words as ever, was there near me. He had come from Navarre, from the university there – that long-time dream of our founder. Juan Jimenez Vargas had contributed to its development for many years as Professor of Physiology in the Faculty of Medicine. José María Albareda had been the first Rector of the university, but he died many years ago. José María Gonzalez Barredo had also lived in Pamplona until his recent death, after having spent years in the United States where he took part at the beginning of the apostolic work there and he had carried out some formidable research work. I was told that he had not been able to come to Rome for health reasons.

Ricardo – Don Ricardo Fernandez Vallespin – who had worked as a priest for many years in Madrid and then over here in American lands, also died some years ago, on 28 July 1988. José María Hernandez Garnica began the apostolate of the Work in many European countries. He was taken by the Lord while our Father was still living, on 7 December 1972. They all, like Paco – Don Francisco Botella – and so many other deceased members of Opus Dei, will have looked upon this ceremony from heaven. Paco, for so long inseparable from me, died on 29 September 1987 in Madrid after many years of fruitful ministry as a priest.

What about Alvaro? That young engineering student of the mid-thirties was now Monsignor Alvaro del Portillo, our Father's successor and Bishop Prelate of Opus Dei. That morning he was up there concelebrating with the Holy Father in the open air in St

Peter's Square, in the solemn liturgical ceremony in which, together with an immense multitude of the faithful, thirty five cardinals were participating and more than two hundred bishops.

The Pope said: "With supernatural intuition Blessed Josemaria preached the universal call to holiness and apostolate untiringly. Christ calls upon us all to sanctify ourselves in the reality of daily life; for this reason, work is also a means of personal sanctification and apostolate when it is done in union with Jesus Christ, because the Son of God, on taking flesh, has joined Himself in a certain ways to the whole reality of mankind and of all creation. In a society in which unbridled desire to possess material goods converts them into an idol and a motive for distancing oneself from God, the new Blessed reminds us that these same realities, creatures of God and human invention, if they are used properly for the glory of the Creator and in the service of our brothers, can be a way for people to meet Christ. He taught, *All earthly things, as well as all the earthly and temporal activity of mankind, have to be taken to God.*"

That day I went through a wealth of emotions which is difficult to sum up. They are best expressed in the words Bishop Alvaro del Portillo spoke during the Mass of Thanksgiving for the beatification, celebrated on 21 May in the Roman Basilica of San Eugenio.

" 'I will give thanks to God with all my heart... I will keep the words of the Lord.' These words of the Psalm, which we will recite in a little while in the Communion Antiphon, sum up the gratitude with which our hearts are invaded today. Yes, 'great are the works of the Lord'. There is nothing so great in the whole universe as the transformation that grace works in the man who has been redeemed. A handful of dust from the earth is raised so high as to be able to participate in the divine Nature, and receive the adoption of children of God in Christ. This admirable vocation of the new man is totally fulfilled in Blessed Josemaría Escrivá. The Church venerates him today on her altars, and presents him to us Christians as an intercessor before God, and offers him to us as a shining example of fidelity to the vocation received in baptism.

As these days of thanksgiving draw to an end, I would like to meditate once more on the teaching which our Lord wished to transmit to us through the life and message of Blessed Josemaria. We do this here before his mortal remains. His body was a member of Christ, and a temple of the Holy Spirit; it was an instrument which our Lord used in order to communicate to men the fruits of the Redemption. His words, his actions, his very loveable smile, the sufferings which he always bore with a contagious cheerfulness, his exhausting work, eloquently spoke a continuous lesson of love and peace. There comes to my mind the exclamation from Holy Scripture which rose up in my soul the day he went to heaven, *Quam speciosi, pedes evangelizantium bona!* How beautiful are the feet, how beautiful are the steps of those who bear such good news.

Several years have passed now since I was able to tell the members of Opus Dei a thought which came to the lips of Pope Paul VI. Expressing his own veneration for our founder, the Pope told me that from then on the founder belonged to the treasure of the whole Church. The extraordinary spread of the private devotion to him demonstrates that, while he continues to be intimately ours, he does not belong exclusively to us. Filled with gratitude and joy, I repeat to you today that the elevation of Blessed Josemaria to the altars represents the beginning of a new expansion of the ecclesial mission for which he was chosen by God. The universality of the task for which God called him – to announce that all earthly realities are a way of holiness – has been confirmed in a solemn and tangible way. His beatification is for all Christians 'a new call to sanctity', a new reason for hope, an example of faithfulness offered to God in the fulfilment of daily work. All of you can remember the words pronounced by the Holy Father on the day of the Beatification. 'How can we fail to see', the Holy Father said, 'in the example, teaching and works of Blessed Josemaria, an eminent testimony of Christian heroism in the fulfilment of ordinary everyday activities... His faithfulness allowed the Holy Spirit to lead him to the heights of personal union with God, the result being an extraordinary apostolic fecundity.' "

On the evening of that same day, after a Mass celebrated by Monsignor Javier Echevarria, then Opus Dei's Vicar-General, now Prelate, the venerated remains of our Father were conveyed in a procession from the Basilica of San Eugenio to the Prelatic Church of Our Lady of Peace.

Dream and your dreams will fall short

There, where I had prayed so many times beside our founder, I knelt down to pray before his holy remains, among the thousands of pilgrims who were appealing for his intercession. For a long time I watched the people filing by: Africans in exotic costumes, Nordic people from the Scandinavian countries, or far away lands like Canada or Poland; people with olive-coloured skins and Indian features with soft Peruvian speech; Carribeans; men and women from all over Mexico; insatiable Asians from Japan or the Philippines, Australians and people from so many other countries. It was like seeing in the flesh the words the Father had spoken to me, when full of faith, he talked about those faraway countries which the seed of Opus Dei would reach.

I thanked our Lord for being able to contemplate this joyful reality and for having had our Father see, right from the beginning, that Opus Dei had a universal appeal and should reach out to all men no matter what their race or station in life.

I also gave thanks to God that the Father had managed to transmit this conviction to the first members from the start. His words were a true channel of God's grace: if they had not been, it is inconceivable that a handful of young men like us, who had never (with some isolated exceptions) even set foot outside our own country, whose experience of life was limited by our age and circumstances, could possible capture the universality and catholicity of Opus Dei. Undoubtedly, God had granted us great faith in the Father's words.

I was grateful to our Lord that what the Father had said to us in those delightful get-togethers on Sunday afternoons in the Ferraz Residence had become a reality in the lives of so many people. He had assured as that if we were faithful to our divine calling, our lives would be converted into the stuff of a marvellous novel. For that to happen we would have to dream. *Dream*, he would say to us over and over again, full of faith, *dream, and your dreams will fall short.*

From the Publisher

Since this book was first published more than a dozen years have gone by and there have been frequent calls for it to be reprinted. In these period there have been a number of historical developments.

The Founder of Opus Dei, Josemaría Escriva, was canonized by Pope John Paul II in Rome on 6 October 2002, in the centenary of his birth.

Fr Pedro Poveda, the founder of the Teresian Institute was canonized in 2003.

Fr Pedro Casciaro passed away on 23 March 1995 in Mexico City, a couple of weeks short of his eightieth birthday. It was the first anniversary of the death of the Servant of God, Alvaro del Portillo. Fr Pedro's brother, José María Casciaro, died in Pamplona, Spain, in March 2004.

Prof Juan Jimenez Vargas died in June 1997.

The Cause of Beatification of the Servant of God, José María Hernandez Garnica, is now in its diocesan phase.

London, 23 March 2008